Hotel Front Office Management

Hotel Front Office Management

Natalie Gilbert

www.statesacademicpress.com

Published by States Academic Press,
109 South 5th Street,
Brooklyn, NY 11249, USA

ISBN: 978-1-63989-273-0

Cataloging-in-Publication Data

Hotel front office management / Natalie Gilbert.
　　p. cm.
Includes bibliographical references and index.
ISBN 978-1-63989-273-0
1. Hotel management. 2. Management. I. Gilbert, Natalie.
TX911.3.M27 H68 2022
647.950 68--dc23

For information on all States Academic Press publications
visit our website at www.statesacademicpress.com

Contents

Preface

The front office of a hotel is its communication hub which is used by the customers to solve their queries, complaints and problems. Most of the front offices are situated near the entrance of the hotel. They play a major role in building a positive image of the organization in front of the guests. Their key objective is to generate revenue by selling hotel rooms through systematic reservation methods. Some of the other responsibilities of front offices include cross selling and upselling of hotel products to increase the net profit. The important software related to a hotel front office are property management systems, accounting systems and hotel computer systems. The topics included in this book on front office management are of utmost significance and bound to provide incredible insights to readers. It is compiled in such a manner, that it will provide in-depth knowledge about the theory and practice of this field. This textbook will serve as a valuable source of knowledge for those interested in this field.

A detailed account of the significant topics covered in this book is provided below:

Chapter 1- Hospitality industry is a service industry which includes lodging, food and drink service, event planning, theme parks, transportation, hotels, restaurants and bars. Hotels are classified into various types on the basis of clientele and location, size, management and affiliation, range of service, ownership and plan offered. This is an introductory chapter which will introduce briefly about the hospitality industry and classification of hotels into various types on different basis.

Chapter 2- The reception area of a hotel which directly gets in touch with their customers or clients is known as the front office. The chapter closely examines the key functions of the front office such as function of reception and registration, function of concierge and function of bell desk, etc. It also discusses the organizational structure of the front office.

Chapter 3- There are various significant aspects of front office operations and management such as tariff structure and plan, room rate and types of room rates, guest cycle, room reservation, source of reservation, types of reservation, procedure of reservation, cancellation/amendments, etc. This chapter discusses in detail the varied aspects related to front office operations and management.

Chapter 4- Front office coordination and communication is an important area of front office operations and management. This chapter explains the role of the front office in interdepartmental communication, and coordination with housekeeping, food & beverage, sales & marketing, engineering & maintenance and safety & security departments. The topics discussed in this chapter will help in gaining a better perspective about front office coordination and communication.

Chapter 5- A front desk usually refers to a space in the lobby area of a hotel. Services of front desk include making direct contact with guests, attending and making calls, foreign exchange, room assignment, etc. The aim of this chapter is to explore the significant services of front desk.

Chapter 6- Accounting functions play a crucial role in front office operations. This includes maintaining guest folios, employee folios, visitors ledger, weekly bills, etc. This chapter closely examines all these functions along with budgeting for front desk operations.

Chapter 7- The application of analytics to optimize price and maximize revenue growth is known as revenue management. This chapter delves into the purpose and importance of revenue management in the hospitality industry. It also discusses the relevant strategies for revenue management.

I would like to make a special mention of my publisher who considered me worthy of this opportunity and also supported me throughout the process. I would also like to thank the editing team at the back-end who extended their help whenever required.

Natalie Gilbert

Introduction to Hospitality Industry

Hospitality industry is a service industry which includes lodging, food and drink service, event planning, theme parks, transportation, hotels, restaurants and bars. Hotels are classified into various types on the basis of clientele and location, size, management and affiliation, range of service, ownership and plan offered. This is an introductory chapter which will introduce briefly about the hospitality industry and classification of hotels into various types on different basis.

Hospitality is the act of kindness related to welcoming and looking after the basic needs and requirements of customers, mainly in relation to accommodation, food and drink. The dictionary defines hospitality as: "The friendly and generous reception and entertainment of guests. Hospitality refers to the relationship process between a customer and a host. In Oxford English dictionary hospitality is defined as: "the act or practice of being hospitable; the reception and entertainment of guests, visitors or strangers". Hospitality can be defined as the generous and cordial provision of services to a guest. The term 'hotel' has common root with the notions of hospitality, hoteliery, hospital, hospice and host. The notion of 'hospitality' can be described as "the spirit, practice, quality or act of receiving and treating strangers and guests in a warm, friendly and generous way without any consideration for the reward and/or return. 'Hospitality' must be internalized throughout the entire system and at all levels of the organization. In other words, by restricting the perception of hospitality metaphor to courtesy and complaint handling skills of front line employees (front office in a hotel), it addresses only to one dimension of host-guest relationship. Hospitality is commonly defined as something related to the friendliness, kindness and hospitableness. The term 'hospitality' is often used in a wider community and organisation in order to describe something related to the friendliness, kindness, and hospitableness provided by the host.

Hospitality industry comprises of companies or organizations that provide food and/or drink and/or accommodation to people who are staying "away from home". Many people have described the hospitality industry in different ways. Some have tried to summarize the scope of the hospitality industry and its characteristics of involving both tangible and intangible features in the service delivery process. Others attempted to describe the industry by exploring the stakeholders involved, mutual benefits generated and the industry's impacts to the society and economy. 'The provision of food and/or drink and/or accommodation away from home'. A difference between private and commercial hospitality, where private is defined as 'acts by individuals towards individuals in a private setting such as the home' and commercial hospitality is defined as 'meals, beverage, lodging and entertainment provided for profit'. The hospitality industry as 'any combination of the three core services of food, drink and accommodation'. A blend of 'tangible and intangible elements-and the service, atmosphere and image that surrounds them.'

The above definitions give clear idea about hospitality and hospitality industry but these definitions define the hospitality industry form consumer point of view not the sector perspective. On basis of above definitions it can be concluded that the hospitality industry is a broad category of fields within service industry that includes lodging, event planning, theme parks, transportation, cruise line, and additional fields within the tourism industry and further hospitality and hospitality industry may be understood as:

- The friendly and generous reception and entertainment of guests.

- The act or practice of being hospitable; the reception and entertainment of guests, visitors or strangers with liberty and goodwill.

- Generous and cordial provision of services to a guest.

- The spirit, practice, quality or act of receiving and treating strangers and guests in a warm, friendly and generous way without any consideration for the reward and/or return.

- Hospitality is commonly defined as something related to the friendliness, kindness and hospitableness.

- Hospitality Industry includes the companies or organizations which provide food and/or drink and/or accommodation to people who are "away from home".

- Hospitality industry is a broad category of fields within service industry that includes lodging, event planning, theme parks, transportation, cruise line, and additional fields within the tourism industry.

- Hospitality comprises a blend of tangible and intangible products, security, physiological and psychological comfort to the guest.

Sectors of Hospitality Industry

Hospitality industry can be categorized into 4 sectors:

- Lodging/Accommodation.

- Food and Beverage.

- Travel and Tourism.

- Sports and Entertainment.

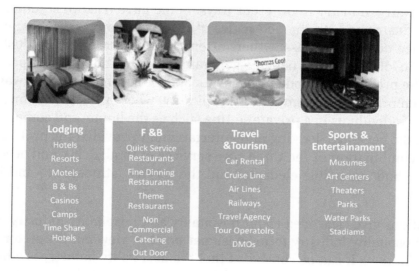

Lodging/Accommodation

Lodging or accommodation is important and broad sector of hospitality industry. This sector of the hospitality industry features from luxurious hotels to exotic resorts and campgrounds. This sector has wide scope ranging from BandB establishments to wide amenities a hotel can offer. During travel the most important facility traveller would require is accommodation. Lodging sector provide wise range of products and facilities to its guest ranging from average room, facilities to luxury suites and peace and calm place to live which is close to nature to hotel in the heart of the city which is near to all important business center.

Types of Hotels

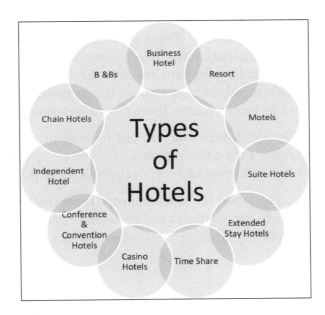

Some important hotels are discussed below:

- Business Hotels: These hotels primarily cater to business travellers and usually located in downtown or business districts.

- Airport Hotels: These type of hotels target clientele are airline passengers who have overnight travel layovers or cancelled flights and airline crews or staff. Some Airport hotels charges the guest by hour instead of normal daily night charges.

- Resort Hotels: Resort hotels are usually located away from cities at exotic location such as in the mountains, on an island, or at beach. These hotels have recreational facilities such as scenery, golf, tennis, sailing, skiing and swimming, trekking, camping and so on.

- Suite Hotels: Such hotels have suit rooms consist of a living room and a separate bedroom. Business men and executives consider suite hotels very attractive as they can work and also entertain in an area besides the bedroom.

- Bed and Breakfast/Homestays: These are houses run by husband and wife. These houses offer rooms for travellers with basic facilities. They are also known as 'Home Stay's'. The owner of the BandB usually stays on the premises and is responsible for serving breakfast to guest.

- Extended Stay Hotels: Extended stay hotels is somewhat similar to the suite hotels. But offers kitchen amenities in the room. These kind of hotels are for those who have long planning to stay specifically wants to stay more than a week and does not want to spend on hotel facilities.

- Timeshare/Vacation Rentals: Another new type or segment of the hospitality industry is the timeshare hotels. These are sometimes referred to as "Vacation-interval" hotels. Timeshare hotels are where the guests who purchase the ownership of accommodations for a specific period. These owners may also have the unit rented out by the management company that operates the hotel.

- Casino Hotels: Hotels with gambling facilities are called casino hotels.

- Conference and Convention Centres: These type of hotels focus on meeting and conferences and overnight accommodation for meeting attendees. They also provide video conferencing facility, audio visual equipment, business services, flexible seating arrangements, flipchart etc. These hotels mostly located outside the metropolitan areas and have facilities like golf, swimming pools, tennis courts, fitness centres, spas etc.

- Independent/Single Owner Hotels: They do not have identifiable ownership or management affiliation with other properties. Example for the same would be family owned and operated hotel that is not following any corporate policies or procedures.

- Chain Hotels: Hotels which are part of a hotel chain and these kind of ownership usually imposes certain minimum standards, rules, policies and procedures to restrict affiliate activities. In general the more centralised the organisation the stronger the control over the individual property.

Food and Beverage

Food and beverage is an important and wide sector of the hospitality industry. People always look forward to food whenever they travel. Moreover people have started visiting other regions for food tourism. People travelling to different countries like to taste local cuisines. It starts with food production and ends at food service on the eating tables, with storage and cooking steps resting in between. Food and beverage sector range from simple local restaurant to a fine dining restaurant. This sector also covers fast food joints, catering businesses, take away, and transport catering etc. Apart from different types of outlets most hotels operate multiple Food and beverage outlets, products and services such as bar, fine dining restaurants, coffee shop, banqueting, lounge etc. Broadly, Food and Beverage sector can be categorized on three basis:

- Quick-service Establishments: These are commercial foodservice restaurants that compete for customers who look for quick snacks, drinks, and meals. Typically, these are self-service eating outlets with few employees. Examples can be McDonald's, KFC, Subway, Pizza Hut, take away restaurants, vending machines etc.

- Catering Businesses: This category provides food and beverage catering services for any special occasion such as wedding party, birthday celebration, anniversary etc.

- Full-Service Restaurants: These are typical speciality restaurants which offer course meals and drinks. These full-service restaurants range from fine dining to casual dining to themed restaurants. These provide highly personalized services to the guest for instance assist the guest in sitting, in taking order, serve food at table.

There can be huge list if we start categorizing food service industry. Some of important types of FandB outlets are listed below:

Food and Beverage Sector

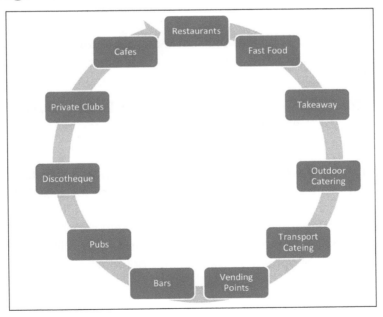

Travel and Tourism

Travel and tourism industry is a one of the important sector of the hospitality industry with lots of opportunities and scope across the globe. This is a complex industry made up of many different businesses, the common theme being that they provide products and services to people who are travelling from one place to another place. The most usually accepted definition of tourism is that provided by the World Tourism Organization: 'Tourism comprises the activities of persons travelling to and staying in places outside their usual environment for not more than one consecutive year for leisure, business and other purposes.' The travel and tourism industry is one of the biggest and fastest growing industries. According to World Tourism Organization that tourism is the fastest growing economic sector, bringing foreign exchange earnings to countries and creating jobs. Tourism is one of the largest and important sectors of external economic activities. This sector brings high growth and development, foreign currency, infrastructure development, new management and educational experience which positively contribute to the social and economic development of the country as a whole. It would not be wrong to say that travel and tourism is most important segment of the hospitality industry and others depend on it. Based on the UNWTO definition on tourism, tourism could be categorized as:

- Domestic Tourism: It is concerned with travelling within the country. It does not need a passport and visa or conversion of one currency into another. Domestic tourism may range from local excursion, regional trips to national level travels. Example: A person, who lives at Delhi, takes a business trip to Mumbai is considered domestic tourist.

- International Tourism: This kind of tourism is the movement of inbound and outbound tourists across the border where tourists are entering into a new country or by leaving their country of origin for experiencing new destinations. An international tourist crosses the boundaries of many countries, uses different currencies, faces different languages and meets different types of people. This tourism requires lot of legal formalities like visa, passport, and currency exchange. International tourism can further be divided in to two types:

  ○ Inbound Tourism: This type of tourism refers to condition where a tourist is entering into a country other than the origin country. For example if someone from Canada visit India he/she is inbound tourist for India, outbound tourist for Canada.

  ○ Outbound Tourism: This refers to tourist who is leaving his/her country of origin for another country. For example if someone from India visits America, he/she is outbound tourist for India and inbound tourist for America.

Travel and Tourism industry is a complex industry made up of many sectors. Travel and tourism sector consists of lodging sector, transportation sector, ancillary services, trade organizations and most important travel agencies and tour operators in a role as "middlemen", who combine tourism activities and work a link between customers and tourism service suppliers (airlines, hotels, restaurants, car hire companies and companies that operate reception services at destinations) and thereby promoting the development of the hospitality industry.

Sectors of Travel and Tourism

1. Attractions: A tourist attraction is a place of interest where tourists visit for its inherent or exhibited natural or cultural value, historical significance, natural or manmade beauty or offers leisure, adventure and amusement. Attraction towards a destination could be climate, culture, vegetation or scenery or specific to a location, such as a theatre performance, a museum or a waterfall. An attraction is a destination that pulls a person to it. Attractions are the main pull factor of tourist flow. Without these attractions, there would be no need for other tourist services. However,

the attractiveness of a destination vary from tourist to tourist. In general, tourist attractions can be categorized into two types: natural attractions and man-made attractions.

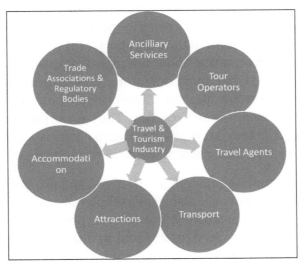

- Man-made attractions are physical structures or events.

- Natural attractions are physical phenomena deemed unusual and/or beautiful (weather, snow fall, hills, mountains, sea).

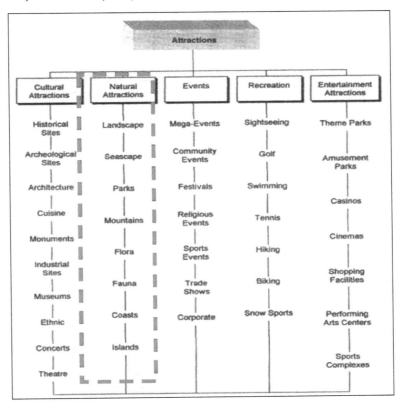

2. Travel Agents: Travel agents help the travellers to plan their trips usually during vacations. They provide assistance to tourists for planning and purchasing of tour components right from airline

tickets, car rentals to resort stays and attraction tickets. Tour operators assembles all the services together and make a tour package which includes everything from arrangement of appropriate transport to hotel stay and restaurant reservations to tours guides, theater reservations, and sports lessons. Most of the essential services are primarily provided by travel agents including transport (road, rail, air and water), accommodation, passport, and visa procuring facilities, foreign exchange and also guidance and information about the places of travel. Many travel agents sell packages on commission basis offered by inbound operators. Travel agent is a retailer and sells the tour package on behalf of wholesaler (tour operator). Travel agent work in horizontal integration with the purpose to gain maximum business and revenue. They act as intermediary between tour operator and customer for selling the tour packages. They earn commission for selling of tour packages of tour operators. They also act as local agent to confirm the services booked by tour operators.

3. Tour Operators: Tour operator links customers (tourists) and primary service providers (Hotels, Airline and Railways). Tour operators are also called wholesaler and they are the destination promoters. They purchase the services in advance from service providers and distribute them through the channel in an organized manner. Services are sold in different price tag to customers directly or through the middlemen (Travel Agent). Tour operators develop travel itinerary and deliver all the services which have been offered in the itinerary. They also customize the packages as per the requirements of customers. They operate in a system. They sign long-term contracts with all the principle suppliers such as air carriers, hotels, cruise liners, and other suppliers. Tour operators may own one or two component of tour (Transport, Hotel). They print brochures displaying each component of services. Package tours are sold through travel agencies or directly to customers.

Connections of Tour Operators

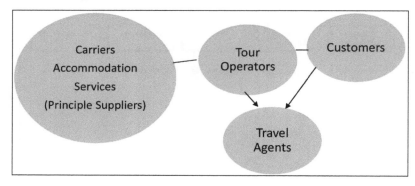

– Sales of goods/services.

→ Arranging a sale for commissions.

4. Ancillary Services: Ancillary services refer to organisations having a supporting role by offering related products and services. Travel agency sells holiday packages and services related to travel such as flight tickets, railway reservation, car rental and so on. But they offer wide range of other services to the travellers and earn extra revenue for example they offer insurance services to the travellers, foreign exchange, car hire, tour guiding, arrangement of theatre or event tickets. Travel companies earn commission on the sale of these services so ancillary services are an important source of extra income. There are a growing number of companies that specialise in offering ancillary services.

5. Transportation: Accessibility is key to success of travel and tourism industry. A transport system acts as a bridge between places of tourist origin and destination. It provides accessibility to its tourist places. Tourism planning is not possible in a region without development of transport system. The system consists of a network of routes or means of transport and the modes of transport. The modes of transport refer to aircraft, ships, steamers, cars, taxies, luxury coaches, buses and the railway trains. Taxies, cars, motor like auto-rickshaws, tonga, mopeds, bicycles and trams are particularly important as items of local transport. These help in carrying the travellers from airports, bus-stands or railway stations to hotels and tourist sites within a city. It is the capacity of a transport system which determines the size of tourist traffic, the increase or decrease in the pace of tourist flows. Beside this the provision of comfortable seats, reasonably high speeds and discounts and offers in air fares are other important criteria for selecting a particular mode of transport.

- Road: Private car, coach, taxi, bus, bicycle, recreational vehicles.

- Rail: Regional services, inter-city routes, high-speed services, steam trains.

- Water: Ferries, cruise ships, yachts.

- Air: Scheduled services, charter flights and air taxis.

6. Trade Associations: There are a number of travel trade associations like TAAI, ICAO, ASTA, IATA, and PATA, WTO, that are quite active in the Promotion of travel trade at global. Tour operation business is governed by government policies and programmes. This business involves handling for foreign tourists, receipt of foreign currency, processing of travel documents and operating in protected areas, including restricted travel areas. Thus, there is a need for travel trade associations to represent the interests and issues to the government or any international tourism or allied bodies. Trade associations are set up to represent the interests of companies operating in particular industry sectors and to make sure that the voice of the sector is heard. Many trade associations draw up codes of conduct which lay down the minimum standards under which member companies are expected to conduct their everyday business with customers and suppliers. An industry trade group is also known as a trade association or sector association. These are the organizations founded and funded by business enterprises to be united to work for the common cause and interest. An industry trade association participates in public relations activities such as advertising, education, political donations, lobbying and publishing. Its main focus is collaboration between companies and standardization of business. Associations conduct conferences, workshops or charitable events or conducting training programmes or distributing reading materials

for creation of human resources. Regulatory bodies exist to make sure that all travel and tourism operators serve the travelling public safety fairly and efficiently. They are found at different levels:

- Global Level: ICAO (International Civil Aviation Organization) and IATO (International Air Transport Organization regulate international air transport services are travel and tourism trade organization who work for promotion and growth of this sector at global level.

- National: IATO, TAAI and FHRAI are national trade organizations who work for the promotion of travel tourism and hospitality trade.

- Local: The local authorities carry out inspections on matters such as restaurants and other food premises, trading standards and inspections of hotels to establish the adequate facilities at destination.

Features/Characteristics/Nature of Hospitality Industry

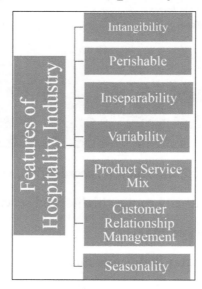

1. Intangibility: Products are tangible and Services are intangible in nature. Hospitality products are services which are intangible in nature. Intangibility is often used to describe the services that cannot be seen, tasted or touched. A service is made and delivered on spot and hence it cannot be measured as easily as a tangible product. We cannot taste the food in a restaurant before we place an order. First we have to order for it and then we expect that it is good in taste. Thus, unlike products, services cannot be touched or felt beforehand. They have to be first ordered and then they become tangible. Basically hospitality products are fundamentally experiences. Besides this intangibility implies that buyers are not sure about the experience they are going to get after consumption of services. That is why consumers ask for detailed information regarding the hospitality product before purchase. Service providers need to focus on each element of the product they offer to their consumers. As they are selling dreams to their consumers. And if these dreams are not fulfilled it will result in poor experience or dissatisfaction. For example – if consumer have paid for an online room booking but he/she has no idea how her/his stay will be. At best, she/he rely on the promise of the hotel that the stay will be an experience to remember. But again, there is nothing tangible about that promise.

2. Perishable/Limited life span: One of the crucial factors/problems faced by marketers is the perishability factor in services marketing. Perishability is one of the most important characteristics of the hospitality industry. The products/services in the hospitality industry are consumed as they are produced. Hotel rooms and air craft seats cannot be warehoused for futures sales. When a hotel room is not booked tonight, it can't be stored today and sold tomorrow. Once the train left the station, unused capacity cannot be sold afterwards for same time period. Hospitality products cannot be stored so, if not consumed they are waste.

3. Inseparability: Products are usually created, stored, purchased and then used, while the hospitality products are purchased first and then produced and consumed simultaneously, at the same place and time. Most travel products are first sold and the produced and consumed at the same time. This is an aspect which clearly sets tourism apart from tangible products. When you buy a new computer it is produced and shipped before you see it on the website or at the retailer's premise. The consumption of that computer – using it – takes place after purchase at your home. You cannot take the hotel room home – only the small bottles of shampoo and toothpaste. And you cannot enjoy the alpine sleigh ride in your living room. Tourism products can only be consumed at the supplier's premise. This implies that services cannot be separated from their providers and, therefore, consumers have to travel to the location of the product, not vice versa.

4. Variability: Hospitality product/services vary from hotel to hotel, time to time as each service is unique. It is onetime generated, rendered and consumed and can never be exactly repeated as the point in time, location, circumstances, conditions. The quality of the product may vary greatly, depending on who provides them and when, where, and how. It happens when the quality of services varies due to that provides them. When there is less number of guests, services are more specific and polite. If there is large number of guests, service provider tend to be busy and might lose some service to the guests. Buyers often give their feedback to others about the service provider. Sometimes two buyers give different feedbacks about the same product consumed by them due to variability.

5. Product-Service Mix: In hospitality industry, customers consume mixture of products and services. For example, one who dines in a restaurant will not only pay for the food and drinks but the services provided by the servers. The bill has covered both tangible and intangible experience. Tangible features, for example, a steak as the main course, a glass of drink, well groomed service staff and decoration of the restaurant. Intangible features such as a comfortable dining atmosphere or the friendly attitude of staff. A successful hospitality business not only delivers its products and services to their customer but also takes care of delivery. The qualities of staff and the way they deliver the service are important than the tangible products in making a hospitality experience satisfactory or unsatisfactory. Hence, the two features can contribute to the total experience in the service delivery process.

6. Customer Relationship Management: Building strong relationship with customer is important for their retention within the hospitality industry. The hospitality industry highly depends on repeated customers for survival. For generating stable revenues building long term relationship with customers can benefit the organizations regardless of the fluctuation in the demand. Not only has this customer relationship helped in strengthen the brand reputation through positive word-of-mouth through repeated customers. In order to develop brand loyalty different methods are currently applied by the lodging and food service sectors, such as membership programmes which give privileges and incentives to frequent customers Such as Marriott hotel rewards.

7. Seasonality: The hotel industry is characterized by seasonality, which plays a major role in acquiring the customers or determining the consumer behavior. Customer demand and expectations fluctuate according to seasons which are categorized as Low/lean and High/Peak. The peak season attracts more tourists than other seasons and its recurrence has resulted to perpetual trends in the hotel industry. In lean seasons consumer demand is very low. Due to fluctuations in demand during the off-season, operators are often challenged to manage their revenues. Hence it becomes essential for hotel operators to understand the seasonality of the regions, so that they can run their operations efficiently by for instance upgrading their infrastructure and facilities well in advance.

Classification of Hotels

Classification on the basis of Clientele and Location

A hotel may target many markets and can be classified according to the market or Clientele and Location they attempt to attract and serve. The most common types of properties based on these criteria include:

- Commercial,
- Airport,
- Residential,
- Resort,
- Timeshare,
- Bed and Breakfast,
- Casino,
- Conference Center,
- Convention Hotels,
- Floating Hotels.

Commercial Hotels

Commercial hotels are situated in the heart of the city. Mostly the businessmen or commercial executives patronize these hotels. Guest facilities at these hotels are – complimentary newspaper, color TV with cable, E-mail, fax connection, car rental, airport pick up, coffee shop, bar, specialty restaurant, swimming pool, health club, room service, concierge, business center, conference room, etc. length of stay in these hotels are from one day to few days.

Airport Hotels

These hotels are situated near the airport and are frequented by businessmen, airline passengers, layover passengers, crew members, etc. The facilities provided are similar to that of commercial hotels but the only difference is that airport pick up is provided from the hotel to the airport and vice versa. The length of stay in these hotels is from few hours to few days.

Residential Hotels

These hotels provide long term or permanent accommodation. Advance rent is collected while other charges are billed weekly. There may be a restaurant serving all types of cuisine and there will be laundry service. These hotels normally work on the European plan. Recently these types of hotels are converted into cooperative hotels or condominiums. The length of stay is from a week to one or more months.

Residence Inn by Marriott Vancouver Downtown.

Resort

A resort may be located in the mountains, on an island, or in some other location away from the crowded areas. Most of the resort hotels provide extensive food and beverage, valet, and room service for the vacationers. These hotels also provide special activities such as golf, tennis, horseback riding, nature hikes, sailing, skiing, swimming, and dancing, etc. resorts also try to be a destination within a destination by providing a wide range of services, facilities, and activities giving guests with many choices. A more leisurely, relaxed atmosphere distinguishes most resort hotels from their commercial counterparts. The length of stay is for one week or more.

Patong Resort Hotel, Patong, Phuket, Thailand.

Casino Hotels

Hotels with gambling facilities are casino hotels. Although the guest rooms and FandB operations may be quite luxurious, their function is secondary and supportive of casino operations. Similar to resort hotels these hotels also cater to leisure and vacation travellers. These hotels attract guests by promoting gambling. A recent trend in casino hotels now days is to provide a broad range of entertainment opportunities, spas, golf, tennis court. These hotels also have specialty restaurants. The length of stay is one week or more.

California Hotel and Casino, 12 East Ogden Avenue 89101 Las Vegas USA.

Conference Center and Convention Center

Most of the hotels provide meeting space and they also offer overnight accommodations and because meetings are their focal point these centers place great emphasis on providing all services and equipment necessary to ensure the success of a meeting – technical production assistance, high-quality audio visual equipment, business center, flipchart, display chart and so forth. These centers also provide extensive leisure facilities like a golf course, swimming pool, tennis court, fitness center, jogging track etc. Guest amenities may not be plentiful at conference centers since these centers concentrate more on fulfilling the needs of meeting planners and organizers then on meeting the needs of program attendees.

Convention Hotels

Convention Hotels are another segment of the lodging industry that has grown significantly in recent years. These hotels have 50,000 sq. feet or more of exhibit hall space plus ballroom and assortment of meeting rooms. These hotels also have sufficient no. of guestrooms to accommodate all the attendees of most conventions. These hotels are primarily directed towards business travellers and offer business services such as secretarial assistance, language translator, fax machines, computer room, teleconference, etc. convention hotels usually attract the convention market from the state, national and international associations and other corporate houses.

Timeshare and Condominium Hotels

Timeshare hotels are referred to as vacation ownership hotels. The concept is that for a set period which may be one week or more in a year the person gets the right to enjoy the stay and other facilities and services in an apartment are any other type of lodging in a tourist complex. It is like an advanced purchase of time in holiday accommodation. Here the purchaser has to pay a one-time capital sum and then an annual contribution towards the maintenance of the property. The fee usually covers services such as cleaning and maintenance of apartment and public areas, electricity, gas, water, etc. Avalon resorts, Sterling resorts, Mahindra holding, etc. are the few time-share hotels.

Condominiums involve joint ownership of a complex. Each owner has the full benefit of a unit and shares the cost that is common to the entire complex such as taxes, maintenance, upkeep of the building, etc. each owner can occupy or sell his unit independently but is obliged under the terms of a contract to contribute towards the pool of common facilities and services. The owner can enjoy recreational exclusive to the complex and the management looks after the unit in the absence of the owner and if permitted by the owner let it out to provide income to him.

Bed and Breakfast Hotels

These hotels are houses with a few rooms converted to the guest rooms. The owner lives on the premises and is responsible for looking after the guest, in these hotels only breakfast is served and meeting rooms, laundry, lunch and dinner, and recreational facilities are offered in these hotels, however, some hotels do offer limited food service.

BandB Hôtel Paris Malakoff, France.

Supplementary Accommodation

It consists of all types of accommodations other than the convention type; it may be described as premises that provide accommodation but not the other services which is provided by the hotels. The main distinctive features of supplementary accommodations are:

- Standard of comfort is modest as compared to that of a hotel.

- They can sell accommodation at a very low price.

- There is an informal atmosphere and freedom regarding dress code.

Supplementary accommodation plays a very important role in the total available tourist accommodation in a country; it caters to both the international and domestic tourist traffic. Types of supplementary accommodations are:

- Dharamshalas or sarai.

- Dak bungalows.

- Youth hostel.

- Dormitories.

- Sanatoria.

- Paying guest accommodation.

- Tourist bungalow etc.

Floating Hotels

As the name implies these hotels are established on luxury liners or ships. These are generally located on river, sea or oceans. On cruise ships, rooms are generally small and all furniture is fixed down. It generally caters to the long-stay guests. It is a complete hotel in itself consisting of all facilities as provided by any hotel on land. It not only provides accommodation but other necessary facilities and services like food and beverage, recreational facilities, swimming pools, etc. Example: AB Celestial Mumbai first floating hotel.

Boatels

A houseboat hotel is referred to as boatels. The Houseboats of Kashmir and Kettuvallam of Kerala are houseboats. which offer luxurious accommodation to travellers. Besides this, all other necessary facilities are taken care of such as food and beverage, etc.

A Houseboat.

Rotels

These novel variants are hotels on the wheel. Our very own "Palace on Wheels" and "Deccan

Odyssey" are the trains providing a luxurious hotel atmosphere. Their interior is done like a hotel room. They are normally used by a small group of travellers. They are costly and hence cater to elite guests providing an elaborate menu and other services to the occupants.

Motel

The term motel has been derived from the word 'motor'. They are located primarily on highways, they provide lodging to highway travellers and also provide ample parking space. The length of stay is usually overnight. These hotels are generally small in terms of the number of rooms.

Classification on the basis of Star

It is the most widely accepted system of rating hotels. The hotel industry follows a star rating system which indicates the number and standard of facilities offered by the hotel. The classification of hotels is done by a central government committee called Hotel Restaurant Approval Classification Committee (HRACC) which inspects hotels for the facilities and services they provide. Different types of hotels according to star classification are:

- 1 Star: These hotels are generally small in size and independently owned. They have a limited range of facilities and the number of restaurants is limited. Basic standard of cleanliness, maintenance and comfort are maintained.

- 2 Star: These hotels are small to medium in size and offer more facilities than 1-star hotels. Standards of cleanliness and comfort are maintained. The reception and other staff have a more professional attitude.

- 3 Star: These hotels are of medium size. Reception and public areas are more spacious, and the restaurants normally cater to non-hotel guests. All rooms have a good standard of comfort and facilities such as room service are provided.

- 4 Star: These hotels are large in size and offer a degree of luxury and equipment in every area of the hotel. The bedrooms offer more space in comparison to lower star hotels. Other features include business centers, meeting rooms, 24 hours room service and laundry etc.

- 5 Star: These hotels are very large in size and offer spacious and luxurious rooms which match the best international standards. The interior designing is very impressive in terms of quality, attention to detail, comfort and elegance. The staff is very knowledgeable in terms of customer care and efficiency.

Different types of hotels.

Classification on the basis of Size

Classification on the basis of size refers to the number of rooms (bed capacity) and should not be confused with the building height, or the area of the property, or the gross sales, etc. The term number of rooms refers to the lettable rooms and does not include those rooms which are convened for other use such as for manager, housekeeper, accounts, etc. and rooms on the ground floor and basement which are generally used for offices, rentals, support services or other operational facilities leased for businesses and associations. Usually, the distribution is:

- A hotel of 25 rooms or less is called a small hotel.

Les Fermes des Petites Frasses, Megève France is the most trending small hotel worldwide.

- One with 26 to 99 rooms is an average hotel.

Castello Banfi – Il Borgo, Poggio alle Mura, Montalcino, Italy.

- From 100 to 299 rooms is called as above average.

Hyatt Regency, Riyadh, Saudi Arabia, contains 261 rooms.

- A hotel of more than 300 rooms is classified as a large hotel.

Located in the Genting Highlands of Malaysia, the First World Hotel is the largest hotel in the world with 7,351 rooms between two towers.

Classification on the basis of Management and Affiliation

Various types of hotels on the basis of Affiliation and Management are:

- Independent hotel.
- Chain hotels.
- Management contract hotels.
- Franchising and referral groups.

Independent Hotel

These are family-owned and operated hotels that are not required to confirm any policy or procedure, they also do not need to adhere to a particular image and can offer a level of service geared towards attracting a specific target market and can quickly adapt to changing market condition. However, these hotels do not enjoy the advantage of volume purchase, advertising exposure, or management insight and consultancy power of a chain hotel.

Chain Hotel

Chain hotel ownership can take a number of forms. Depending on the association that the chain organization has with each property. These hotels usually impose certain minimum standards, rules, policies, and procedures, which is to be followed by other properties of the same chain. These hotels are usually classified as operating a management contract or as a franchise or referral group.

Marriott International, a renounced hotel chain worldwide.

Management Contract Hotel

These hotels are the properties owned by other entities. Under this type of contract, the owner or developer usually retains the financial and legal responsibility for the property, the management company pays its expenses and in turn, receives an agreed-upon fee from the owner or developer and the remaining cash goes to the owner who also pays for debts, insurance, taxes.

Franchising and Referral Group

Franchising is simply a method of distribution whereby one entity that has developed a particular pattern or format for doing business. The franchiser usually provides a strong brand name, national and international central reservation system, management training programs, advanced technology, and central purchasing services.

Referral groups consist of independent hotels, which have joined together for some common purpose. While each property in the referral system is the same but there is no similarity in the quality of service and guest expectations. Hotels within this group refer their guests to other affiliated hotels. With this kind of approach, a hotel may gain a much greater level of exposure.

Classification on the basis of Range of Service

- World class service: These are also called luxury/Five Start hotels; they target top business executives, entertainment celebrities, high- ranking political figures, and wealthy clientele as their primary markets. They provide upscale restaurants and lounges, Valet, concierge services and also private dining facilities.

- Mid-Range Service: Hotels offering mid-range or otherwise 3 to 4-star hotels service appeal the largest segment of the travelling public. This kind of hotels does not provide elaborate service and have an adequate staffing. They also provide uniformed service, food and beverage room service, in-room entertainments and also Wi-Fi etc.

- Budget/Limited Service: These hotels provide clean, comfortable, safe, inexpensive rooms and meet the basic need of guests. Budget hotels appeal primarily to budget-minded travellers who want a room with minimum services and amenities required for the comfortable stay, without unnecessary paying additional cost for costly services.

Classification on the basis of Ownership

- Proprietary Ownership/Independent Hotel: Owners' hotel Proprietary owner ship is the direct ownership of one or more properties by a person or company. Small lodging properties are owned by family and large properties are owned by major international hotel companies. No affiliations or contract with other property, No tie up with other hotels. Owner has independent control. Profit goes to the owner. Quickly respond to market changes. Work with limited finances.

- Management Contracted Hotels: Management by others and properties owned by individuals or partners, operated by external professional organization for management fee.

  ○ Adv: International recognitions, operating systems, training program, marketing, international expertise, profitable operations, advertisement, reservation system, staff.

- Chain Hotel: A group of hotels that are owned or managed by one company is called chain hotel.

  ○ Adv: Large central organization providing central reservation system, management aids, financial strength, expertise, manpower, specialties, promotions.

- Franchise Hotels/Affiliated: It is the authorization given by a company to another company or individual to sell its unique products and services and use its trademark according to the guidelines given by the former, for a specified time and at a specified place. Franchise owner (franchisor) grant another hotel (franchisee) the right use its methods and system, technical services, marketing trademark, signs etc. for fees.

  ○ Adv: Opening assistance-architectural, interior designs, Systems and procedure, Staff training, Financial assistance, Advertising and global marketing, Central reservation and Central purchase

- Referral Chain: A referral chain is made up of independently owned and operated hotel and provides shared advertisement, joint reservation system and standardized quality. Virtually there is no shared management or financial functions.

- Time Share/Vacation Ownership/Holiday Ownership: Each room is owned by several people for different time period. Each owner gets a stay of specific period for a number of years. One time purchase is made by paying purchase price and payment of a yearly maintenance fee. Generally located at dream sites like beaches, hill, waterfall etc.

  ○ Adv: Long term accommodation, comfort homes, economical, good location, international exchange possible.

- Condominium: Joint ownership of a complex. Type of accommodation where owner of a room or an apartment in a complex, of several such accommodations, furnishes it and informs the management of the times when he will be using it. He permits to rent out the apartments at other times and the rent goes to the owner. The owner pays the monthly maintenance fee.

Classification on the basis of Plan Offered

- European Plan: It is a plan where only the lodging that is bed is offered. Thus the charges are made for lodging facilities only. The guest is free to take or not to take teas, breakfast, and meals in the hotel. He has a choice of eating out at any other good restaurant. The guest is booked to pay for lodging only and is charged separately for all other things or services he enjoys or consumes. This system is generally followed by youth hostels or hotels which are situated in metropolitan cities. Most of the hotels are being run on European plan. Almost all the public sector hotels are run on this basis.

- Continental Plan: In the case of continental plan, bed and breakfast are included in the tariff charges. Thus bed is offered along with breakfast and the guest is, however, free to take his meal and tea as he likes. Thus the guest tariff includes lodging and 'bed and breakfast' and for other he is separately billed.

- American Plan: Hotel where American plan is prevalent, boarding and lodging is provided in the charge. The tariff fixed includes board and lodging. It is an all-inclusive full board tariff. Accommodation and three meals daily are included in the price of the room. It includes bed, breakfast and two principal meals and evening tea. It does not include early morning tea or coffee after lunch, or dinner. The needs are usually 'table d'hôte menu'. It is also known as 'full pension'. This analysis is mostly used at those tourist resorts, which are not situated in big cities.

- Modified American Plan: The tourists mostly prefer this plan, as it is comparatively more flexible. It is offered in most of the good hotels and is normally by arrangement. It includes hotel accommodation, breakfast and either lunch or dinner in the price of the room. Thus, in this type of accommodation bed and breakfast and along with it one principal meal, lunch or dinner at the discretion of the guest is also included. It generally includes continental breakfast and either 'table d'hôte lunch or dinner in the room rates. It is also known as 'demi-pension'. However, and the western style hotels operating which cater the foreign tourists, operates on the American plan.

Computers and Front Office

Every organisation requires computers to run its operations smoothly and hotels are not an exception. And hotels working world over have been revolutionized by new innovations in information technology and adoption of computers. Computers have long been a part of hotel industry offering a way organized data in doing business transactions. Front office is the core back bone of the hotel where computers are well equipped with dedicated software called property management system. Computer applications are central to front office operations in today's modern hotels. For new properties, computers are standard pieces of equipment; for existing hotels, computers are being integrated into everyday operations to assist in providing hospitality to guests. Computer applications include routinely processing reservations as well as handling registrations, guest charges, guest checkout, and the night audit. Interfacing, electronic sharing of data, of hotel departments such as food and beverage and the gift shop through point-of-sale, an outlet in the hotel that generates income (restaurant, gift shop, spa, garage); maintenance through monitoring of energy and heating and cooling systems.

The positioning of the hardware at workstations is based on the same work flow analysis used for any new process or equipment. Considering the needs of the guest (who will be the end user), the employee who will operate the equipment, and the other staff who will want access to information. The information one has gained from the needs analysis will assist in explaining particular needs to the computer consultants who will install the required property management system. The installations of the electronic cables that connect all of the hardware need also to be analyzed. Installation and replacement of cables that run through walls and floors can be costly for a hotel property. The requirement for air-conditioned atmospheres for proper computer functioning should also be investigated; in guest service areas, this may not present a problem, but in other areas, it may pose difficulties. Computer system – consists of 3 interrelated and interdependent components namely:

- Hardware
- Software
- Users

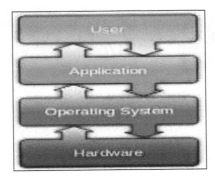

Computer Application in Front Office Operations – replacing manual, mechanical work or use of electric devices.

Choosing Hardware

Choosing hardware for a PMS is not as difficult as choosing software. Today most available hardware is compatible with standard computer operating systems (such as Microsoft Windows). This consideration is essential because most software programs are written to run on these standard operating systems. Hence one must choose hardware based on its ability to handle the software that needs to be checked with the hardware vendor.

Other technology factors to consider include the following working concepts:

- Processor speed: It helps to know, how fast a central processing unit (CPU) makes calculations per second; expressed in MHz (the abbreviation for "megahertz").
- Disk drive: It's a place in the computer where data is stored or read; hard or floppy—3½-inch versus Zip drive.
- Megabyte: 1,024 kilobytes of formatted capacity.
- Gigabyte: 1,024 megabytes of formatted capacity.

- Access time: The amount of time required for a processor to retrieve information from the hard drive; recorded in milliseconds.

- Internet: A network of computer systems that share information over high-speed electronic connections.

- I/O ports (input/output devices): Keyboards, monitors, modems, mouse, joystick, light pen, printers, and track balls.

- Monitor: It's a television screen with color or monochrome capacity to view input and output data, control column width and line length of display, adjust height of character display, and allow visual control.

Adoption of Computers in Front Office

The steps involved in selection of a Property Management System are:

Step 1: Identification of Need

Firstly an analysis is done by hotel operators/management to determine whether there is a need of computerized system or not. The following steps are followed in this process:

- Selection of a team is done, comprising the representation from all the departments at all levels from all the shifts to analyze the needs.

- Analyze the flow of guests that could be done by an analysis of the guest cycle.

- Analyze the flow of information from other departments to the front office e.g. billing information, room status information etc.

- Analyze the administrative paper work produced in other departments.

- Evaluate the needs that have been identified in terms of importance.

- Combine the needs to determine the desired applications.

Step 2: Software Selection

- Today, software is available in modules to cater to different areas in a hotel.

- Based on requirement, a hotel may go in for the entire PMS or parts thereof.

- Proper software selection is very important, as it involves a, heavy investment.

- Configured or customized as per the need of the hotel.

Step 3: Hardware Selection

- The hardware should be selected to run the needed software. The basic factors to consider here are the Processor speed, Disc drives, I/O Port for connecting peripheral devices & for networking, Monitors/touch screens, Keyboards, Printers, Modems and Supplies: paper, forms, ribbons, ink, toner, cartridge, floppies, DAT, CD-RW etc.

The other factors to be kept on mind while selecting the hardware are:

- Positioning of hardware: Based on the workflow analysis done during needs analysis.

- Does it benefit the guest, who will operate it, who all will require access to the system at that position?

- Climatic condition: Whether air-conditioning required/not especially in back-of-the-house areas.

- Ergonomics: Psychological & physiological effect of computers on people.

Step 4: Other Considerations

- Vendor Claims: Before selecting a PMS, claims made by the supplier need to be enquired. That could be done by inquiring about the product from the current users of the same; whether they are satisfied using the system, problems faced by them in using the system.

- Installation plans: Proper planning of installation is essential for maintaining guest services & one must have a complete plan laid out for installation of hardware & cabling in different areas of the hotel; also, who shall be installing the hardware & who shall be installing cables.

- Training: One needs to enquire about the classroom & on-the-job training provided by vendor or not.

- Back-up power sources: Provision of UPS.

- Maintenance agreement: The cost of repair and replacement of hardware & software should be known.

Step 5: Financial Considerations

- The decision regarding purchase or rental of a PMS needs to be taken because of heavy investment that could tie-up the cash flow of an organization.

- And if the cost benefits are not realistically projected, profits may difficultly to be achieved.

- Analyze the savings in terms of overtime paid to the employees, losses due to late charges, cost of marketing database collection, wastage of energy.

- Advantages of outright purchase, discount for full payment in cash, finance charges, depreciation.

- Advantages of lease: Continuance of cash flow, application of lease payments to purchase price, tax advantages of leasing etc.

Computer Application in Front Office

The Computers are used in various sections of Front Office in a Five Star Hotel from pre arrival to the post departure of the guests in following ways:

- Reservations:
  - Guest data,
  - Room inventory,
  - Deposits,
  - Special requests,
  - Blocking,
  - Arrivals,
  - Departures,
  - VIP,
  - Projected occupancy,
  - Travel agents,
  - Guest messages,
  - Reports.
- Registration:
  - Reservations,
  - Guest Data,
  - Room inventory,
  - Room status,
  - Security,
  - Reports,

- Self-check-in.
- Room status:
  - Room inventory,
  - Availability,
  - Reports.
- Posting:
  - Point of sale,
  - Room,
  - Tax,
  - Transfer,
  - Adjustments,
  - Paid out,
  - Miscellaneous charges,
  - Phone,
  - Display folio,
  - Reports.
- Call Accounting:
  - Guest information,
  - Employee information,
  - Post charges,
  - Messages,
  - Wake-up calls,
  - Reports.
- Checkout:
  - Folio,
  - Adjustments,
  - Cashier,
  - Back office transfer,

- ◦ Reports,
- ◦ Guest History.
- • Night Audit:
  - ◦ Guest charges,
  - ◦ Department totals,
  - ◦ City ledger,
  - ◦ Cashier,
  - ◦ Financial reports,
  - ◦ Housekeeping.
- • Inquiries Reports:
  - ◦ Reservations,
  - ◦ Registrations,
  - ◦ Checkouts,
  - ◦ Housekeeping,
  - ◦ Credit balances.
- • Back Office:
  - ◦ Accounts payable,
  - ◦ Accounts receivable,
  - ◦ Payroll,
  - ◦ Budgets,
  - ◦ General Ledger.

Reservations

The reservations module in computers consists of subsystems that can receive individual guest or group data, check a guest's booking request against a data bank of available rooms, and store this information for future usage. The guest data are received through a personal phone call or through another computer in the referral system. All of the possibilities or room types and locations, room rates, and special requests can be matched with the existing room inventories. This information can be stored for up to 52 weeks (or more) in most systems.

Information concerning guarantees with credit cards or confirmed reservations is captured at time. Details on deposits, blocking, times of arrival and departure, VIP guest lists, projected occupancies and reports on these reservation functions assist the front office manager. The guest who is checking out of the Ritz-Carlton, Los Angeles, and wants to make a reservation at the Ritz-Carlton, Florida for that evening can have the reservation confirmed within seconds. The guest information already available in the data bank, and through electronic transmissions, the request is verified (via a check of the existing room inventories held in the data bank for the Ritz-Carlton, Florida) by a central computer. Similar procedures can be followed by other referral agencies.

Registration

Computerized guest registration modules have greatly improved the check-in process. Because information is already been captured at the time of reservation, hence less time is required for registration. The front desk clerk need only verify the guest's request for room type, location, and rate with room inventory and room status. Similarly provisions for walk-in guests without reservations are even handled. Method of payment is also established easily. The hard-plastic key can be issued after the security module has changed the entrance code for the room. The guest registration procedure can also be completed by the self-check in process, a procedure that requires the guest to insert a credit card having a magnetic stripe containing personal and financial data into a self-check-in terminal and answer simple questions concerning the guest stay.

Call-accounting

The call-accounting module of a property management system automatically posts telephone charges and a predetermined markup to a guest's folio. The individual subscriber to the telephone system (the lodging property) can charge a service fee for any local or long-distance call. The hotel can now use the telephone system to generate profit rather than to simply supply service to the guest. Further, the ability to make a profit through adding service charges, combined with the increased frequency and accuracy of electronic posting, has made the call-accounting option very desirable.

Checkout

The PMS has played a commendable job during checkout procedure. The inconvenience of guest checkout (long lines, disputes over charges) is greatly reduced with the PMS checkout feature, which prints out an accurate, neat, and complete guest folio within seconds. Disputes over guest charges still occur at the time of checkout, but not as often. The posting of a long-distance telephone call to room 201 instead of room 209 is less likely to occur with a PMS, because the PMS interfaces with the call- accounting system and the phone charge cab are automatically posted to the guest's electronic folio. Efficiency at time of checkout is also improved when the desk clerk retrieves a hardcopy of the folio and presents it for review to the guest. The PMS monitors already indicated method of payment made by guest at check-in, an imprint of the credit card, the floor limit, an amount of credit allowed by the credit-card agency, and house limit and an amount of credit allowed by the hotel. These controls help to avoid high debit balances; the amount of money the guest owes the hotel. Last-minute purchases of products or services are automatically posted at the point-of-sale terminals.

Night Audit

The night auditor acts as a desk clerk and posts the room and tax charges, the night auditor even balances the guest transactions of the day. To extend credit to guests, debits and credits, the amount of money the hotel owes the guests, must be balanced on a daily basis. The debits originating from the various departments must be checked against the totals posted to the various guest folios. The credits, in the form of guest payments, must be accounted for by reviewing the guests' outstanding balances.

Inquiries/Reports

The inquiries/reports feature of the property management system allows management to retrieve operating or financial information at any time. The front office manager may want to check the number of available rooms in the room inventory for a particular night, the status of the number of guests to be checked in, the number of guests to be checked out for the day, the current room status from the housekeeping department, or the outstanding balance report, a listing of guests' folio balances. These reports can be produced easily on a PMS. The inquiries/reports feature of the PMS enables management to maintain current view of operations and finances.

Back Office

The hotel's accounting office, known as the back office, uses the accounting module of a property management system, which assists in the overall financial management of the hotel. PMS simplifies the accounting processes. These include: the labor-intensive posting procedure of accounts payable, which is the amount of money the hotel owes vendors; the transfer of accounts receivable, which is the amount of money owed to the hotel.

Different Systems used in Front Office by Hotels

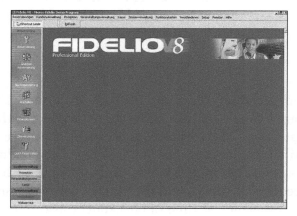

FIDELIO is one of the world's bestselling front office systems, and it is the system of choice for many hotels like Hilton International, Inter Continental, Mandarin Oriental, Forte and many other chains and independents around the globe. Fidelio was able to create the original electronic room rack. Complete, graphical plan illustrations of each floor allow front office staff to monitor and control the occupancy of every room in the building. Using a system of twelve different colour codes, the status of each room is visible at a glance – either currently, or at some future date. Yellow indicates a room is "clean and vacant", blue is "dirty and arrival expected", and so on. Reservations data can also be shown in tabulated form to give an overall occupancy picture for any specified day. For group bookings, from the most complex convention to airline allotments, the group and block management functions handle it all. Master billing, split rates, staggered arrivals, package plans, group history, room type control, block forecasts and traces – they all help to optimize group business, without the time consuming paperwork. As well as handling room management, FIDELIO Front Office maintains all guests' accounts, and offers numerous other facilities such as mailing, word processing, and customized printout of confirmation letters, guest messages and other documents.

Micros

Hotel Property Management Systems and Point of Sale Solutions

One of the oldest and leading software developers can help in operating a single boutique hotel or an international hotel chain, MICROS hotel property management systems are robust enough to handle all of the elements involved in hotel revenue management with the flexibility one needs for day-to-day operations. Point of sales systems integrate with the OPERA Enterprise solution, allowing to link Point of sale transactions, back office functions, and guest management capabilities in a single system. All of the systems are modular, so one can take the solutions required.

Host

The-Host Hospitality Management System will transform the way one manages hospitality business for good. It is powerful, feature-packed, user-friendly hotel management software that empowers staff to take complete control of inn keeping business - no matter the size. The software can handle from 300 room Hotels to small cozy Bed & Breakfast retreats. Moreover, onsite-training ensure that staffs have the tools and confidence to use the system to its absolute maximum. The-Host Hospitality Management System provides the following: Reservations, real time online web reservations, front desk, and back office, guest billing, reporting, point of sale and a lot more. Everything one would require as an hotelier, innkeeper or lodging provider. It is a business management system, not just a reservation system. The-Host not only successfully covers every aspect of conventional guest and property management systems, but goes beyond with features only associated with systems costing many times more.

Optima Property Management Systems

Optima PMS is a state of the art; Windows based Property Management System that incorporates the latest in advanced technology. It is designed to provide all the features of a sophisticated Front Office system linked with other computerized hotel applications on the same relational SQL database.

Optima PMS places all the vital information needed for optimum operation at the manager's fingertips. All information can be viewed on-line, printed in a large variety of reports or shown on graphs. Advanced icons and color-coding give the managers an excellent overview of all hotel operations and allow them to maintain precise management controls. It is a profitable marketing tool, as it captures a wide range of data needed to make the correct marketing analysis. Information analysis is simple, quick and precise, emphasizing revenues, budgets and yearly comparisons in combination with data of occupancy, segmentation and other guest information.

The Optima Property Management System enables maximum performance, utilizing the latest technology. Together with the use of a modern GUI it offers the ultimate system for any Front Desk. Optima is a most powerful and advanced Front Office system based on years of experience and on highly sophisticated development and focus teams, including superior hoteliers, engineers and front office specialists. These teams have researched and 'brainstormed' to meet the highest standards of the hospitality industry for the next century.

Advantages of Computer Applications in Front Office

- Data Storage.
- Guest History.
- Call Accounting.
- Express Check in and Check Out.
- Night Audit.
- Time Saving.
- Storing Of Guest Preference and Sharing with Chain Hotels.
- Less Paper Work.
- Better Coordination with Other Departments.
- Personalized Service.

Technological Advancements in Front Office

The computers have made the job of the front office employee very easy just by the click of a button the room reservations and room status can be checked by hotel front office employee. It has become easy to remember the guest choices and preferences who are regular visitors thus improving the quality and experience of service by the guest. In the recent years technological advancements have changed the way the front office works. Here are some of the technological advancements that have taken place in front office of a hotel.

The Cloud based PMS

The PMS of the hotel is such which has the interface of the cloud. It is easy to use and install and has many benefits like cost savings and increased guest satisfaction. When PMS and POS are integrated to the Cloud, It becomes easy for the staff of the hotel to do day to day operations directly from the tablet or a mobile devise. The service delivery of the guests are looked after at ease and at the place they want. Thus the service level of the hotel is elevated.

The Cloud PMS helps the hotel staff to check the room status, from a remote place. The front office employee can at sit in a cafeteria and do the bookings of the guest. They can also upgrade the guest rooms and check the VIP status of the hotel. The cloud helps the management to check the reports and performance from anywhere thus it helps the managers to be in-front of the guests more and interact with them rather than just sitting at the back office.

Mobile Device as Door Key

The information technology has advanced so much that everything is now available at your finger tips. Gone are those days when high end hotels used to give heavy metal key or electronic key cards to the guests to open their rooms. Now a days a simple mobile app can do the wonders of opening the lock of the door for you therefore it provides the guest with more security. Just by scanning the code on the door the lock of the guest room will get unlocked. Thus the guest feels more secure and they do not have the hassle of carrying the electronic key cards wherever they go as the guest room key is in their smart phone.

Service Automation

Due to the advanced of technology, travelers will make use of their mobile device as one of the platform for booking directly with the hotel. By the raising rate of the smart phones users and tablet, mobile may replace the importance of PCs in the future—according to the Forrester Research. The property management system of the hotel may need to be investigated on this field so to meet the demand of the customers. Many guests prefer to do their tasks themselves, thus self service is very much in today. A simple task like remote Check-in and Check-out, in room dining orders, housekeeping services are being made available on the guest mobile through different Apps. A wide range of services can be automated by the hotel for the guest, thereby freeing the staff of the hotel to perform other activities that will lead to guest satisfaction and will give them a totally different experience. Service automation has helped the guests save their time and have helped them to move directly to their rooms without standing on the long queue at the front desk.

Fixed-mobile Convergence

The in room phones that were used in the hotels are having very less role during the guests stay but the in room phone now a days is more of an interactive device for the guest. The guest just needs to pair his smart phone with the hotels interface and he would be able to tasks control of TV, Sound-system, Wakeup calls, laundry and other hotel services.

Location-Based Services

Imagine a situation that just by a click of the button you are able to locate all the employees of your hotel, this technology of now a day's being used by high end hotels wherein the management can keep a track of the effectiveness of the hotels employees. Location based services will help the management to understand the exact amount of staff required during a particular shift and it will also keep a tab on the leaves of the employees.

Tech Lounges

The guest lounges and business areas have become totally Wi-Fi enabled. The corporate world of today of very busy, an employee carries his office work even when they are travelling thus the access to internet has become a dire necessity now a days. Therefore the hotel lobbies and business centres have been transformed as a wireless hub where free Wi-Fi facilities are available. Number of guests when searching for a hotel room online keeps this as a criterion for selection of a hotel and in case any hotel is not offering the Wi-Fi services the room occupancy for such hotel is supposed to go down.

Tech-Enabled Meeting Spaces

The old concept of meeting spaces were just a collection of table and chairs but in the modern world this concept has become ineffective. The modern day business hubs have transformed themselves into a smart meeting room where along with sitting space multimedia services along with videoconferencing facilities is being made available to the guests. They provide limited catering disturbance during the long meeting and these rooms are highly advanced in technology and no require a dedicated engineer throughout the meeting hours. Along with it for larger gatherings the guests often demand these kind of services from the hotel thus the hotel should be ready with portable equipments so that the needs of the guest can be catered to.

Social Listening

A word of mouth can do wonders to the image of the hotel. Guests have a lot to say about their experience about the hotel but sometimes they don't say it directly, they take the help of social media. Social media has become an integral part of almost everybody's life, guests now a days share their experience along with pictures on social media thus social media has indirectly become a biggest mode of companies advertisement. Therefore the hotels have to give their best and have to provide excellent service to the guests as if in social media the image of a hotel starts going down, the hotel may loose on the business. Social media also helps the hotel to find out about the guest need, wants and complaints and further help the hotel to keep an eye on the competition.

Hotels are Offering Customized Experience via Technology

By the use of the technology the service delivered by the hotels can be customized even before checking in to the hotel. Just by sitting at the comfort of your room the guest needs to login to the user interface of the hotel and has to select the options available like room temperature, artwork, music selection etc. The guest when arrives at the hotel will get the exact services as was selected by him. Thus every guest can have a unique experience staying at the hotel as the hotels now days are looking forward to provide tailor made service options to the guest according to their needs and in return enhancing the service experience of the guest during the stay.

Front Desk Elimination

Imagine a hotel where there is no front desk at all how would it be, front desk free hotels have been a hot topic of discussing in the hospitality industry now a days. Since the technology has advanced so much that from the remote places the guest can do the front desk activities like check-in,

Check-out, Settling of bills etc. Thus the future hotels will be free from front desk and the guests can directly walk into their rooms. But the elimination of front desk means the elimination of the personal touch from the hotel front office area, since front desk serves the first point of contact between the guest and the hotel, therefore it helps the customer to get an idea of the hotel services and its brand image further in case of any problem the guest first calls the front desk, therefore if the front desk goes from the hotel so will go the personal touch from the hotel which in maximum number of times has been a necessary elements in the repeat guests.

Front Office: Functions and Organizational Structure

The reception area of a hotel which directly gets in touch with their customers or clients is known as the front office. The chapter closely examines the key functions of the front office such as function of reception and registration, function of concierge and function of bell desk, etc. It also discusses the organizational structure of the front office.

Front Desk is a very important department in the hotel, making direct contact with guests. The main function of this department is Reservation, Guest service, Check-in, Check-out, Telephone, Finance and Cashiering, Foreign Exchange, Room Assignment, Inquiry etc. The Front Office is also called the nerve centre of a hotel. It can be defined as a front of the housing department located around the foyer and the lobby area of a hospitality property. As this department is located around the foyer area of the hotel and is visible to the guests, patrons and visitors, they are collectively called "Front Office". Should guests have any problems or require to appreciate or comment, they would normally go directly to the Front Office, because it is convenient to contact and converse with other departments. Therefore, this department is the direct delegate to link the work and report the consequence to other departments. This department is one of the major operational and revenue-producing departments of the hotel which generates two-thirds of the revenue earned by a hotel from the sale of the guest rooms. It involves in providing valuable services to the guests during the entire guest cycle consisting of pre-arrival, arrival, occupancy and departure.

Importance of Front Office Department

Traditional Front Office functions include reservation, registration, room and rate assignment, guest services, room status, maintenance and settlement of the guest account, and creation of guest history records. The Front Office develops and maintains a comprehensive database of guest information, coordinates guest services, and ensures guest satisfaction. These functions are accomplished by personal in diverse areas of Front Office Department. The front office is also known as the face of the hotel. It is the first guest contact area and also the nerve centre of the hotel. All the activities and areas of the front office are geared towards supporting guest transaction and services. The operational function of the front office department:

- Guest Registration: Does all guest registration-related activities like Check-in, room assignment, welcoming, room rate etc.

- Guest Service: Fulfils any Guest Services related activities.

- Guest History and Records: Creates and maintains a guest profile, history, likes and dislikes, collect feedback etc.

- Guest Database: Develops and maintains a comprehensive database of guest information.

- Updates Room Status: Responsible to update the correct room status like CI, CO, DNCO, DND etc.

- Reservation: This section is responsible in registering the room reservation from various sources, with recordings, filing of reservation records, and revise on the appropriate time to make sure that guests would have their rooms upon entering the hotel.

- Postage and Parcels: This section is to facilitate guests pertaining to the posting of letters, telegrams, and parcels.

- Telephone: This section is to facilitate guests pertaining to the telephone both internally and externally, and to wake guests up in the morning upon request.

- Finance and Foreign Exchange: This section relates with the Accounting Department, through the collection from guests through their services, and also give the foreign exchange service.

- Inquiry: This section is to answer questions and inquiries of guests. Therefore, this section would have to be alert with all the movements of the hotel.

- Bell Desk and Concierge: Provide all services related to Bell desk and Concierge.

Staffing the Front Office Department

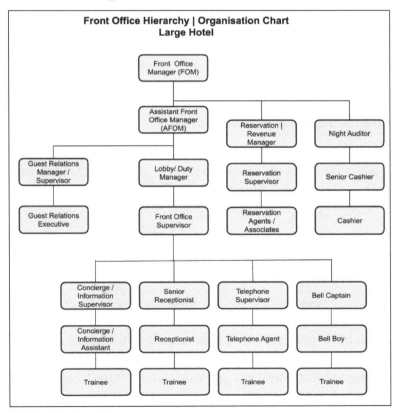

In order to carry out its mission, goals and objectives, every company shall build a formal structure depicting different hierarchy of management, supervision, and employee (staff) levels. This very structure is referred to as an organisation chart. Moreover, the organisation chart shows reporting relationships, the span of management, and staff/line functions. The organisation chart for the front office department differs as per the size of the hotel.

Typical Staff Positions under the Rooms Division Department

- Front Desk Agent: Registers guests, and maintains room availability information.

- Cashier: Maintains and settles guest folios, and properly checks out guests.

- Night Auditor: Controls the job of the accounts receivable clerk, and prepares daily reports to management (ex: Occupancy report and revenue report).

- Mail and Information Clerk: Takes messages, provides directions to guests, and maintains mail.

- Telephone Operator: Manages the switchboard and coordinates wake-up calls.

- Reservation Agent: Responds to reservation requests and creates reservation records.

- Uniformed Service Agent: Handles guest luggage, escorts guests to their rooms, and assists guests for any bit of information requested.

Functions of Front Office

The front office department in a hotel performs quite a few important functions. To achieve the operations of front office need to have a well-defined organizational structure. The organizational structure of the front office depends on many factors:

- Size of the Hotel: The size of hotel (number of rooms) will actually decide the staff requirements to achieve front office objectives in an effective and efficient way. The bigger the size of hotel the more specialised staff is required. On the other hand in smaller hotels less staff member may be able to perform a wide variety of duties.

- Standard of Service: Luxury hotels usually provide various products and services and more personalised services may be provided to guests and hence the requirement of more specialised staff would be required to perform such duties.

- Type of Guests: Every hotel has its own clientele and generally combination of various guests depending on the purpose of visit like business, recreation, religious purposes, etc. The needs of the guests even differ accordingly. A business client prefers less time to be spent on checking in and checking-out and it is quite possible they won't mind carrying their own luggage. And guests visiting for recreation will demand more luxurious and personalized services.

- Type of Hotel: The category of hotel on the basis of location even plays a vital role in number and specialisation of staff members. A resort may require limited staff members as the length of stay is more compared to a hotel situated on transit location. Such hotels on transit locations may require staff readily available at all times for arrivals and departures.

The front office can be divided in two major operations:

1. Front-of-the-House: Operations that take place in front of the guest is termed as front-of-the-house. It involves either direct interaction with the guest or being conducted in front of the guest. Activities like check-in and checkout take place in front of the house, wherein guest interacts with the hotel staff. Guests with prior reservation or walk-in's are handled directly by front office staff at the arrival. Sections of front office like car valet, bell desk, travel desk, reception, lobby, business center, concierge deal directly with guests as the requirement of procedures followed at various stages of guest cycle.

Front office is considered as the first and last section of guest interaction. The activities form luggage handling, reception, registration of guests, escorting a guest, providing information related to hotel and city, handling guest complaints, handling business center activities need direct interaction and are handled by front office staff and all these section and the interactions happen in the front of the guest. The staffs at the front-of-the-house need to have pleasant personality.

The role of front office staffs do not confined with only sale of rooms but even creating a lasting impression and further enhancing the brand image of the property are also important responsibilities of front office.

2. Back-of-the-House: The name suggests that these operations and activities do not take place in front of the guests. These operations do not require direct interaction with the guest. They act as ancillary sections, but are helpful in meeting objectives of front office operations. One of the important back-of-the-house responsibilities is taking the reservation of room for guest. The PMS systems nowadays keep the updated record of guests and such personal information of guests helps in customizing the product as per guest requirements. The other activity involves tracking of guest transaction and accounts. The financial transaction includes room rent, laundry, food and beverage, room service used by the guest during their stay with the hotel. The night auditor helps the back of the office department in the hotel in maintaining the guest accounts. Telephone is other section which is involved in taking care of telephone calls and directing them eventually. The coordination with other departments is also essential in the hotel for efficient functioning of hotel operations. The coordination with the departments such as housekeeping, maintenance, security is directly related with safety and security of the guest and also ensures comfortable stay to guests.

Function of Lobby

The lobby space type includes foyers, entries to halls, and security screening areas at or near the entrance to a building or demarcated space, and are meant to welcome and direct tenants and visitors, control access, and provide exit ways from buildings. This space type is often designed with both secure and non-secure areas. The lobby space type does not include elevator lobbies; however, they may be adjacent or connected physically or aesthetically. Building lobbies often serve as the "public face" of building interiors and are becoming more interactive spaces that provide an enhanced user experience.

The lobby of this office in Washington DC was transformed through the use of a bright and colorful motion-activated mural.

Space Attributes

The character and function of a lobby space often influence a visitor's first impression upon entering a building. Key design concerns for this space type include balancing aesthetics, security, sustainability, and operational considerations.

Accessible

Accessibility should be planned early in the process. Various types of disabilities should be considered, including those with visual, learning, mobility, speech, and hearing impairments. Staff should also be educated and informed regarding how to provide an appropriate service or accommodation that might be requested or required. Physical features to address in the lobby space include:

- Doorway openings at least 32 inches wide and doorway thresholds no higher than 1/2 inch.

- Aisles kept wide and clear for wheelchair users. Remove or minimize protruding objects for the safety of visually impaired users.

- Connect levels of the lobby via an accessible route of travel, or provide procedures to assist patrons with mobility impairments.

- Provide ramps and/or elevators as alternatives to stairs.

- Make information desks wheelchair accessible.

- Provide ample high-contrast, large print directional signs throughout the lobby.

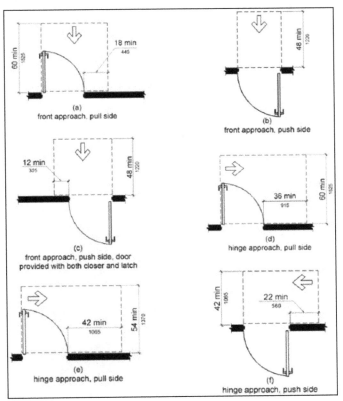

Required door clearances.

Aesthetics

- Utilize appropriate finishes, furniture, signage, and art to reflect the public nature of the space as well as the image of the organization(s) housed within the building.

- A spatial compression/release experience can enhance the aesthetic experience (outside approach, compression thru entrance doors/vestibule, release in lobby/atrium).

- Well-designed lobbies provide workers/occupants with a relief opportunity, such as breaks, from more confined spaces.

These two lobbies have achieved a powerful aesthetic through the use of large-scale artwork, high-end materials and finishes, and the overall volume of the space.

Functional/Operational

- Consider combining employee and visitor entrance to spaces.

- Design space to accommodate peak loads.

- Design the space for flexibility to accommodate different use configurations or expansions.

- Equipment that must be installed in lobbies should be of a low profile variety and consolidated with other equipment to minimize bulk.

- Consider air pressurization and entrance door design to mitigate stack effect at tall building entrance and elevator lobbies.

- Specify durable finishes to accommodate maximum pedestrian traffic.

Dolcezza Coffee and Gelato at Hirshhorn in the redesigned lobby of the Hirshhorn Museum and Sculpture Garden.

- Public buildings will often have historic features in lobbies and hallways, requiring and deserving special design treatment in renovations.

- Maintain the historic character of spaces while modernizing for enhanced security, accessibility, sustainability, and general circulation.

- Equipment that must be installed in historic lobbies should be placed carefully to avoid altering the original spatial configuration of the lobby. Place security equipment in ancillary spaces where possible.

The lobby of Building 33 in Washington, DC. The building, which houses the Naval Facilities Engineering Command offices, is an adaptive reuse of a warehouse dating to the late 1800s. The project incorporated a number of recycled materials, day lighting to reduce energy use, and occupancy sensors and dimming controls to enhance lighting efficiency, while maintaining the historic integrity of the structure.

Productive

Interactive signage in lobbies provides ease of access to information for building users.

- Lobby spaces requiring 24-hour operation should be provided with a dedicated HVAC system.

- For lobby spaces at the exterior of a building, a dedicated air-handling unit should be provided to maintain positive pressurization.

- Design lobbies to provide workers/occupants with a relief opportunity such as breaks from more confined spaces. Whenever possible, incorporate views to nature or incorporate elements such as a water feature, plants, and natural materials.

- Incorporate technology into lobby spaces to improve the building users' way finding experience, provide interactive experiences or visual enhancements, and even provide real-time readouts of building energy use and other features.

Security and Safety

- In higher-risk facilities, separate secure and non-secure areas with turnstiles, metal detectors, or other devices used to control access to secure areas. A control desk and bag checking area should be located within the secure area. Mechanical ductwork, piping, and main electrical conduit runs should not extend from one area to the other. Traffic separation devices should be flexible and portable to allow for changing traffic patterns.

- Design control points such that secure areas cannot be bypassed. Ensure that security personnel can properly observe all areas of control points.

- Larger security screening areas should be located in conjunction with art installations, visitor seating, and exterior entrances. Adequate space should be set aside for queuing. If queuing will occur, the area should be enclosed in blast resistant construction.

- Avoid installing features such as trash receptacles or mailboxes that can be used to hide devices in non-secure areas.

- Avoid using raised floor systems in non-secure areas.

- Location of fire command center and emergency elevator control panel requires design integration with lobby wall finishes, BAS systems, fire protection systems, and building communications systems.

- Design of lobby doors to the street(s) must account for egress from higher floors if stairs exit into lobby, and not directly to the outside.

- Incorporate CPTED principles into the design of the space in order to reduce the opportunity for theft of materials and other acts of violence. This will entail the systematic integration of design, technology, and operational strategies for the protection of people, information, and property.

Sustainable

Designing a sustainable lobby space should be part of an integrated process that takes into account: the materials, operations, and health and well-being of the users.

- For lobby spaces at the exterior of a building, utilize daylighting through the appropriate placement of windows and skylights to reduce electric lighting needs Utilize features such as shading devices to decrease direct solar gain.

- Provide insulation in roofs and walls in order to reduce energy use and heat gain in the space.

- Incorporate natural ventilation to lower utility costs.

- Address healthy indoor environmental quality through appropriate airflow and filtering of air. Use low-emitting materials, furnishings, and finishes that do not off-gas.

- Use durable products in the lobby space and plan for products with reduced packaging and recyclability potential to minimize waste.

- Consider air lock or vestibules at entrance doors to prevent loss of heating/cooling.

Function of Reservation

Reservation is a process of booking and blocking rooms in advance for the prospective guests. It is the hotels ability to equate the guest's inquiry with the room availability. Approximately 70% of room sales business comes from reservations. Various reservation records are maintained so that the reservation section is able to provide the guest with efficient service and also deal with the guest inquiries regarding room availability, rates, discounts, food plans and services and facilities offered.

- Ensures room on arrival: A guest who makes prior reservation is ensured of the required type of room, no of rooms for his entire stay in the city. This saves him from the difficulty of finding accommodation on arrival especially during peak seasons when most of the hotels are full.

- Budgeting: As he is informed of the tariff at the time of reservation, he is able to budget his holiday or tour, taking in account the amount he spends on his stay, food, entertainment etc.

- Other facilities: The guest is ensured of certain facilities offered by the hotel which can be confirmed by making the reservation e.g. sightseeing tours, business center offering secretarial services, entertainment etc. He is also able to give the hotel address to his associates for any meetings, correspondence transfers to and from the hotel.

Importance for the Hotel

- Prior reservation gives the hotel an indication of the level of business likely to be encountered during any particular period. The reservations manager knows the amount of business ensured during that period from the confirmed reservations. It enables him to forecast future revenue generation and take necessary action to improve the amount of revenue expected.

- Guest satisfaction: The hotel is able to plan its activities and be prepared to receive an expected guest. They are able to provide the necessary services and facilities like security, transfers, preference of rooms to known guests, providing compile entries and any particular service asked by the guest at the time of making the reservation.

- The front office manager is able to make the necessary decision regarding the no of walk-instant that can be accommodated on a particular day. Rooms requiring be repairing or taking off for redecoration can be blocked during the slack period as shown by the reservations.

The no of rooms to be blocked for such purposes will also be determined according to the expected guest arrivals.

- Scheduling of staff: Hotel staff may be scheduled more accurately to void under staffing or over staffing problems.

Main Functions

- Taking reservations for hotel rooms: This is the main function. They receive and process the requests for bookings from prospective guests and after checking the various charts on the room availability position for the required dates the booking may be confirmed. In case the room availability position is negative, alternate accommodation is suggested and alternate dates may be offered.

- Information regarding various services and facilities may be given if asked for. It may be volunteered when alternate room and dates are suggested.

- Amendment of booking: Guest wishing to change the type and no of rooms and/or dates of stay booked earlier would be amending their booking. This is also done through the reservations department.

- Cancellation: This releases more no of rooms for sale for the dates specified and reservations must keep track of this in order to sell the rooms to other guests.

Group Reservation

Reservations of rooms form the largest percentage of business of a large hotel. Out of this total business the group business is maximum in many hotels. Hence the hotels getting their maximum revenue from the group business should be extra careful while dealing with group reservations.

Guaranteed Reservation

This kind of reservation is which the hotel does not have to worry about the loss of room revenue even in the event of no show of the guest. The guarantee can be given by a company for a company guest, or by credit card Company for a guest paying by credit card or by travel agent for travel agency bookings. So the hotel is assured about the business and the guest is assured about the room since the room for such reservations will not be released at the time limit but will be blocked till the end of the day.

Walk-In

This is a very common term. This term refers to those guests of the hotel who arrive without any prior notice or reservation in the hotel. These guests arrive at the hotel hoping that there will be some room available for them. The hotel has to be very careful while dealing with the walk-ins. If the guest is paying by cash, then it is preferable for a hotel to ask for some advance from the guest. The advance should be sufficient enough to cover at least one night stay and some extra expenditure in the hotel. Such guests should be referred to the lobby manager and authorization should be taken from him on the registration cards of such guests. It also important to inform the other revenue centers about the PIA (Paid In Advance) or Cash only guests. These guests will not be allowed credit for any services or amenities provided to them. The desk agent should try and sell higher priced rooms to such guests.

Function of Reception and Registration

The reception counter is situated in the bobby and is the first departments were guests contact. Reception, registration, occupancy are the responsibilities of this section. This section also handles reservations that may come before 9 am and after 6 pm. They also provide information about the location of rooms and the facilities offered by the hotel. The registration section put effort in up selling and cross selling of hotel facilities to the guest. Employees at registration counter pursue the guest to purchase more highly priced room that had actually desired or requested for. The registration section also takes care that all the formalities associated with the registration of the foreigner are duly completed such as filling up of form C and dispatching the same to the concerned authorities. Registration section also assigns the room keys to the guest after registering the guest. Keys are another important responsibility of front office department is the safeguarding the keys of guest rooms of the hotel. Front office department stores the room keys at its proper place and assigns the rooms' keys to the guest after fulfilling all the formalities of registration.

The main functions of reception and registration are:

- Welcoming of the guest according to the time of the day.

- Making registration cards, key cards, on the start of the new day by the night auditor.

- Guest registration cards once prepared are slotted alphabetically in room racks.

- Check-in procedures, registration card is filled, rates are fixed at the time of reservation but for walk in' rates are fixed at the moment of arrival only.

- Check-out procedures are done, billing process is executed.

- Slotting of supporting bills (laundry, room service, etc.).

- Currency board is maintained.

- C-forms are filled and sent to FRRO/Police station for foreign guests.

- Electronic keys are prepared on spot for FIT'S and in advance for groups/crews.

- Guest feed-back register is maintained.

- Guest comments card is given for knowing the experience of guests and to analyse the performance of employees.

- Some complementary coupons which are provided by them are:

  ◦ Meal coupons (Breakfast, Lunch, Dinner) to coffee shop.

  ◦ Flower requisition coupons prepared and sent to housekeeping department.

  ◦ Champagne requisition vouchers prepared and sent to food and beverage department.

  ◦ Bar requisition vouchers are prepared and sent to bar of the hotel.

  ◦ Food amenities requisition voucher.

Functions of Concierge

A hotel concierge is typically the first image that comes to mind when the word concierge is mentioned. A hotel concierge is available to make a guest's overnight stay a positive and memorable experience. They often recommend and make reservations to nearby restaurants, arrange transportation and help secure tickets to special events.

Facilitation Travel

Some concierges double as private or for-hire chauffeurs. These individuals do more than just drive people around, however; they're also commonly relied on to act as personal assistants. As such, they could be responsible for arranging tours and excursions or transferring passengers from airports and other transportation hubs to cities. Concierges who also drive passengers might have to develop deeper relationships with their clients. For instance, a travel enthusiast who's accustomed to ritzy treatment may expect their chauffeur-concierge to have their favourite newspaper or beverages on hand when they meet up. In some cases, concierges who actively perform travel services require special licensing and training.

Improving Hospitality

Hotel concierges perform services that define the modern hospitality experience. At a basic level, their work includes tasks like taking reservations, checking guests in and fielding requests for items and amenities. They commonly act as the first point of contact for patrons. Behind the scenes, a hotel concierge may perform tasks like overseeing cleaning services, managing resource inventories, compiling reports on maintenance jobs and other office work. While the highest-level decision-making is often left to management staff, concierges are critical cogs in the business-process machine, and higher-ups commonly delegate vital tasks to these key players.

Assisting Visitors

In hospitals and other large-scale healthcare facilities, concierges routinely handle the front-end tasks associated with patient occupancy and family-member visitation. Hospital concierges may schedule overnight occupancy for a patient's loved ones, pass on treatment requests from relatives to nurses and care teams and provision specific amenities prior to patient stays. Many also provide on-demand services, such as fulfilling special dietary requests or securing entertainment. A healthcare concierge could even be responsible for high-level resource management and planning. Some have been known to oversee construction and administer improvement projects, like upgrading habitability features.

Keeping Patrons Informed

Regardless whether they work in hospitals, hotels or other institutions, one common task nearly all concierges perform is answering questions. Patrons may want to know about nearby tourism sites, regional cuisine, entertainment and a host of other issues that impact the quality of their visits. To field these questions accurately, concierges need more than prior knowledge. Some also have to complete additional training to learn about their company's unique offerings or branding. Those who work in special-interest facilities, such as hotels near national landmarks, may also improve their career skills by brushing up on local histories. In certain situations, it may be to their advantage to be multilingual.

Guest Services

Nightclubs and restaurants commonly employ concierges to control access, greet guests and oversee daily operations. These individuals have to be sufficiently capable to keep an eye on multiple affairs simultaneously without losing track of issues like crowd control, security, emergency response and patron requests. Concierges and other front-of-house staff usually handle reservations, large parties and seating arrangements. During high-volume periods, they may move to assist with expediting kitchen or bar services.

Function of Bell Desk

Bell desk is an extended arm of front desk. There are many activities at the time of arrival, during stay and at the time of departure of guest which cannot be carried out from the front desk but are to be carried out essentially, in order to provide services to the guest. As the name suggest it is a small desk /counter in the lobby near the main entrance of the hotel. The bell desk should be situated in clear view of the front desk, cashier and particularly the doorman standing outside the lobby, so that the doorman may signal for a bellboy at the arrival of a guest. Further, it is also important that the bell desk is situated near the luggage centre and luggage entrance.

- Luggage Handling: Luggage handling of the guest is done at various occasion such as arrival, during stay (change of rooms) and at the time of departure. At the time of arrival when the luggage of the guests moved from car/taxi to the lobby and further to the allotted room, the activity is called "Up bell activity". When the luggage of the guest is moved from room to lobby and further to the car/taxi at the time of departure the activity is called "down bell activity".

- Paging: Apart from luggage handling the bell desk is also responsible for paging a guest. The paging is a system of locating the guest in the hotel. Many times the in-house guest expects a phone call or a visitor but decides not to wait in the room, and might decide to go to public area such as bar, restaurant, swimming pool, lobby or lounge etc. of the hotel or may go out of the hotel. In such cases hotel request the guest to tell about his whereabouts through a location form. This proforma may be kept in the stationery folder in the room as well as at the information section of the counter. Usually it is filled in by the guest but many times it may be filled in by the hotel staff on the instructions of the guest.

- Mail and Message Handling: The bell desk's function is also to handle and distribute mail and message received by the front desk in the absence of the guests to their respective rooms. Also distribution of newspapers and magazines etc. to various rooms and the areas of the hotel and keeping a record of the same is done by the bell desk.

- Delivery of Newspaper: As per the hotel policy all hotel guests receive a copy of hotel newspapers each morning. The bellboys in the night shift are responsible for delivering the newspapers to all occupied rooms.

- Collection of Room Keys at Departures: Another very important function of the bell desk is the collection of room key from a check out guest and depositing the same at the information desk.

- Miscellaneous Jobs: Miscellaneous jobs such as postage stamps handling, taking care of outgoing mail of the guest, carrying out outside errands for the guest and hotel such as buying of cinema tickets, moving of files and documents etc. for the guest as well as going to banks, post office and FRRO police station for delivering of 'C forms' etc.

Procedures and Records

1. Left Luggage Procedure: At times guest find it inconvenient and expensive to carry their luggage to a place where they are going for a few days. Guest is expected to check out by check out time (12 noon) even if their fight is in the evening and they find it too expensive to retain the room for extra day just to keep the luggage. Mostly hotels offer the left luggage room facility free of cost but some hotels do charge for it. Left luggage facility may also bring back the guest to stay in your hotel on his next visit. The procedure for receiving luggage is as such:

- Before accepting the luggage, it is checked that whether guest has settled his bill or not.

- Check the baggage of the guest if it is properly locked or not. In case the baggage is damage than the guest must be informed and note for the same must be made in the receipt.

- Luggage stickers should be pasted on all luggage pieces. A proper receipt must be made, signed by both guest and bell captain and handed over to the guest.

- Enter the details in the left luggage register with the expected date the luggage will be picked up by the guest.

- Keep the luggage in the left luggage room under lock and key. Before accepting the luggage, it is checked that whether guest has settled his bill or not.

- Check the baggage of the guest if it is properly locked or not. In case the baggage is damage than the guest must be informed and note for the same must be made in the receipt.

- Luggage stickers should be pasted on all luggage pieces. A proper receipt must be made, signed by both guest and bell captain and handed over to the guest.

- Enter the details in the left luggage register with the expected date the luggage will be picked up by the guest.

- Keep the luggage in the left luggage room under lock and key.

When the guest comes to pick up his luggage pieces from the left luggage room then the following procedure is carried out:

- The guest is requested to give the receipt. In case guest has lost the receipts than guest is requested to sign in the left luggage register.

- Check the receipt and bring out his luggage pieces from the left luggage room.

- Make an entry in the left luggage register entering the date luggage pieces delivered.

- Stick hotels stickers for publicity.

2. Scanty Baggage Procedure: Scanty baggage means no baggage or a light baggage consisting of brief case or air bag. Guest with scanty baggage is normal skippers from the hotel. Skippers are those persons who check out of the hotel without settling their bills. The scanty baggage guests also normally go out with their light baggage and hotel never knows that if this guest is going out with an intention to come back or not. To save guard the hotels interest, normally guest with scanty baggage are requested to pay in advance. There is a set procedure adopted by hotels to keep a control on guests, with scanty baggage.

- Lobby manager and the reception are notified immediately on guest's arrival about the scanty baggage.

- Arrival errand card is stamped with scanty baggage.

- Guest registration card's all copies are stamped with 'scanty baggage'.

- The scanty baggage register is filled up by the bell desk.

- Get the guest registration cards and the scanty baggage register signed by the lobby manager.

3. Luggage Handling Procedure in case of Groups' Arrival and Departures: In case of a large group arrival, usually there are many number of luggage pieces to be carried to the guests' room. Usually each suit case has the guest name printed. A copy of the rooming list is supplied by the tour operator, which contains the names of all the residents. The room are allotted by the receptionist. The bell boy puts the luggage tags and hotels stickers on each suit case. On luggage tags the bell boy writes

the room number of the guest. The bell boy ensures that each suit case is delivered to the respective guests' room as early as possible. At the time of check out, the guest is requested to keep their luggage outside their room or they are picked up from their rooms and brought down to the lobby. After getting the luggage pass from the cashier, the bell boy take their luggage to the waiting cars/buses.

Function of Telephone Section

The section is situated at the back of the office. All incoming and outgoing calls are tracked, diverted and handled. They even handle telephone messages received during the day.

Function of Cash and Night Auditor

The cash section of the front office department plays a vital role in recording and maintenance of various transactions held at front office and other point of sales in the hotel. The section also verifies the guest and non-guest accounts of the front office. The section is responsible to post charges to guest accounts, receive payments at check-out and during the stay. This section coordinates the billing of credit card and corporate and bill to company guest accounts with the accounting division. All guest accounts are balanced by the cashier at the close of each shift. He/She normally entail answering guest inquiries regarding fees and services. The section also conducts periodic reviews of various accounts of the guests to make sure that the departmental accounts are balanced against the guest accounts. Night auditing is responsible to check the accounting records on daily basis. The auditor summarizes and compiles information for the hotel's financial records. Moreover, he/she tracks revenue, occupancy percentage and other important front office operating statistics.

The auditor works at the graveyard shift and prepares the summary of cash and credit payment activities, reflecting the hotels financial performance for a day. Posting of room charges and room taxes to guest accounts including guest transactions not posted during the day by the front office cashier is even done by the auditor. Front office prepares and updates the folio of the guest. Guest folio consists of all the statement of transaction that has taken place in a single account. All the bills are presented to the guest at the time of departure. These bills are all of those items of expenditure that had been incurred by the guest during his/her stay at different sections of the hotel. Each transaction between hotel and guest must be recorded and updated properly and accurately so that guest is neither overcharged nor undercharged. The front office staff records and maintains all the transactions between the guest and the hotel on the folio. The folio is initiated with zero balance. Depending upon the transactions the balance in the folio gets increase or decrease. After the settlement of the folio balance must return to zero.

Complaint Handling

Front office plays a vital role in handling guest complaints during the stay in the hotel. Front office staff should be prepared to handle all types of complaint. Front office staff should try to solve the complaint with his/her skills and techniques. When guest approaches to the front office with a complaint, front office personnel should listen guest complaint patiently. Right body language is very important at this time. Front office employee should take notes of every single point of information. All the guest complaints should be dealt with seriousness and guest are apologize by front office personnel no matter how small or insignificant that issue was. Front office personnel who handles the complaints offers the clear solution to the guest and if he is unable to offer a solution, than manager should be informed immediately. At last guest is enquired about whether he is satisfied and problem has been revolved or not.

Communication with Other Departments

To achieve the overall objective of front office operation that is sale of rooms and maintaining brand image of the property, the front office need to communicate and coordination tend to be important. The coordination for sale of rooms includes housekeeping which cleans and keeps rooms ready for sale and even helps in day to day services provided to the guests. In case of any maintenance problems in the room is handled by the engineering and maintenance department. Security department coordinates in keeping the hotel premises secure for hotel guests. All such departments that are a part of guest services need to have smooth coordination with front office.

Front Office Organizational Structure

There are lot of staff working under front office manager. The structure of the front office department changes according to the size of the hotel business, physical size of the hotel, and the hotel management policies. Following is the general structure of the front office department:

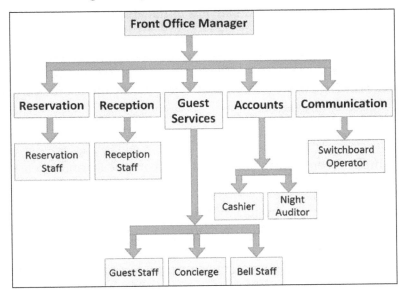

Organisation is a group of people working together to achieve a particular objective/goal. Organisation is the process of understanding the job, grouping responsibilities and authority among staff, establishing relationships in the activities and staff for the achievement of common goal. Moreover 'Organisations are social units deliberately constructed and reconstructed to seek specific goals. A hotel is a company which may have hotels in numbers called chain hotels and even could be an individual property. The hotel is generally managed by Board of Directors. If the company is operating worldwide or nationwide then the company could have regional heads and further an individual property headed by a general manager. The organisation of hotels differ from hotel property to property and from chain to chain. A huge change due to technological advancements and management techniques is slowly reducing the labour required to perform particular tasks. Yet hotel industry is considered to be the most labour intensive industry and the most important human touch cannot be eliminated to extend personalised services to the guests.

The hierarchy structure, the number of staff required differs from large to small property. Business cannot be managed by a single person, and hotel industry is not an exception to it. When the organisation have many people to achieve objectives/targets, it becomes important to know what, how, when, why they have to work to get the maximum use of resources and in less time. To achieve the goals, organisations involve division and subdivision of departments. The organising of departments means understanding the job, dividing the job into small components, grouping responsibilities, establishing relationships in the activities and staff for the achievement of a goal. The departments of hotels are divided in revenue generating and non-revenue generating departments. Moreover, the department coming directly in contact with the guest is called as 'Front of the House' while the departments which do not come in contact with the guests directly are called as 'Back of the House'.

Job Description of Lobby Manager/Duty Manager

- The lobby manager reports to the front office manager.

- Responsible to greet the VIP/CIP guests of the hotel and performs special services for VIP/CIP Guest's.

- Assists in VIP's/CIP's arrival and departure in the absence of guest relation executive.

- Responsible for cleanliness of lobby area and public areas and looks for orderly appearance of front office staff.

- On times checks the registration cards of arriving guests and ensures all information should be filled and signed by the guests.

- Assists in sending guest messages, parcels to guest room.

- Instructs the night receptionist, regarding: Walk-in guests and release room blocked because of no-shows.

- He/she assists in handling room lock problems.

- On times prepares and checks for VIP's arrival and escorts such guests to rooms.

- Co-ordinates with all other departments concerned in order to run smooth operations of front office.

- Checks switchboard and makes sure appropriate wake up calls are made.

- Handles guest complaints and other related problems and reports on the Assistant Manager's log book.

- Coordinates with sub section like reception, business centre, cashier, concierge and bell desk.

- Approves and sign for allowances, rebates etc., as required by Front Office Cashier.

- Responsible to authorise charges to be made for late departures.

- Promotes and maintains good public relations.

- He/she motivates and maintains good relation with staff.

- Maintains and be guided of hotel policy on credit/lost and found hotel guests properties.

- Has to follows up in credit check report and liaise with credit manager.

- Head of front office operation during the absence of front office manager.

- Discusses all matters that needed to follow up with the next shift reception manager.

- Approves the working schedule of front office attendants and submits the same to front office manager.

Job Description of Reservationist

- The reservation agent reports to the front office manager.

- Keeps track and processes reservation requests by mail, telephone, telex, cable, fax or central reservation systems.

- Should have the knowledge of all type of rooms available and their location and layout.

- Should be updated with the selling status, rates, and benefits of all packages plans.

- Processes and updates reservations from the hotel sales office, other hotel departments, and other sources of reservation (travel agents, corporates, intermediaries, etc.).

- Knowledge of the credit policy of the hotel.

- Prepares and sends letters of confirmation to guests.

- Creates and maintains reservation records by date of arrival and through alphabetical listing.

- Has to communicate reservation information to the front desk, especially for next day or same day.

- Has to processes cancellations and amendments if any and promptly communicate this information to the front desk.

- Should understand the hotel's policy on guaranteed reservations and no-shows.

- Forecasts room revenue and occupancy.

- On times assist reception duties when required.

- Has to be fully aware of health and safety, fire and bomb threat procedures.

- Responsible to process advance deposits on reservations.

- Tracks and establishes future room availabilities on the basis of reservations.

- Opens and closes the availability when required in all the GDS channels and on the hotel website.

- Should be aware on property management system and configuring rates on the hotels property management system.

- Has to ensure that the room sale target is achieved.

- In its managerial role he develops room revenue and forecasts occupancy.

- Has to prepare expected arrival list for front office use on daily basis.

- Has to assist in preregistration activities whenever required.

- Handles daily correspondence related to bookings.

- Keeps the reservation files updated.

- Getting information about areas of interest in order to target more clients in particular seasons.

- Helps in making arrangements for clients travel programs.

- Determines room rates based on the selling tactics of the hotel from time to time.

Job Description of Receptionist

- The receptionist needs to report to the manager front office.

- The duty of receptionist is to receive, inquire about guest requirements and making allotment of rooms.

- Registers the guest after ensuring the reservation or availability of rooms in case of walk-in.

- Opens guests bill/folio.

- Allot room after referring to room status chart.

- Has to prepare arrival and departure (AandD) register.

- Hands over the key and asks the bell boy to escort the guest to the room.

- Prepares C' form for international guests and sends the same to foreign regulatory registration office (FRRO) or local police station within stipulated time.

- Has to prepare arrival notification slips and notify to concerned departments.

- Receives messages on behalf of the guest and hand over to the guest once in the hotel.

- Should be able to provide information related to hotel, city, state, country, shopping, etc.

- Keeps room racks updated.

- Prepares various meal and complimentary amenity coupons for the guests.

- Keeps track of any scanty baggage guest and takes advance from the guest accordingly.

- Prepares various reports from time to time.

- Maintains log book for important events.

- Maintains discount register.

- Updates the currency exchange board.

Job Description of Night Auditor

- Trains front office cashier in night auditing.

- Verifies all postings and balance.

- Checks and posts room charges and taxes to guest accounts.

- Processes vouchers like guest charges voucher and credit card vouchers.

- Post charges to the guest accounts that have not been posted or were incurred at the graveyard shift.

- Transfers charges and deposits to master accounts.

- Checks to see that all charges are assigned to the appropriate departments.

- Verifies that all transactions performed at the front desk are supported by documentary evidence and signatures as necessary and that they have been correctly posted and allocated in to PMS system.

- Verifies that all charges posted from the POS Software reached the correct guest folios and even not missing.

- Prepares for the end of day procedure.

- Follows the night audit checklist.

- He must have complete knowledge of emergency procedures.

- Balances the day's charges, making corrections as necessary.

- Prints up and files reservations for the next business day.

- Verifies that room rates are correct and posts those rates to guest accounts.

- Monitors the current status of coupon, discount, and other promotional programs.

- He should be able to function as a front desk agent especially in terms of check-in and checkout procedures.

- Tracks room revenues, occupancy percentages, and other front office statistics.

- Prepares a summary of cash, check, and credit card activities.

- Checks figures, postings, and documents for accuracy.

- Records, stores, accesses, and analyzes computerized financial information.

- Prepares important management reports which details the results and further summarizes results of operations for management.

- Runs end of day process in property management software (PMS).

- Operates PMS and other front office equipment's.

- Responds to guest needs, special requests and complaints and informs the respective manager.

- On times helps in performing check-in and check-out.

Job Description of Cashier

- The cashier reports to night auditor.

- The cashier operates front office posting software.

- Obtains the house bank from accounts section and keeps it balanced.

- Helps in completing guest check-in procedure.

- Performs variety of banking services for guests, like check cash and foreign currency exchange.

- Keeps follow up on all deposit dues/deposit to be paid by the guests.

- Posts the charges to guest account and non-guest accounts.

- Handles paid-out transaction if any during the day.

- Transfers guest balances to other accounts as and when required.

- Helps in completing guest check-out procedures.

- Settles guest and non-guest accounts.

- Dispenses guest records after the guest checkout.

- Handles various modes of payment like cash, traveller's cheque, credit cards and bill to company.

- Front office cashier assumes responsibility for any cash used in processing front desk transactions.

- Adjustments of discounts is done by the cashier wherever applicable.

- Clarifies customers question or concerns about the charges on their bills.

- Maintains adequate supplies of outlet stationery for cashiers.

- Assists with distribution of month end reports as directed by accounts or front office manager.

- Maintains a track of all high balance guests.

- Checks and follows up on all bills on hold.

- Checks the billing instructions that should be correct for all expected departure guests.

- Provides on-the-Job training to new staff members.

- At the close of the shift balances department total.

- At the close of shift balances cash.

- Issues and manages safe deposit boxes.

- Assists front desk staff on check-in as and when required.

Job Description of Bell Boy

- Bell boy reports to the bell desk or to the lobby manager.

- Carries luggage at the time of arrival for both FIT's and Walk-in guests: The bell desk staff performs important function of greeting the guests at the time of arrival and helping them in unloading luggage from the vehicles. The bell boys further escort the guest to the room after registration and transport the luggage from lobby to the guest room. While escorting the guest, it is expected that the bell boy will inform the guest about various other facilities the hotel offers as an approach of suggestive selling. Once the guest reaches the room, the bell boy makes guest comfortable and gives details about different facilities in the room and the usage of various electronic/electrical gadgets.

- Carries luggage at the time of guest departure for FIT's and Walk-in guests: The bell desk is responsible to transport luggage of the guests from rooms to vehicles at the time of departure. Care needs to be taken while transporting luggage looking at the nature of luggage being carried as could be fragile.

- Luggage handling for groups at the time of arrival and departure: Handling luggage of groups becomes little complicated as the number of luggage could be high. And the important part is transporting luggage to different rooms allotted to group members after identifying the correct luggage of every individual guest. In this process, a rooming list is handed over by the front desk staff to the bell desk clearly indicating the guest name and room numbers allotted. Further the bell boy puts luggage tags on all the luggage items and makes a note of that separately. It becomes easy as the group members are informed to attach name tags on every luggage which is otherwise also recommended by tour operators for travel purposes. And then the bell desk transports the luggage to every guest room. The process of carrying luggage from porch/lobby area to guest room is called as Up-bell. On the other hand, at the time of group departure the luggage is collected from each dedicated room to a group and is brought down and loaded to the vehicle of the groups. The bell boys need to be careful for the same because on times a two or more groups may be checking-out at same time. The process of transporting luggage of group from rooms to porch/lobby is termed as Down-bell.

- Paging service for the guests: Another important function of bell desk is to provide paging services to guests in order to locate them for any message and mails delivered looking at the urgency of the message received on behalf of the guest by the hotel. A paging board is used for the purpose which shows the name and company of the guest.

- Newspaper/Magazine delivery in guest rooms: The bell desk staff is also responsible to deliver complimentary and requested newspapers and magazines in guest rooms. The process starts early in the morning as hotel receives them from the assigned vendor. The bell boys check from the register for the newspapers and magazines to be distributed in the guest rooms. The newspapers/magazines are packed in newspaper bags and are then distributed by bell boys' floor wise for speedy distribution. The bags are hung on guest room door knobs.

- Postal services to guests: The bell desk even acts as mini post office and provides various types of postal services like postal stamps, postcards, envelopes on guest requests. The bell desk also arranges for courier services for the guests for any urgent mails.

- Helping in housekeeping services: The bell desk staff also assists housekeeping staff in conducting light housekeeping services in lobby and reception area. The services may be light dusting and wiping of entrance door. The bell boys sometimes even help housekeeping staff in making rooms in case of urgent check-ins or due to lack of staff on times.

- Others: Bell staff even purchases various items requested by guests like cigarettes, drinks or may be some eatables if not available in hotel and asks reception to prepare visitors paid outs in case guests does not pay for the same at that moment of time.

Qualities of Front Office Employees

The front office is a critical department in a hotel in view of its revenue generating capacity and influence in image- building, the staff working in it assume a special importance. The staff selected to perform duty at front desk must reflect these following characteristics:

- Should have a warm personality and smart appearance.

- He/she must have keen interest in people, and of polite and courteous nature.

- Must have an ability to poise under pressure, keeping his cool and acts as a problem solver.

- Should have a desire to be helpful, but also diplomatic and tactful on times.

- He/she must have the ability to listen, hardworking and punctual.

- The staff member should be team worker and should have the ability to get along with co-workers, and pleasant approach and good motivation and coordinator. A Desire to be liked, with good public relation qualities.

- Every front office staff should have the ability to help another employee without resenting it or showing irritation.

- As they have to deal with different natured guests, should be confident, analytical, intelligent and a good salesman.

- They need to have neat personal habits, so that no one gets irritated by such a habit.

- Good memory is one of the important key factors as he/she should be able to remember names of regular guests for personalised service.

- He/she should have knowledge of languages and especially local and one foreign language.

- The front office staff deals with the transaction of the guest from arrival till departure and so need to have numerical ability.

Working at front desk requires reserve of energy as he/she have to deal with many problems that arise in hotel for time to time. Hence, by following simple rules of living can reserve built to act continuously in same mood and efficiency:

- One should sleep plenty to meet challenges in the day.

- One should not drink to be moderate. In fact if a person smokes one should not do that at least at working hours.

- A person working at front desk need to have positive nature because as on front office one has to meet the guest and form a lasting impression. So make sure that the guest gets a positive impression from the moment he walks in.

Attributes of Front Office Employees

To be a successful front office employee, one needs to have following attributes to deliver best services to guest with delight:

- Salesmanship: A front office staff should be able to motivate guests to spend more on the hotel facilities rather than only guest room.

- Problem Solvers: Guest most of the time approach the reception staff in case they have a problem or a complaint. The front office staff must be diplomatic and resourceful to solve the problem at the shortest possible time. The guest should feel nicely heard and with a hope of getting the problem solved.

- Knowledge of the Products: No service provider can be expected not to have knowledge about the product and services an organization is providing and hotel front office is not an exception.

- Reference Point: Being the communication center of the hotel, guests who wants information comes to the reception with their queries. The perception of guests is to get solution of every query or problem is with the front desk employees.

- Image Builders: Front office staff is considered as image builders of the hotel as they are the first and last contact of guest. Every phase of guest stay has to be made comfortable and consideration has to make guests delighted. They can definitely generate a good image for the establishment in their manner of dress, communication, personal conduct and efficiency.

- Personal Grooming and Hygiene: The front office staff is mostly exposed to the guest at all times, a clean image helps to portray a good image. They should have a very high sense of personal grooming and hygiene at all times.

- Physical Fitness: Being the busiest departments of the hotel, the staff members should be physically and mentally fit to provide 24x7 services with delight.

- Self-Confident: It is usually as front office personal meet guest of different countries, states and cultures. They should feel comfortable and confident while dealing with these people.

- Quick Decision Making: Guest often approach the front office with problems and requests front office must be able to decide quickly a converse of action that satisfies the guest at the same time keeping the interacts of the establishments alive.

- Good communication Skills: The front office staffs speech must be clear and language must be correct. It is desirable that front office staff knows more than one language but the local language is mostly preferred. Knowing foreign languages is an added advantage as it helps in dealing with foreign guest in their own language.

- Diplomacy and Tactfulness: This is a great attribute required often, because there are situations when guests are irritated over a particular situation or a problem. A diplomatic dealing helps in diffusing the problem instantly.

- Ability to remember names and Faces: One of the important attribute of front office staff is to remember names and faces of guests for more personalized services and that decides the good from the average, amongst the front office staff. Every individual has self-esteem and his/her name is most precious to him or her. If front office staff can call most of the guest by their names this can flatter them and even the guest is retained for coming future. It may be considered as one of the major aspects related to image building.

- Good Manners: As a hotel is a meeting place for social elites all the grace and etiquette association with good society come into play. They're wishing the guest at all times and thanking them is the basic etiquette.

References

- Front-office-introduction-operations-functions, front-office-training, train-my-hotel-staff: setupmyhotel.com, Retrieved 17, March 2020

- The-lobby-space-type-includes-provide-exit-ways-from-buildings: wbdg.org, Retrieved 22, January 2020

- The-functions-of-reservations-tourism-essay, tourism: ukessays.com, Retrieved 27, May 2020

- 5-functions-of-a-concierge: besthospitalitydegrees.com, Retrieved 12, February 2020

- Front-office-management-structure: tutorialspoint.com, Retrieved 20, June 2020

Front Office: Operations and Management

There are various significant aspects of front office operations and management such as tariff structure and plan, room rate and types of room rates, guest cycle, room reservation, source of reservation, types of reservation, procedure of reservation, cancellation/amendments, etc. This chapter discusses in detail the varied aspects related to front office operations and management.

Tariff Structure and Plan

Hotels have to decide the rack rate of different category of rooms and have to strategically allot discount to be offered during different category of seasons and clients (travel agents, corporates, etc.). Hotels have different category of rooms and each type of room have different tariff depending upon the size of the room, its location, view from room, etc. and accordingly the individual category of room is assigned a standard rack rate. The rack rate is fixed and tariff card is printed and is approved from Department of Tourism. The tariff fixed is further shared with all sources of reservation and uploaded on the hotel website. Resort hotels may print an additional tariff card for off seasons. Front office is expected to sell rooms at the rack rate and any guest who is provided discount depends on sales strategies adopted like company volume, frequency of visits, etc. These special rates/discounted rates are offered to clients such as groups coming through travel agents, corporates, crew or even direct. Moreover to promote business promotional rates are offered to group leaders, travel agents, crew, embassies, etc. Incentives are even offered to guests depending upon potential referral business they generate for hotels. The special rates are authorized by higher management depending on the policy and strategies adopted from time to time.

Room Rate and Types of Room Rates

Basis of Charging Room Rent

1. Check-in Time: This is the time when a guest arrives in a hotel for the purpose of stay only.

2. Check-out Time: The time when a guest leaves or vacates his room is called check-out time.

There are three ways or basis of charging room rents:

- 24 Hour Basis: The guideline under this basis for the purpose of calculating the room rent is the check-in time. A guest has to pay for one day or 24 hours calculated from the check-in time. Under this basis and other basis as well, whether the guest stays for a full period or a part of it; the minimum charge will be for a day. Usually this basis is being adopted by Resort Hotels.

- Night Spent Basis or Night Basis: Under this basis the guideline for the purpose of calculating room rent is the number of night spent by the guest. This basis is usually adopted by

Motels. The time of night is specified in such a case. In fact only the numbers of nights are taken into consideration with respect to the check-in time. Even if a guest does not spend a night, but stays during the day time, then also he has to pay one day's room rent.

- Check-Out Time Basis (COT Basis): This is the most popular basis mainly adopted by Commercial Hotel, Transit Hotels and sometimes Resort Hotels. Under this basis the guideline for the purpose of calculating the room rent is the check-out time, which is fixed by the hotel, by which time a guest will have to vacate the rooms or else he is charged for another day. Under this basis guests are allowed to stay during the hotel day only. Hotel day is a cycle of 24 hours that starts from the check-out time. The selection of check-out time depends on the time when maximum number of flights, long distance trains and busses arrive. It is popular because both guests and hotel are benefited. It is beneficial for a walk-in guest as he can expect a vacant room at the check-out time. Adopting this basis, a hotel can deploy rooms to more number of guests and plan its schedule. As per this system, a particular time of the day is fixed as the check-out time. The most common is a 12 noon check-in/check-out system. According to this, the day starts at 12 noon daily and ends at 12 noon the next day, immaterial of the time at which the guest checks-in. If the guest has checked-in in the morning before 12 noon and intends to stay overnight, then from the point of his check-in, till 1200 hrs. That day makes one day and from 1200 hrs. till the next day, becomes another day. As a result, when the guest stays sometimes for 24 hours or lesser, he could be charged for more than a day. In other words, the same room may be sold twice in the same day. Since it is not practical for any guest to check in at exactly 1200 hrs. Most hotels permit a grace period (of about 2 hours), before and after checkout time. Though the system is good for the hotelier, many guests may think of this system as unreasonable.

- Day Use Basis: This is also known as Day Basis. This is not an independent basis of charging room rent. This basis is adopted by hotels in combination with some other basis of charging room rent. Under this basis, guests are allowed to use rooms during the day time only and maximum for a period of six hours. Day use basis is adopted by Transit Hotels and Commercial Hotels along with check-out time basis generally, during lean season. Under this basis, guests are offered a maximum discount of 50%.

Food Plans

Food Plan is a scheme or package through which we offer accommodation as well as food to the guest against a fixed rate. Following are the food plans commonly available in hotels:

- European Plan (EP): Under this plan, guest is offered only accommodation. Early Morning Tea (EMT) is optional.

- Continental Plan (CP): Under this plan, guest is offered with accommodation and Continental Breakfast. Early Morning Tea (EMT) is optional. All additional charges are considered extra.

Continental Breakfast

- Fruit Juice (fresh/canned).

- Bread/Toast (served with butter and preserves).

- Tea/Coffee.
- Bermuda Plan (BP): Under this plan, guest is offered with accommodation and American Breakfast. Early Morning Tea (EMT) is optional. Also known as BandB plan. All additional charges are considered extra.

American Breakfast

- Fruit Juice (fresh/canned) -----Cereals (served with hot or cold milk) ----- Eggs to Order----- Bread/Toast (served with butter and preserves) ----- Tea/Coffee.
- American Plan (AP): Under this plan, guest is offered with accommodation along with two major meals and two minor meals. Early Morning Tea (EMT) is optional. This plan is also known as 'all inclusive plan' or 'full board' or 'enpension'.
- Modified American Plan (MAP): Under this plan, guest is offered with accommodation along with one major meal and one minor meal. Early Morning Tea (EMT) is optional. . It is also called as 'demi pension' or 'half board'. This facilitates the guests to eat out for one meal. It is usually used for groups where meal coupons are provided to the guests (coupon is valid only for a day) and the coupon cost is included in the room rent.

The use of these Plans

Commercial hotels prefer EP/CP/BP because:

- Commercial hotels are situated in the urban areas, there are bound to be numerous restaurants in the vicinity. Hence the guest will prefer to keep his option open as far as meals are concerned. Moreover the hotel may not have a particular cuisine which the guest likes.
- On the other hand hotel being situated in an urban area would get plenty of chance guests in their restaurants. Thus their FandB income is not restricted to only hotel residents. They do offer meal inclusive plans but only to groups sent by travel agents and company bookings for conventions, seminars, etc.

Resort hotels prefer AP/MAP because:

- They may be situated in an isolated area with hardly any restaurant in the vicinity. Guests therefore prefer to have meals in the hotel. For the tourists wishing to go sight-seeing during the day, an MAP will be more appropriate.
- The hotel itself benefits from this plan since the hotel relies only on the resident guests for their food and beverage income.

EP, CP, BP are the popular plans adopted in Commercial and Transit Hotels. They mostly get businessmen as clients, who normally have their major meals in independent restaurants. The Commercial hotels also get plenty of walk-in guests.

- Go Plan: This is not a food plan in true sense, but is a kind of service provided by chain hotels. In this plan a guest is provided with temporary credit facility and they can settle their bills at their last unit (stay) of their tour program. Guests who come through Travel Agents attached to that hotel and Regular guests can avail this facility. It is an adjustment made in the settlement of accounts. If a guest stays in different hotels of the same chain in the course of his tour, his bills will be forwarded to his next destination every time he changes the place of stay. The guest can make the payment at the last hotel he visits belonging to the same chain.

Factors Affecting Room Tariff

- Cost: The total expenditure that is incurred in providing service and product to the ultimate consumer of the hotel service is the cost. The higher the investment that has been made in a hotel property, the higher would be the room rent.

- Level of Service: A hotel offering the best services or more services like spa, gymnasium, banquet, specialty restaurant, etc. will charge a higher room rent in comparison to other hotel offering limited services.

- Amenities: Hotel providing more amenities in room will charge higher price for their rooms.

- Food: What all meals are provided in room package (food plan) will also affect room prices.

- Competition: The higher the competition in the market lower the prices.

- Target Market: The target market governs the rack rate of a hotel. Hotels are priced on the basis of the spending power of the target guest.

- Location: Location of the hotel effect the room tariff e.g. downtown hotels or hotels near tourist destinations or sea facing are more expensive than other hotels.

Room Tariff

Room rates of hotels are technically known as Tariff. It is statutory on the part of the hotel to display its tariff to the guests. There are two ways to display a tariff structure:

- Through Tariff Card.

- Through Tariff Board.

A tariff card is used in large and medium sized hotels. They use the tariff card with details of their rooms. These are available at the Reception Desk and also in each and every guest room. A tariff board on the other hand is used in small sized hotels. The board is placed behind the Reception Counter where it will be visible all the guests. Following are the information obtained through a Tariff Card:

- Room rates against each plan.

- Government taxes as applicable, e.g. Expenditure Tax, Entertainment Tax etc.

- Other charges levied by the management of the hotel, e.g. Service Charge.

- Basis of charging room rates.

- Brief description of the facilities available in the hotel.

The various taxes applicable, varies from place to place depending on government policies.

Hotel IHM	Accommodation	Rates
A super deluxe hotel set amidst lush green landscaped lawns, in the heart of the city.	Single Occupancy	
	EP	Rs. 4000.00
	CP	Rs. 5000.00
	AP	Rs. 8000.00
The hotel has 350 rooms and suites, centrally air-conditioned, direct dial telephone, mini bar and internet, in all rooms. It has five restaurants serving Indian, Oriental and European cuisines and two Bars.	MAP	Rs. 6500.00
	Double Occupancy	
	EP	Rs. 7000.00
	CP	Rs. 8500.00
	AP	Rs. 10000.00
Other facilities provided are Swimming Pool, Secretarial Service, Health Club, Travel Desk, Car Rental, Bank, Chemist, and 24 hours Business Centre.	MAP	Rs. 9500.00
	Suites	
	EP	Rs. 12000.00
	CP	Rs. 14000.00
	AP	Rs. 18000.00
Arrangements can be made for Golf, Tennis, Surfing, Horse Riding and C	MAP	Rs.16500.00
(Above rates are excluding taxes) Luxury Tax - 10% Expenditure Tax - 10% For Group Booking please contact the Front Desk.		

Packages, plans and discounted rates can be negotiated at the time of reservation. Each hotel has different room rate categories based on room size, location, view, furnishing and amenities. Each category is assigned a rack rate based on the number of pax occupying the room.

1. Rack Rate: Rack rate is the standard price determined by the management. Hotel design a standard rate for each category of rooms offered to the guest. These are the highest possible rate for each category of rooms.

2. Special Rates: There are certain circumstances when special reduced rates or discounts may be offered on rack rates during the low occupancy period. The special rates are: The room rate which is printed on the tariff card/board is called the Rack Rate and is the highest quoted rates offered generally. The special rates are:

- Corporate Rates: These are the promotional rates to attract the corporate market segments. These are generally 10 to 20 % below the rack rate.

- Package Rates: It covers all expenses of accommodation, food, transportation, sight-seeing, entertainment, etc. These are normally for a fixed period of time, e.g. 4 days and 3 nights. These can be meeting, marriage or holiday's package.

- Seasonal rate: Depending on the desirability of a location at a particular time of the year, destination may have a high or a low season and rate also change accordingly.

- Advance purchase rate: It is a new concept; heavy discounts are given on room booking done in advance. Discounts depend upon advance period and number of rooms booked.

- Week day and week end rates: Hotel occupancy change with regard to the days of the week and rate goes low with decrease in occupancy and goes up with increase in occupancy, e.g. down town hotels are busy on week day whereas resorts are busy on weekends.

- Day and half day rate: Rates offered to guest using room for few hours.

- Group Rate: Groups (G.I.T-Guest in Transit) are given special rates due to the number of rooms taken by them at a time. A group under standard stipulation comprises of 15 guests or more. Based on the discretion of the Management, the group leader may be given a complimentary room for a minimum of 15 paying customers. Guests who do not come into any of the above groups are called as 'F.I.Ts' or Free Individual Travellers. i.e., they are not part of any group or company enjoying special rates. When these are Domestic clientele, they are referred to as 'D.F.I.T'. or 'Domestic Free Individual Traveller'. Similarly, if the guest is not a domestic traveller i.e., if he is a foreigner, then he is called as 'F.F.I.T'. or 'Foreign Free Individual Traveller'.

- Tour rates: These are special discounts that are given to wholesalers who operate series of tours for groups arriving and departing together.

- Company Guaranteed Rates (CGR): Companies which give regular guaranteed business to the hotel are given discounts.

- Company volume guaranteed rate (CVGR): Based on the room night potential of different companies, certain hotels give a special rate to those companies which contribute a large volume of room nights. This special rate offered came to be called as the 'Company Volume Guaranteed Rate' (C.V.G.R) or 'Company Guaranteed Rate' (C.G.R.). The higher the volume of business, the higher was the percentage of discount given. For this purpose, all those companies which offer a large quantum of business could be 'A' rated. As the contribution figure dipped, the company rating would also drop to 'B' or even 'C' for those with a relatively poor volume of business. Many hotels today, in order to accommodate all categories of employees from one particular organisation, have gone ahead and offered very low rates to the lower down officers, and higher rates to the top brass of the company, based on their entitlements and expenditure capabilities. A record of the room night contribution (R.N.C.) of individual companies is maintained either on a computerized system or manually by an alphabetically indented register. Periodically, the companies are informed of their volume contribution. If the expected room night contribution was not maintained by any one company, they would fall to a lower rating or even be left out of the C.G.R. list after the total period of assessment

- Employee rate: Employees of major hotel chains have a special employee rate for all employees at their member hotels within the chain. This is however based on the availability of space and policy of the individual hotel.

- Travel agent rate: Travel agents provide substantial volume of business to hotels; hence hotels offer them special discounts and commissions.

- Government rates: These are the discounts given to the government official travel for official purpose.

- Educational rate: These are the special rates offered by hotels to students and educationists who have a limited travel budget. They provide a large chunk of repeat business to hotels.

- Membership rate: Rates offered to the guests who are the member of influential organization or memberships offered by hotel that provide volumes of business to hotels.

- Introductory rate: Rates offered by new hotels or hotels providing new services to the market.

- Complimentary rates: These are rates where hotel does not charge the room rent from a guest, these are provided to tour or group leaders, tour operators, travel agencies, local dignitaries, and media personnel's.

- Promotional Rates: For publicity and promotion special discounted rates are offered to CIP's. These discounts are authorized by senior staff members.

- Off Season Rates: Resorts usually have separate tariff for peak season and off season, the off season rate being much lower.

- Staff Discount: In chain hotels, employees may be given discounts on room rates for hotels belonging to that chain. This is given on space available basis.

- Airline/Crew Discount: For their crew members, airlines are given a fixed discounted rate. Most airlines enter into a contract with hotels in different cities where its flights commute, wherein staff of the airline (crew) is given a very special rate for a fixed period. Their duration of stay may be a few hours up to a maximum of 24 hours. There is also another special rate negotiated for the lay-over passengers. The food-plan applied would be based on the requirement, but the food element computed is also on a discounted basis.

- Crib Rate: Reduced rates are applicable for children below five years.

- Extra Bed: A fixed charge generally one fourth of the room rate. As most five star hotels today do not have single rooms, but have only double rooms which could accommodate a minimum of two guests, a third person if present, is given an extra bed and charged. This charge is in most hotels levied even if an extra bed is not given. The rate charged could be approximately 20 to 25% of the room rate.

- Other rates: Besides the above, special rates may also be given to a hoard of other category of people based on the discounting policies of the management. Some of these might be commercially important persons (C.I.Ps) for publicity and promotion purposes, influential persons like company directors, decision makers, top executives, travel writers, etc. Such discounts have to be authorised by a senior member of the management.

Room Tariff Fixation

A hotel fixes the room tariff on the following two bases:

- Cost Based: Cost based pricing is a room rent determination technique that covers the basic cost of operations at a given level of service, plus the pre-determined % of return on investment.

  Cost + fixed profit % = selling price

- Rule of Thumb: This is also known as cost rate formula or 1:1000 ratios. This is the oldest method of determining the room rent of any hotel. According to this approach, the room rent should be fixed at the rate of Rs. 1 for each Rs. 1000 spent on the construction and furnishing of the room (cost per room or room cost), assuming that the average occupancy is 70% for the year.

Cost per room or room cost = cost of (land + construction + fixture + fitting)/Total number of rooms

Drawbacks associated with rule of thumb approach:

- Consider only cost incurred in constructing rooms but does not consider other factors like inflation, competition, fixed expenses.

- Does not consider return on investment (ROI).

- Consider average occupancy at 70% which is not always achievable.

- Does not consider depreciation of fixed asset and elevation of land cost.

- Approach fails to consider unexpected expenses, and contribution of other department.

- If the property is new, construction cost will be high in comparison to their hotels, that will affect profitability.

- Approach does not take care value of property into consideration, if the property is new, amenities are new.

- Local market and competition rules your rates.

Hubbart Formula

Also known as bottom up approach. This is a scientific way and most recent approach, of determining the room rent, was developed by Roy Hubbart in America in the 1940s. It resolve all the problems of the rule of thumb approach. To determine the average selling price per room, the approach consider operating cost, desired profit and expected number of the rooms sold.

Steps of Hubbart Formula Approach

- Calculate the hotels desired profit by multiplying the desired rate of return by owners' investment.

- Calculate pre-tax profit by dividing desired profit by 1 minus the hotel tax rate.

- Calculate fixed charges and management fee. The calculation includes estimating depreciation, interest expenses, property tax, insurance, amortization, building mortgage, land, and rent and management fee.

- Calculate undistributed operating expenses. The calculation include estimated administrative and general, data processing, HR, transportation, marketing, property operation and maintenance and energy cost.

- Estimate non room operated department income and loss, that FandB, and other departments income or loss.

- Calculate the required rooms' department income. The sum of pre-tax profit fixed charges and management fee undistributed operating expenses, and other operated department income less other operated department income equals the required room department income.

- Determine the room department revenue. The required rooms department income plus room department expenses of payroll and related expenses, plus other direct operating expenses, equals the required room department revenue.

- Calculate the average room rate by dividing room department revenue by the expected number of rooms to be sold.

  Doubles sold daily = double occupancy rate * total number of rooms * occupancy %

  Singles sold daily = rooms sold daily – number of double rooms sold daily Singles sold daily * x + doubles sold daily * (x + y) = (average room rate) * (total number of rooms sold daily)

  where x = price of singles; y = price differential between singles and doubles; x + y = price of doubles.

Market Based

Market based pricing is setting a price based on the value of the product in the perception of the customer. In this case, the hotel works backwards as it first makes an accommodation product available at a price that a guest is willing to pay, and then it tries to cut down on the cost to achieve a reasonable rate of return on that basis. Some common methods of market based pricing are:

- As per Competition: In this approach market looks at comparable hotels in the geographical market and sees what they are charging for the same product.

- Market Tolerance: Checking competing hotels' best available rates for a room, by calling up the competitive hotel without disclosing your identity.

- Rate Cutting: Lowering of rates to increase occupancy levels, especially during off season.

- Inclusive and Non-Inclusive Rate: Charging rates on the basis of meals provided.

- Guest Requirement: Varying room tariff as per guest requirement, e.g. early check in on CO basis or late check out on MAP basis.

- Prestige Pricing: Product and prices are fixed much higher than other hotels, it works on the mentality that if it is expensive it must be good.

Guest Cycle

Guest cycle refers to the distinct stages of guest interaction between the hotel and guests. On the basis of the stage of interaction and activities involved, the Guest Cycle is broadly, classified into four main stages based on the activity type. These are: Pre-Arrival, Arrival, Stay and Departure.

Pre-Arrival Stage

As the term suggests, Pre-Arrival Stage comprises of all the guest activities and interaction that arises between the guest and hotel much before the guest actually arrives at the hotel. Though, physically the two entities might not meet, rather there is an absence of a face-to-face encounter and also it is the first interaction between the two. These conditions make the Pre-Arrival Stage an important first impression of the hotel establishment. In the Pre-Arrival Stage, Reservation is the most important activity that takes place. This is because during this phase, the guest makes a choice of a particular hotel for stay. There are many factors that cohesively come together and guests' choice about a particular hotel is affected by varied factors such as quality of website, advertisements in print, hoardings and media, experience of self and others, reputation and goodwill, location advantages, reviews, ratings recommendations, budget and pricing etc. Hence, managing the quality of all these activities and co-ordinating them is essential work towards influencing the guests' decision of selecting the property.

Once the hotel is shortlisted by guest to make a booking, the guest himself or the booker, which is the person designated by him, contacts the hotel by means of mail, phone, fax for making room reservation. This interaction is also important. How the call is received, how the guest is spoken to, how promptly his requests are reverted, accuracy of information, eagerness to please and politeness, terms and conditions and flexibility in approach, these are a few instances of interactions at this stage that need to be positive in order to make the booking. The reservation request is received by the reservation department. Once the details of reservation are taken and confirmed with the guest, the reservationist requests for an advance payment. With the online payment options, it is much easier and time saving to transfer funds. As soon as payment is received a guest folio is opened and rooms are "blocked". The management of room inventory at this stage is very important. Yield Management, which is based on the dynamics of market demand and rooms supply, rooms rates for that period are firmed. This is called Revenue Management, which is fluid pricing based on demand to optimize revenue and minimizing unsold rooms. Thus the function of front office in the pre-arrival phase include the following:

- Confirmation of the room reservation request of the guest.

- Receipt of advance payment and creation of guest folio.

- Confirmation and blocking the room for the guest.

- Taking note and communicating special arrangements required, if any (extra bed, crib, wheelchair, amenities etc. if required).

There is a lot of data collected during the process of reservation. This is utilized during further Front Office and sales activities' interactions and operations. A reservation system which is well organized and managed maximizes room sales and revenue by closely and constantly monitoring the room status and forecasting the room revenue.

Pre-Arrival Procedure for FIT guests

In hotel terminology, FIT refers to a Free Individual Traveller, and in Tourism the same term is expanded as Free Independent Tourist. Both mean the same. It refers to those travellers who travel independently, that is not in a group. They make their own hotel bookings and other travel arrangements. They are direct bookers and may make their stay arrangements through pre-booked reservations, or as walk-ins. The following is the pre-arrival procedure for FIT is simple. Only reconfirmation of booking is the important task.

- If the guest presents a confirmation letter, the Front Desk Associate verifies to check the date and the name of the hotel; the guest may have arrived on a different date at the wrong hotel.

- Check with the guest if the reservation was made by another person, it is possible that the reservation agent might have entered the reservation under the booker/caller name.

- Re-verify the reservation by searching the hotel software by last name, first name, reservation number, partial name search, mobile number, Booker name, company, travel agent, etc.

- If the guest had booked from the travel agent ask the guest to call up the travel agent and get more details of the booking.

Pre-Arrival Procedure for VIP guests

The term VIP refers to Very Important person. All hotel guests are VIPs, but within all guests, based on certain traits a few are selected by the management and termed as VIPs. These include celebrities, film stars, sport personalities, ministers, media personnel, top managers of key corporate accounts, sports, fussy guests and also regular guests. VIPs are Handle with Care (HWC) guests and demand special attention. The process of identifying a guest a VIP takes place before their arrival.

- A VIP status is often approved by the General Manager, Rooms Director/Director of Operations, or Director of Sales. Because all VIP's guests are pre-registered, the person approving the VIP status also assumes responsibility for the guests' credit status. The decision of qualifying a guest as VIP is with the front office department. Also, Sales department provides with inputs on whom, especially in case of corporate guests who may be classified as a VIP.

- The VIPs may be categorized into various sub categories and named as VIP A, B, C D or any other nomenclature. The type of guest and amenities is pre-determined against each category and the staff can easily provide services accordingly.

- The preregistration formalities are to be already completed in advance by an authorized representative of the hotel, and for registration the guest should take minimum time and only crucial details like signature should be asked for/In case of very high profile VIPs like film stars or industrialists, registration formalities may be carried out in the comfort and privacy of the guest's room.

- On arrival, the hotel if so required by the VIP guest, may arrange for a pickup from the airport. The pickup may be in various categories of luxury cars, depending on the status of the VIP. When a VIP guest arrives at the hotel, everyone should be alert, wish and the front office personnel should extend a warm welcome (ATG).

- The General Manager or Front Office Manager should escort the VIP guest to their room, and while allocation an upgrade may also be offered. Presidential Suite is often given to Heads of States.

Pre-Arrival Procedure for Groups

A group refers to a collective booking for at least fifteen or more number of rooms. It may be a corporate, social or leisure business, and has a group leader or group co-ordinator. The rate and inclusions along with the billing is pre-determined. Owing to the volume business that a group assures, the rate is special and discounted, but they also assure for guaranteed business especially lucrative during times of low demand. The check-in procedure for a group requires specialised preregistration activity as a group consists of a large number of people who have to be registered at the same time. The following steps are undertaken one or two days prior to group arrival:

- Duty roster be prepared for adequate staffing and allocation of duties. It is approved by the Front Office Manager.

- Read, understand and execute Group Contract and brief all staff accordingly. Consider all arrival guest profiles, history and special remarks, if any. Also, ascertain arrival and departure time of Group and make note of all relevant guest requirements and special needs. After cross checking the arrival and departure dates, the same are fed into the Group payment master folio. Cross check also the billing instructions on the Property Management System (PMS) for all group rooms in Group payment master.

- Check is group reservation details such as for rate code, room rate, meal packages, inclusions, instructions are correctly picked up in accordance to the group contract.

- Create Routing instructions on all group rooms to group payment master (If the billing instruction is Room + TAX to travel agent). This will also help to have a smoother check out experience for the group members and also cashiers.

- The front office makes a rooming list as per the list of guests as sent by the Travel Agent/ Company. An important detail is to check the number of occupants per room. If so needed, prepare a separate sharer guest folio accordingly. This will help at the time of checkout, if guests wish to pay separately. The rooming list is shared with other departments and serves as a reference with other departments like Housekeeping, Room Service, Coffee Shop, Finance etc.

- Print group arrival report for the date of group arrival and check room allocation. Allocation is based on room status and availability and needs of the arriving guests. Take special note and allocate rooms suited to special needs, Honeymooners, wedding anniversaries, birthdays, type of occupancy etc. Check for requirements like extra bed, baby cot requirement and send notification to the housekeeping department. Prioritize group early arrivals and specific room type requirements like suite rooms, interconnecting rooms, single lady guests etc.

- Ensure that housekeeping/Room service/Engineering is aware of any special needs of the group. Send a requisition form to this department and also create a trace on PMS.

- Call up the group coordinator and reconfirm the arrival time of the group.

- The front office should prepare a guest arrival list, which contains details of each guest in the group. The list contains details such as name, address, passport details in case of foreigners, Government Identification details, purpose of the visit, arrival and departure details, duration of stay, preferences for meal, and any special instructions.

- Key cards are pre-prepared, tagged and kept ready to be issued on arrival.

- A separate temporary counter may be set up in the lobby, away from the reception counter. This helps in managing the flow of the guests and avoids overcrowding. This also ensures that the group is attended to and so are the other FIT guests. Ensures prompt service without delay or queues.

- Once the type and number of guest rooms is confirmed, the front office should block the rooms for the group, preferably on the same floor. This confining adds to the convenience of not only group guests, but also other guests staying in the hotel.

Pre-Arrival Records

- Pre-Arrival List (Expected Arrival List).
- Notification to other department using the Notification Slip.
- Amenities Voucher.
- Welcome/Welcome back letter with a mention of hotel inclusions in room rate.
- Preparation of Guest Registration Card.

Pre-Arrival Records for VIPs

In addition to the standard pre-arrival records discussed above, also includes:

- VIP List (Expected VIP Arrival List).
- Amenities Voucher.
- Information to other departments.

Pre-Arrival Records for Groups

In addition to the standard pre-arrival records discussed above, also includes:

- Meal coupon.
- Separate check in counter.
- Key Cards.
- Rooming List.
- Personalized welcome letters and envelopes.

Room Reservation

- Separate check in counter.

- Key Cards.

- Rooming List.

- Personalized welcome letters and envelopes.

Arrival Procedure for various Categories of Guests

Registration

Each service encounter is a moment of truth. It starts much before the guest actually lands at the reception or at the hotel for that matter. Valet, doorman, bell boy, receptionist-all service personnel greet and welcome the guest (with standard phraseology and appropriate body language). On his arrival at the hotel, the guest usually goes to the reception area, which is manned by Front Office Associate or Receptionist. This is the first face-to-face long interaction of the guest. The registration activity which is also called as check-in, takes place at the reception. This procedure involves the guest to fill up the required details on the Guest Registration Card (GRC) or make entries in the hotel register. This is called as registration. Registration is the process of gathering information from the guest that is mandatory as per the laws prevailing in that country. According to Foreigners' Act 1946, and Registration of Foreigners Rules, 1992, the hotel establishment should keep the records of the guest staying in his premises as per Form F (of the Registration of Foreigners Rules, 1992). Registration is the formalization of a valid contract between the guest and the hotel, in which the hotel offers safe and secure boarding and lodging facilities to the guest and who accepts to pay for the same. Additionally, as part of the registration process, in case of foreigners, the front staff should also fill Form C and verify passports and visas of the guests. The Registration procedure incorporates seven distinct steps. These are:

- Pre-registration: Pre-registration refers to all those activities that are undertaken by the front desk agents before the arrival of the guests to the hotel. Doing this helps to plan and prepare for impending arrivals and helps accelerate or speeden the process of guest registration.

The Expected Arrivals List (EAL) is prepared on a daily basis. It mentions the names of all guests who are expected to arrive the next day, other details of their arrival and stay like time of arrival, date of departure, rooms requested reservation status special requests, and instructions are also mentioned. This report is printed the evening prior and is the basis of planning of operations. Rooms are also allocated against this report.

Expected Arrival List								
HOTEL ABC								
Arrival Date:								
S.No	Guest Name	Room No.	Expected Arrival time	Date of Departure	Room Rate	Pax	Billing instructions	Remarks

- Another important part of the inventory management plan, is calculation of the Room Position. It is the room availability status for the following day and is based on the expected arrivals and expected departures. It also includes factors such as overstays, under stays, no shows, and out of order rooms.

- Amenities Vouchers are also prepared for the arriving guests, and these are sent to the concerned departments such as housekeeping and FandB service. These vouchers instruct the type of amenities to be placed in each arrival room. Details of placement of amenities in guest room such as cookies, fruit platter, flowers, is done prior to guest arrival.

HOTEL ABC		
DATE:		DAY:
PLEASE SEND COMPLIMENTARY		
Tick	Tick	Tick
_____ Flowers	Single_____	Double_____Special_____
_____ Fruits	Single_____	Double_____Special_____
_____ Cookies	Single_____	Double_____Special_____
_____ Soft drink Bar/Full Bar		
To		
Mr/Ms_____ Date of Arrival_____ Room No Card to be attached: Remar ks:_____		

- The FO agent prepares the Guest Registration Card (GRC) in advance as part of pre-registration. The information that is required to be filled in the GRC is gathered from two sources: the reservation form and the guest history card. When this is done, it enables guests to experience a quick check-in when they arrive at the registration desk. This is because they only are required to verify information already entered in the registration card, and once done, guests have to only sign the registration card to check-in.

- In case of a walk-in guest, since the details are not present and a GHC has to be made afresh, all guest details are taken over the counter, hence the walk in guest takes comparatively longer as it is not supported by pre-registration.

- Depending upon the hotel's system, preregistration may be carried out either manually in manual and semi-automated systems, or fully automated Front Office system. The task is essentially transfer of guest data from reservation and guest history directly onto the registration form. In case of manual system, it can be a laborious process.

- The pre-registration process is crucial for inventory management function as it reflects the expected arrivals and the room availability status. This allows the front desk staff to make necessary arrangements and welcome walk-ins. Apart from that, preregistration makes check-in for guests faster.

- Creating the registration record: After the guests' arrival at the hotel; it is important for the front desk agent to create record registration which is a collection of important guest information and is mandatory as per the laws of the country. It requires the guest to mention his/her details, such as: full name, address and other information. The formats used during the check-in of the guests are:

1. Guest Registration Card (GRC): Registration card is filled by the guest during check-in. It is a very important document, maintained in hard copy from where a front desk agent gets all the

information about the guest. It consists of details of guest like name, address, organization name and address, nationality, arrival time and date, expected date of departure, purpose of visit, room number, number of person, room rate etc.

Hotel ABC Guest Registration Card
No. _____
Name of the guest: _____ Date of birth: _____
Company: _____ Designation: _____
Address of the guest: _____
Passport No. : _____ Nationality: _____
Passport: Date of Issue: _____ Validity: _____
Date of arrival in XYZ Country: _____ Proposed duration of stay in XYZ Country: _____
Proceeding to: _____ Purpose of visit: _____
Whether employed in XYZ Country: [ ] Yes [ ] No Registration certificate no. _____
Date of arrival in hotel: _____ Time of arrival: _____
Room No: _____ Room Type: _____ Pax: _____ Plan: _____
Date of departure from hotel: _____ Time of departure: _____
Mode of payment: _____
Credit/Debit card no.: _____ Expiry: _____
I agree to abide by the hotel rules and regulations:
Guest's signature: _____ Receptionist's signature: _____
Check in noon; Check out 10 a.m.

Guest Registration Card

2. C Form: A foreigner is any person born in or coming from a country other than one's own. He holds a passport for a country. C Form is a legal document which has to be filled by all foreign nationals. Children up to 16 years and diplomats from other countries are also exempted from filling C form. All places of accommodation, including hotels, guest houses, dharamshala, universities, hospitals, institutes, hostels or any other place that provides accommodation to foreigners, must submit the details of the residing foreigners in Form C. This helps registration authorities in locating and tracking the foreigners. The hotel is liable to send the information in the C form to the nearest (Foreigners' Regional Registration Office (FRRO), mostly located only in metropolitan cities. or in case of absence of FRRO in the city, it must be sent to Local Intelligence Unit (LIU). In smaller cities or towns, the C form has to be sent to the local police station. This is to be done within 24 hrs of arrival of any foreigner national; in case of Pakistani, Bangladeshi and Chinese nationals, this information should reach within 12 hours of the guests' arrival in the hotel premise. Pakistani forms are directly sent to special branch of FRRO called Pakistan Cell. The C Form is made in triplicate, whereby the first original top is sent to the FRRO, the second copy is sent to the local police station, and the third copy is kept as office record with the hotel. With

digitalization, the same information can be now uploaded on the official website. This is speedier and convenient.

Hotel ABC Form C (Rule 14)

S. No. _____ Date:

Name of the Hotel: _____ Complete Address of Hotel: _____

Name of the foreign visitor: _____

(In full in block letters, surname first)

Date of birth: _____

Company: _____ Designation: _____

Passport No. : _____ Nationality: _____

Passport: Date and Place of Issue: _____ Validity: _____

Address in XYZ Country: _____

Date of arrival in XYZ Country: _____ Arrived from: _____

Whether employed in XYZ Country: [ ] Yes [ ] No

Registration certificate no. _____ Date and Place of Issue: _____

Proposed duration of stay in XYZ Country: _____ Proposed duration of stay in the hotel: _____
Proceeding to: _____ Purpose of visit: _____

Manager's signature: _____

Form C

- Passport: The Front Office staff should verify the passport of foreign nationals. A passport is a document issued by the government to allow its citizens to travel abroad, and requests other governments to facilitate their passage and provide protection on reciprocal basis.

- Visa: Foreign nationals visiting XYZ Country need to possess a valid passport and a valid XYZ Country visa. Visa is an endorsement on the passport, allowing the holder to enter the territory of the issuing country. It is a document or more frequently a stamp, authorising the bearer to visit a country for a specific length of time. However, the issuance may not be treated as a guarantee to enter into the foreign territory. The bearer may be subjected to inspection at the port of entry and may be asked to produce the documents presented at the time of procurement of visa. Types of visas: Immigrant/Permanent, Temporary/Non Immigrant which include Tourist, Student, Business, Work and Transit Visas.

- Arrival and Departure Register: It is a register maintained by the Front Desk Agent which monitors all the arrivals and departures on a particular day. It monitors the rooms allocated and those just vacated for helping the Housekeeping department for making rooms ready again for guests. It also helps to find out the number of people checked in so as to calculate the house count.

- Assigning the room: Assignment is an important part of the registration process. It involves identifying, blocking and allocating available rooms in a specific room category to a guest. Room and room rates may be pre assigned on the basis of information as confirmed during reservation. Room assignments assigned as part of pre-registration, but finalized only during registration.

- Establishing the method of payment: Hotels insist that all reservations be paid for in advance, preferably fully or at least partly. Especially in case of periods of high demand, it is important to confirm bookings. There are various modes by means of which a guest may choose while making a payment both in advance as well as on departure or end of the stay. These are:

  - Cash: Cash is the best method of payment especially for the scanty baggage or no baggage guest. These guests are required to make cash deposits at least for the first night.

  - Credit Cards: Nowadays most of the guests prefer to pay through their credit cards, as they get the advantage of credit payment depending upon their payment cycle, and also earn loyalty points. It safer and less bulky and may be used across borders. The front office agent must verify some credit card details such as expiry date, credit card number and should also check whether the card is accepted by the hotel.

  - Debit Cards: This is another type of card used by the guest. In this method the amount is directly deducted from the guest's bank account.

  - Miscellaneous charge orders/voucher: These are payments made in advance to Airline Reporting Corporations (ARC) or Travel Agents for the hotel services. The ARC or travel agent issues an MCO or voucher respectively which is presented to the hotel to adjust charges. The MCO/voucher is redeemed later by the hotel from the ARC/travel agent.

  - Special Promotions Payment Methods: Some guests may present vouchers, coupons, gift certificates, or special incentive awards received from businesses, airlines or other authorized agencies. The front desk agents must be aware of hotel agreements to honor such vouchers and take care because such documents may differ in value, conditions or terms.

  - Bill to Company: For the bills to be sent to the company for settlement involves deferred payment and also a risk of delayed payment, sometimes leading to a bad debt. This facility is offered to companies that are approved by the Finance department, after studying their financial standing and historic payment record. Also, the Front Office Agent must confirm that a billing letter is received for each such booking.

  - Personal Checks: Most hotels have a strict policy against accepting personal checks, though some may accept them. Hotels may accept checks only during standard banking hours to allow the front office staff to obtain bank verification of the check if necessary.

- Verifying the guest identity: It is mandatory nowadays for the guests to provide photo identification in the form of a passport or a citizen card to ensure positive identification of the guest's name, address, signature and photograph. Verifying the guest's identity is compulsory in all hotels. The type of identification and identification number on the card or passport should be recorded in the guest record. As an additional security measure, if the guest does not speak the local language, it should also be noted in the guest's record. This information helps the hotel staff to identify guests requiring foreign language translation and is also helpful in emergency situations.

- Issuance of Room Key:

  - By issuing a room key the front office agent completes the registration process. For the security of both the guest and the property, room keys must be very carefully controlled.

  - Also for safety and security reasons, the front desk agent should never announce the room number when handing a guestroom key to a guest. If the hotel provides bell service, the front desk agent should introduce the bell attendant to the guest, hand the guestroom key to the bell attendant and ask him or her to show the guest to the room.

  - On the way to the room, the bell attendant should familiarize the guest with hotel information such as special feature, locations of emergency exits, emergency procedures, restaurant locations, retail outlets and their hours of operations, and other appropriate information.

  - Once inside the guestroom, the bell attendant should explain the features of the room, answer any questions and hand the room key to the guest.

  - If the guest is displeased with the room, the bell attendant should listen attentively and bring the matter to the attention of the front desk agent for immediate action.

- Fulfilling Special Requests: During registration, the front office agent must make sure that the special requests made by the guest during the reservations process are acted upon. Some requests may be:

  - Location – E.g. close to or far from elevator,

  - View (pool, city, direction),

  - Bed Type,

  - Smoking/non-smoking,

  - Amenities,

  - Special furnishings for disabled guests such grab bars in bathrooms,

  - Special rooms for single lady travellers,

  - High-speed Internet access,

  - Entertainment systems.

Check-in of FITs with Reservation

- FIT Check-in: At the bell desk:

  - The doorman greets the guest.

- The bellboy receives the guest, carries his luggage and leads the guest to the front desk.

- The bellboy returns to bell desk and keeps the guest luggage at the bell desk and waits until the guest completes registration.

- He then fills out an arrival errand card.

- He hands over the errand card to the receptionist.

- After the guest has been registered and the room is allotted, the receptionist will write the name of the guest and room number on the bell boy errand card and give it back to the bell boy along with the room key.

- The bellboy carries the guest luggage from the bell desk and escorts the guest to his room.

- At the room the bell boy unlocks the door, switches on the lights, explains the functioning of all appliances in the guest room, asks the guest if he needs assistance with unpacking his luggage, he wishes the guest good stay and returns to the bell desk.

- He hands over the errand card to the bell captain.

- FIT Check In: At the Front Desk:

  - When the guest with reservation arrives at the front desk, the front office receptionist must ask for the guest reservation status, which may be a confirmation letter or confirmation number.

  - In some hotels pre-registration may be done for all guests with reservation. If pre-registration is done then registration form is given to the guest, who checks the details entered are correct and sign the form. If the pre-registration is not done then the guest must fill up the registration form and the Front Office Assistant should provide assistance in filling the form.

  - After the guest has signed on the registration form, the receptionist will verify the method of payment.

  - A room is assigned to the guest and the room number is written on the registration form and on the errand card.

  - The receptionist then hands over the room key to the bellboy or the guest.

  - After the room is key is given and the guest has been escorted to the room, the Front Office cashier must open a folio under the guest name and his room number.

Walk-in Guest Check-in

- Walk-in Guest Check-in: At the bell desk:

  - The doorman greets the guest.

  - The bellboy receives the guest, carries his luggage and leads the guest to the front desk.

  - The Front office assistant checks the room status.

- If the room is available, then the bellboy returns to bell desk and keeps the guest luggage at the bell desk and waits until the guest completes registration.

- He then fills out an arrival errand card.

- He hands over the errand card to the receptionist.

- After the guest has been registered and the room has been allotted, then the receptionist will write the name of the guest and room number on the bell boy errand card and give it back to the bell boy along with the room key.

- The bellboy carries the guest luggage from the bell desk and escorts the guest to his room.

- At the room the bell boy unlocks the door, switches on the lights, explains the functioning of all appliances in the guest room, asks the guest if he needs any assistance with unpacking his luggage, he wishes the guest good stay and returns to the bell desk.

- He hands over the errand card to the bell captain.

- Walk-in Guest Check-in: At the Front Desk:

  - In the case of a walk in guest, the Front office assistant must first find out what the guest needs.

  - After ascertaining guest requirement, the Front office assistant must sell the rooms and facilities of the hotel to the guest.

  - When the guest has decided on the type of room, the Front office assistant must give him a registration form and helps the guest in filling the form.

  - The method of payment of the guest must be determined; if the guest is paying through a credit card then the credit card number is taken. If the guest is paying through bill to company then Front office assistant must check if the company is approved by the hotel.

  - After the method of payment has been determined the guest signs on the registration form and give the form back to the receptionist.

  - Front office assistant writes the room number on the form and hands over the room key to the guest or bellboy.

  - Front office cashier opens a folio under the guest's name and his/her room number.

Check-in of a Group

- The evening before the date of the arrival of the group reservation section send the details of the group expected to arrive to the reception. These details include the name of the group, name of travel agent or company, date of arrival/departure, arrival details, type of accommodation required, meals plan, rooming list from these details the receptionist will carry out pre-registration of the group, prepare key envelopes with room keys and meals coupons, if required a separate group arrival counter may be set up to receive and register the group. The bar is informed for the welcome drink and the HK department is informed to check for a confirmed availability of rooms. The bell captain is informed in order to arrange for the required number of bellboys at the time of arrival of groups.

- Luggage handling during check in is also important. The luggage of the group is identified, individually tagged and transferred to the rooms. The bell boys carry the luggage of the group together.

- Requisition given to Room service for group welcome drinks and hot/cold towel. These are pre-prepared and kept ready to be served promptly on arrival.

- The group leader completes the registration process for the entire group and fills GRCs and take signature on them.

- Group Welcome letter is prepared, neatly folded and kept in envelope. Apart from rest, inclusions and incidental charges are mentioned.

- Guests may proceed to their respective rooms and the group leader confirms meal preferences, wake up calls, day's activities and special needs.

- Check-in of a Group at the Bell Desk:

    ◦ The bellboys unload the guest luggage and bring them to the bell desk.

    ◦ At the bell desk the baggage of individual group members is separated, nametags are put on the baggage in order to separate them.

    ◦ The bellboys then load the luggage on to the luggage trolley and the errand card is filled.

    ◦ After registration of the group is completed, the bellboys will transfer the luggage to respective guest rooms.

- Check-in of a Group at the Front Desk:

    ◦ On arrival group is welcomed by the GRE and the group members are seated in the lobby. A welcome drink is provided.

    ◦ The group leader is taken to the check in counter where he is asked to sign on registration form and to confirm the rooming details.

    ◦ All the group members are given the pre-registered registration from to verify the details and to sign on the form.

    ◦ After all members have signed in the registration form and group leader has checked the rooming arrangements, the FO assistant will hand over the key envelopes to the group leader.

    ◦ The group leader distributes the key envelope to the group members and the bellboy escorts them to rooms.

    ◦ The FO cashier opens a common master folio for entire group and individual folios for each group member.

Check-in of Crew Members

- Crew members are staffs of Airline companies. They normally have a tie up with a hotel and promises regular business. The Lobby manager and bell desk usually handle check in of a crew guest.

- On arrival the crew members will bring with them a crew sheet or the airline office may have sent the crew sheet to the hotel before the arrival of the crew. The crew sheet contains names of all crew members and their ranks and passport details with their signatures.

- The lobby manager allots rooms to crew members after they have signed on registration form.

- The lobby manager fills a wake-up call sheet.

- The bellboy escorts the crew to the room. The wake-up call time is informed to the telephone department.

- The Front office cashier opens a folio for the crew.

HOTEL ABC

CREW CHECK-IN SHEET

CREW .... DATE OF ARR .... TIME OF ARR..........

Roo m no.	Designa tion	Name	Nation ality	Passpo rt	Dt. Of is sue	Plac e of issue	Signat ure	Dt. Of depart ure	Rema rks

Departure : Date ....   Front Office Asst. ....

WAKE CALL ....   ASST. MANAGER ....
PICK UP ....

Criteria for Taking Advance (Walk-ins, Scanty Baggage etc.)

Scanty Baggage Guest

- A guest who arrives at the front desk requesting for accommodation and is carrying very less or no baggage is known as scanty baggage guest.

- In case of arrival of such a guest, the bell boy should inform about the same to the front desk. The bellboy keeps the guest luggage at the bell desk and fills out an arrival errand card. He writes SB (Scanty Baggage) on the errand card and hands over the errand card to Front office assistant.

- For registering a scanty baggage guest, the FOA should take authorisation from the Duty Manager.

- All The registration formalities should be completed just as in case of walk-ins. After the registration is completed the Front office assistant writes the room number on the errand card and hands over the room key along with the errand card to the bellboy.

- Ensure that an advance payment for the entire duration of stay is asked from the guest.

- The Front Office Associate should imprint the "Scanty Baggage" stamp on the GRC.

- The Front Office Associate should prepare APC (All payment cash) slips and send it to all Points of Sale (POS).

- The FOA should allot a room and hand over the room key to the guest. A bellboy should escort the guest to the room.

Check in Procedures in Hotels and Company Guest Houses

Similar procedure for check in and registration is carried in all types of accommodation establishments. In case of smaller places of stay, the system may not be fully automated. In such cases, formats are made and preserved in hard bound registers.

Room Reservation

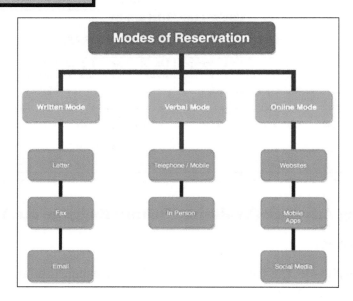

Reservation section plays a pivotal role in room sales and may be considered as backbone of front office department in hotels. Room reservation section reserves room for all future dates and for the current day reception takes care of booking rooms. Luxury and other hotels at prominent places are sold one year in advance and sometimes more before that keeping in view all instructions from the guest with any special requests, billing instructions, etc. of the guest and further pass on the information to reception for easy and comfortable check-in of the guest on the date of arrival. In present times the computerized reservations systems and the property management system makes the task easy as the information is easily shared by all the point of sales in the hotel such as housekeeping, room service, etc. Room booking generally is considered to be confirmed after the advance payment for the guest. When the hotel receives the advance same is acknowledged with a receipt and the confirmation letter.

The utmost importance of reservation section is giving a hotel chance to equate the guest inquiry with the rooms' availability on a particular day and thus gives hotel sufficient time to get most suitable guest rooms ready. The section is also able to forecast the business that the hotel would get in future and the revenue generation respectively. The forecast of business also allows the hotel to plan for human resources. The reservation of room is taken on a reservation form manually, taking down each instruction and any preferences accurately. The reservation/cancellation/amendment is further updated in computerized system for easy communication. Sometimes hotels are even overbooked to achieve 100% occupancy and to achieve the same rooms need to be overbooked keeping in mind certain considerations such as no-shows, cancellation, amendments, etc. Overbooking means to confirm more number of rooms than available on a particular day and is a deliberate act by the hotel.

Duties of Reservation Personnel

The number of reservation personnel depends on the size of the hotel. The major duties and responsibilities of reservationist are:

- Receive and handle enquires related to booking through various modes of communication. The personnel needs to be well versed with new technological advancements adopted by industry form time to time.

- Coordinate and communicate with sales and marketing division for any reservations and updating of the same respectively.

- Have knowledge and information about the product and the availability of the same in the concerned and other hotels of the chain with the help of system of reservations adopted by that organization.

- Possess knowledge of various plans, packages, and seasonal rates to be offered to the guests during their request for booking.

- Creates and maintains the reservation record of the guests and send the confirmation number to the concerned guest.

- Communicate the reservation policy of the hotel and the reservations agreement guidelines for better understanding and maintaining brand image in the market.

- Communicating reservation records with the reception/registration for easy operations.

- Maintain company volume guaranteed rate.

- Maintain discount registers as and when required and refer the same at the time of booking.

Modes of Reservation in Hotel

The mode of reservations tells the hotel management how the reservation has reached the hotel. For example, a reservation request may reach the hotel through traditional methods like a written mode such as letter, fax, telex or e-mail or through a verbal mode like telephone or in-person etc. In this modern era, the majority of the reservation is via online modes like website, OTA, mobile apps, social media etc.

- Written Mode:

  ○ Letter: This mode is commonly used by travel agents, tour operators, companies and corporate houses who send in their reservation request to the hotel on their company letterheads. The hotel will make the reservation as per the details are given in the letter.

  ○ Fax: Fax or facsimile transmission uses electronic scanning technique to send copies of a document over an ordinary telephone line over a special machine that prints identical copies of the document. This makes it possible to send a reservation request instantaneously. Hotels process the request as per details and send the confirmation letter to the guest.

  ○ Telex: Telex or Tele Printer Exchange involves the use of specialized telephone lines, where the message is communicated in a written form.

  ○ E-mail: The most common method of communication E-mail is an electronic mail that makes it possible to contact the hotel instantaneously. The hotel will process the reservation request on the basis of the details given. This mode of reservation is fast and very convenient.

- Verbal Mode: Reservation requests may also reach the hotel through verbal mode or oral communication i.e. in person or over the telephone. The advantage of oral communication is that it generates immediate response and feedback and is very fast and convenient. Additionally, the guest can get complete information and clear any doubts through oral communication. The disadvantage of the Verbal mode is that it does not provide a permanent record or correspondence of the agreed booking terms and conditions.

  ○ In-Person: If an individual or a representative goes to the hotel to book rooms for future it is termed as an In-Person reservation. When an individual comes to the hotel and requests a room for the day it is termed as a Walk-In Reservation. The hotel processes the rooms according to the details given by the guest and issues a confirmation number and a letter if the reservation is made for future and assigns a room if the guest requests for one for the same day.

  ○ Telephone: The most common method of direct reservation communications, a prospective guest may telephone the hotel directly. The reservation assistant takes the information sequentially as per the script. Most of the hotels these days have high-end systems that record a call which can be used later on for training purpose.

- Online Mode: The online mode is the preferred mode of booking in this era of internet, web and mobile. The main advantage of the online mode is that the hotels are always available for reservations and generate an instant confirmation voucher as per the real-time availability. Other advantages with the online mode are that the hotel can also ask the guests to make a prepayment for the reservations well in advance and reduce the chance of no-shows.

  ○ Web: Guest making a booking via a web browser like hotels website or booking engine, different online travel agent - OTA's, review sites like Trip Advisor etc.

- ○ Mobile App: Bookings delivered via hotels own or third-party mobile apps.

- ○ Social Media: Bookings made via different social media like facebook, twitter, Instagram etc.

Source of Reservation

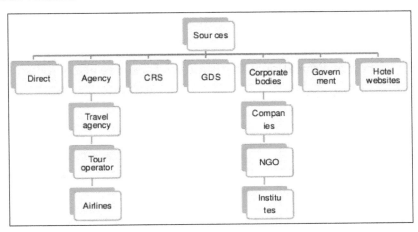

The reservation in of accommodation in a hotel is usually generated through the different organization as they are determined to get the stay and take delivery of the service facilities. The various sources through which the reservations come to the hotel are listed below:

- Travel and Tour Organization:

  - ○ Tour Operator: These are wholesalers who coordinate with different mode of transportations, hotels, tour, associations, tourist offices etc.

  - ○ Travel Agencies: Travel agencies are the backbone of the tourism industry and potential source of business for any hotel. They are the generator and creator of the hotel business. They collect travel and tour information regarding purpose of visit and develop new idea and promote new destinations as well.

  - ○ Trekking Agencies: Trekking is simply defined as foot travel on mountain, trails or walking on foot in discomfort areas. They are the source of reservation in hotel for accommodation and food.

  - ○ Rafting Agency: Rafting agencies organize trip on fast flowing river water by boat/dug out/rafts/canoe for short or long distance. It is one of the most sought after water sports which is full of adventure. In Nepal wildlife watch, fishing trip are very popular offered to the guest in the form of package.

  - ○ Mountaineering Agencies: It is related to the show covered high altitude mountains. The duration of stay in the hotel is very short due to camp out programs.

- Airlines: The role of airlines, whether international or domestic is to provide quick transportation to the masses. Airlines promote tourism growth and help in earning considerable amount of foreign exchange.

- Companies and Commercial Business Role uses: The companies and commercial business role uses reserve rooms for their clients or guests, participants, employees, etc. When they are out of station on deputing.

- NGOs and INGOs: The organization provides accommodating reservation and other facilities for their guest and employees.

- Embassy and consulate offices: They are good source of reservation. They reserve the room for the expatriates and officials from their country.

- Universities and other Educational Institutions: These are also good source of reservation students associations, professors, technicians and employees are the reliable reservation source to hotel.

- Ministries and Government offices: They reserve the room for their guest, diplomats or government employees. Usually they are sent for official programs. Participation in international conference/summit, seminars or sports events is the main objective of these groups.

- UN organization and Banks: These are valuable source as they come for special mission for short duration. Special packages rates are offered at high discounts on rooms and food and beverages.

- Free Individual travellers (FIT): A group coming to a hotel as an individual and not as a part of a group is typically referred to as an FIT. They don't seek the service of travel agencies.

- Chain Hotel and Referable from other hotels: Through the channel of group hotels, rooms are booked for guest mostly on confirmed reservation request. These guests from chain hotels or other individual hotels usually come under guaranteed reservation.

- Global Distribution System (GDS): GDS is a network of providers that bring products and services that are geographically spread to the doors representation of costumer anywhere in the world.

- Central Reservation System (CRS): CRS are another expanding phenomenon to make booking easier. They provide toll free telephone number to encourage travellers to use their facility.

Types of Reservation

Guaranteed Reservations

The hotel assures a guest with a guaranteed reservation that a room will be held for him or her until check-out time of the day following the day of arrival. In return, the guest guarantees payment for the room, even if it is not used, unless the reservation is cancelled in accordance with the hotel's cancellation procedures. The term no-show refers to a guest who made a room reservation but did not use it or cancel it. Guaranteed reservations protect the hotel's revenues even in the case of a no-show. Variations of guaranteed reservations include:

- Prepayment: A prepayment guaranteed reservation requires a payment in full made before the day of arrival. From the perspective of the front office, this form of reservation guarantee is generally the most desirable.

- Credit Card: Major credit card companies have developed systems to guarantee participating properties payment for reserved rooms that remain unoccupied. Unless a credit card guaranteed reservation is properly cancelled before a stated cancellation hour, the lodging property will post the charge to the guest's credit card account and the card company will subsequently bill the card holder. This is the most common method of reservation guarantee.

- Advance Deposit: An advance deposit guaranteed reservation (or partial prepayment) requires the guest to furnish a specified amount of money I in advance of arrival. The deposit is typically large enough to cover one night's lodging plus taxes, but may be larger if the reservation is for a longer stay. Should a guest holding an advance deposit reservation fail to show or cancel, the hotel may choose to retain the deposit and cancel the reservation for the entire stay.

- Travel Agent: Although travel agent guaranteed reservations were quite popular before the 1980s, they are becoming less common since both travel agents and hotels tend to prefer credit card or deposit guarantees when possible. Under this guarantee method, the hotel generally bills the travel agency after a guaranteed reservation has been classified a no-show.

- Corporate: A corporation may sign a contractual agreement with the hotel in which it agrees to accept financial responsibility for any no-show business travellers it sponsors. The use of corporate contracts is often popular in hotels with large transient markets.

- Non-Guaranteed Reservations: In the case of a non-guaranteed reservation, the hotel agrees to hold a room for the guest until a stated reservation cancellation hour, usually 6:00 p.m., on the day of arrival. The property is not guaranteed payment under this type of reservation. If the guest does not arrive by the cancellation hour, the hotel is free to release the room for other use; it is effectively added to the list of rooms available for sale. If the guest arrives after the cancellation hour and rooms remain available, the hotel will accommodate the guest. Hotels approaching full occupancy may choose to begin accepting only guaranteed reservations once a specified number of expected arrivals has been achieved. In full occupancy situations, the efficiency of the reservations process is especially critical.

- Tentative/Provisional Reservation: Provisional reservation is done when a request from prospective guest is received for some future day arrival and the hotel blocks the room for this guest, provisionally in the hotel records such as charts and diaries and racks or computer and sends a letter of offer to the prospective guest. The offer has a cut-off date by which the guest should send his confirmation which may be in the form of a letter, guarantee by company, credit card or deposit whichever the hotel may request. Once the confirmation from the guest is received by the hotel within the cut-off date, the hotel makes the tentative booking into confirmed booking. Otherwise the tentative booking is cancelled and the records updated.

Group Reservation

Group reservations can involve a variety of contacts: meeting planners, housing or convention bureaus, tour operators, and travel agents. Group reservations typically involve intermediary agents and require special care. Usually when a group selects a hotel, its representative deals with the hotel's sales division. If space is available, an agreed-upon number of rooms, called a block, is set aside for the group's members. As reservations are received from group members, they are applied against the rooms held in the group's block, thereby reducing the number of rooms available within the block. Rooms reserved for specific guests are referred to as booked; hence, as group members reserve rooms, their status changes from blocked to booked.

Reservation Availability

Once inquiry data are received, they are compared to previously processed reservations to determine the availability of remaining accommodations Processing a reservation request results in one of several responses. These responses include:

- Acceptance of the reservation as requested.

- Suggestions of alternative room types and/or rates.

- Suggestions of alternative hotel properties.

In any reservation system, it is necessary to keep a close check on reservations to avoid overbooking-that is, accepting reservations that outnumber available rooms .A hotel may certainly try to book for a full house, but avoiding overbooking makes good business sense in several, ways: Most important, it helps maintain good customer relations and encourages repeat business. In addition, hotels may be subject to law-suit when they fail to furnish agreed-upon accommodations. To avoid overbooking, hotels must monitor room availability through reservations coordination. A reservations control book, wall chart, computerized system, or some other control device must be established and maintained.

Procedure of Reservation

Identification of the Sources of Business

The hotel normally identifies two major sources of business: Free Independent Travellers (FIT) and associated Travellers (Groups). The FIT component is simply a non-group affiliate seeking overnight accommodations. Regardless of whether a request is made by an individual, a family or a collection of friends, a request may still be termed as FIT reservation if it meets certain qualifications. When meeting groups, convention groups, and the like are seeking guest room space in the hotel, these types of requests are referred to as group reservations. The groups are differentiated from the FIT reservations based on 1.) Whether a group coordinator is involved. 2.) Whether the group will pick up some or all of its member's charges. 3.) Whether special room rates, services and/or room types apply. Group reservations typically require that a block of rooms (allocation) be initially reserved for the group with a specific rooming list following at a later date. It should be noted that if a group does not have all of its blocked rooms booked by a reasonable date, most hotels will release the uncommitted rooms from the group's block. FIT reservations; however usually allow for both blocking and booking taking place simultaneously. Regardless of its source of business, a reservation request begins the hotel's reservation process read more about different source of reservation.

Communication with the Hotel

There are numerous ways a hotel can learn about the guest's request for available space. The potential guest can connect with the hotel via a telephone, email, online, Social Media, other devices or referral systems may all become important, communication links between the sources of business and the hotel property. It is important that the potential customer be aware of how to contact the hotel in order for lodging management to maximise guest room sales. A property receives reservation inquiries in a variety of ways. The reservation request may be made in person, over a telephone, in a mail, via facsimile or telex, though the internet or online, social media, mobile apps, instant messaging systems (Whatsapp, Telegram, Facebook Messenger) through a central reservation system, global distribution system or through an inter sell agency.

Formulation of the Reservation Request

Once a hotel is contacted by a guest about reserving space its staff must intelligently formulate the reservation request and complete a reservation record. The reservation record is the permanent file form used to store all the information pertinent to a specific reservation or in current era creating a computerised reservation record in the hotel management software or PMS. In formulating the reservation request, the three most important factors are a) the expected date of arrival and departure b) the desired room type c) the number of rooms needed. Using this information the hotel staff can search the room availability file via the designated arrival date. If the date is not closed the reservation agent proceeds by checking room type and the number of rooms available. Along with this preliminary data, a reservation record will usually be judged complete when it includes the following information:

- Guest's Profile Data.
- Guest's group/company affiliation.
- Arrival date and time and departure date.
- The number of nights.
- Number of Pax.
- Room type requested.
- The number of rooms required.
- Type of bed.
- Rate quoted/Rate Code.
- Date reservation received.
- Reservation Status.

- Billing Instruction.

- Pickup Details.

- Any other Details or special remarks.

- Source Code.

- Market Code.

Reservation Acceptance

A reservation can either be accepted or denied or turned away based on the availability of rooms in the day(s) in question. An acceptance would lead the receptionist into the confirmation phase, while a denial or turn away could cause a series of other options to be exercised like for example recording the turn away reason etc.

Confirmation Notification

The acceptance of the reservation is followed by a notification confirming the blocking of a room or group of rooms. The reservation confirmation is sent to the booker or guest by email, fax, SMS, social media or online chat (Instant messenger). The confirmation establishes:

- A check on the entered reservation request data and satisfaction of the reservation request.

- An agreement of room rates.

- An agreement of method of payment.

- A statement of the hotel's cancellation procedure.

Modification and Pre-Arrival Activity

Once the reservation has been accepted and confirmed many changes to reservation record can occur prior to the guest's arrival. Changes in the arrival or departure dates, number of rooms required, adding pickup details, reconfirmation, updating deposit status, number of pax and outright cancellations are examples of common pre-arrival activities. Any time a change in a reservation record is required; the reservation record must be pulled and updated according to the guest request to keep the reservation-related data up to date. Also searching and retrieving the correct reservation record for any modification and cancellation request is crucial to an effective reservation process. Also, while processing the cancellation below details need to be updated on the reservation record for any future reference.

- Caller Name.

- Caller contact details.

- Reason for Cancellation.

- Cancellation reference number.

- Date of Cancellation (Recorded automatically by the hotel software or enter manually).

Front Office: Operations and Management

- User or Reservation Agent Name who processed the cancellation (Recorded automatically by the hotel software or enter manually).

Cancellation/Amendments

A guest actually does a service to the hotel when they take time to cancel a reservation instead of not informing and then the reservation becomes a no-show. A reservation cancellation informs the hotel that a previously reserved room is once again available, and helps the front desk more effectively manage its room inventory. Hotels should make processing cancellation easy and efficient. Reservation Cancellation, like any guest service, requires the hotel staff to be polite, courteous and effective as possible.

Cancelling a Non-Guaranteed Reservation

Following points to be taken with care while cancelling a non-guaranteed reservation:

- Obtain the guest's name and address.
- Number of reserved rooms.
- Arrival and departure date.
- The reservation confirmation number if available.
- Name and contact number of the Person calling for cancelling the booking.
- Reason of cancellation.

These information will ensure that the correct reservation record is accessed by the reservation agent and then cancelled. After recording the cancellation, if available the agent can give the cancellation number to the guest/caller who had cancelled the booking. Reservation agent must ensure that the correct reservation has been cancelled and also may ask the guest whether they would like to make an alternate reservation for any other dates.

Cancelling a Guaranteed or Credit Card Guaranteed Reservations

While cancelling a guaranteed reservation, along with the points mentioned above the reservation agent should also take care of the following points:

- Communicate to the caller that according to the hotel cancellation policy their credit card would be charged along with the total amount which is going to be charged.
- After processing the cancellation the reservation agent should give the cancellation number to the guest, this would be retained by the guest as proof of cancellation int he event of erroneous credit card billing.
- Make the reservation record as cancelled, properly initiated and documented and add the cancellation number to the reservation record.
- Most credit card companies support no-show billing only if the hotel issues a cancellation number.

- If a non-automated property then update the room availability, returning the reserved room back to availability status.

File cancelled reservation documentation for future references as per the hotel policy. In a non-automated hotel the reservation record is kept until the expected date of arrival just in case the reservation was cancelled by mistake.

Advance Deposit Policy

Polices related to cancellation of reservations with advance deposits may always very among hotels. The reservation agent should treat cancellation of reservations with advance deposit with much care as they do with other types of reservation cancellations. According to the hotel policy of some hotels the advance deposit charges are refunded back to the guest after deducting the applicable cancellation charges.

Systems of Reservation

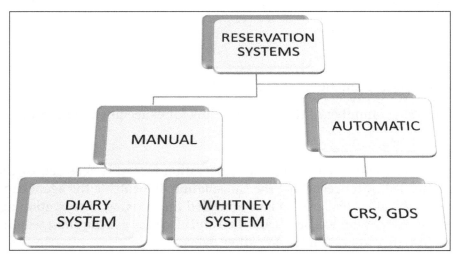

All reservations received in hotels are entered and updated somewhere so that the same is retrieved in shortest possible time. The recording of the reservations in a particular method is called system of reservation. The system of reservation is dependent on types and sizes of hotels. The methods are:

Non-Automated

The non-automatic or manual systems of reservation were common before automation in hotels. Two manual systems were generally used by hotels depending on the type/size of the hotel.

- Diary System: The hotel diary system of reservation is found in small sized hotels having limited number of guest rooms. A diary is used in this kind of system that consists of 366 pages to mark the days of year. The reservation is recorded on reservation slip/form and then later transferred to diary according to the arrival of the guest. The diary consists various information such as room types, plans, PAX, mode of payment etc. The biggest advantage of diary system is that it is easy to understand. Even a new recruit will learn the system in short time independently. All the advance reservation is entered in the diary and less risk of losing the particular reservation. It is a cheapest system of reservation. This system requires less space as the diaries can be stored one over the other. The only limitation of diary system is that its time consuming, difficult to move, only one person can use the diary at a time and it might untidy.

Table: Room Reservation Diary.

S. No .	Name of the guest	Type of Accommoda- tion	No. of Pa x	Arrival Time	Date and Time of depar- ture	Purpose of Visit	Billing In- structions	Ad- vance	Booked by	Signa- ture

- Whitney System: It is one of the popular systems of processing reservation in large hotels not automatized. The Whitney system of reservation consists of large wooden racks called Whitney racks having 14 to 16 columns. The first columns are the broadest and stores res- ervation of the present month of the present month. The next 11 columns denote the forth- coming eleven columns of the present and next year. The last two columns are for the subsequent years to come. The information on the Whitney slips is transferred from the reservation form. The main advantages of Whitney system is that it's adjustable, able to provide instant information and time saving. The disadvantages of this system are that it requires more space; slips may lose, could have typing errors and be costly.

Table: Whitney Slip.

Name	Type of Room	No. of Pax	Date and Time of Arrival
Booked by	Billing Instructions	Remarks	Date and Time of Departure

Fully Automated

The fully automated or computerized reservation system or central reservation system ids most popular system of reservation in hotels used globally. This system operates through the principles of WAN (wide area network) and is connected to sales department of hotel around the globe. The system receives records and updates the reservations made from any reservation office of the chain hotel. The advantages of computerized system is that it is time saving, easy to retrieve information whenever required, can be used for multi purposes, operatively is perfect with minimum errors or no errors and saves space. On the other hand some properties, especially individual may find the system expensive, some may find it difficult to understand, requires computer training, may be reason for unemployment. The central reservation system is of two types:

- Affiliate System: This is a system formed by the properties belonging to one chain. A guest is connected form one central point and is shared among all hotels belonging to the chain. A guest can book his/her reservation form any city.

- Non-affiliate System: This system is used by association of various individual properties to gain benefits as gained by chain hotels in case of affiliate system of reservation, as it works in the same way.

Semi-Automated

This is a system of reservation which uses combination of both manual and computer system due to lack in trained staff, lack of budget to purchase costly software. A single computer may be used by hotels in such system without any more terminals in the hotel, supported by well-designed charts providing legible information about the availability of rooms. The systems and software's can be tailor made as per the requirement of individual hotel property and will certainly save hotels capital expenditure.

- Density Chart: The density chart helps to know how many rooms are available on a particular day or how many rooms have been overbooked. This chart is designed on the principle that each booking request reduces the availability of the rooms or increases the over booking of the rooms and each cancellation increases the availability of rooms. All rooms of same category are grouped together irrespective of location in the hotel.

- Room Status Chart: The density chart controller makes a room status chart which shows the request and closed dates. The closed date's means that no rooms are available on these dates but in case of on request means few rooms are available for sale. In case of group reservations it's always advised to contact controller before confirming the reservation of group. Room status chart is even termed as year perpetual planner.

Bell desk is a section of front office department providing uniformed services. Bell desk is preferably located on left hand side of the lobby area from the entrance to generally ease up the operations of front office. The bell desk is headed by a bell captain and has a team of bell boys according to the size of hotel property. Bell desk primarily helps in transportation of guest luggage at the time of arrival and departure.

Role and Functions of Bell Desk Operations

Organization

The various duties and responsibilities of bell desk are handled by team headed by bell captain and followed by number of bell boys and trainees depending on the size of hotel. The bell desk works

24x7 and so work in three shifts to provide service to the guests. The bell desk is located mostly on the left side of the lobby area while entering in the hotel. And is considered to be the first department to come in contact with the guests on their arrival.

Organizational Structure of Bell Desk

Bell Captain

↓

Senior Bell Boys

↓

Bell Boys

↓

Trainee

Duties and Responsibilities

Bell Captain

The bell captain is a supervisory job and is responsible to lobby manager. His main duties include allocation of tasks to bell boys and trainees, inspection of tasks given, welcoming regular guests on times. He implements any instructions received from management. He listens to the grievances of his staff and tries to resolve. A bell captain heads one shift generally of eight hours and is directly responsible for the smooth functioning of department. The main duties and responsibilities of bell captain are:

- He/she records the attendance of the bell boys and trainees at the beginning of each shift and takes briefing of staff and passes on special instructions to them about their activities and conduct during the shift.

- He is even responsible to ensure grooming and personal hygiene of bell staff for providing proper service.

- Assigns errands to bell boys.

- Left luggage room is controlled by him/her and maintenance of register.

- Message distribution has to be supervised by him/her.

- Distribution of newspaper and magazines is also supervised.

- To control the moment of bellboys by maintaining the control sheet to summarize the activities of bell boys.

- Any arrivals with scanty baggage are to be recorded in log book, arrival register and scanty baggage register and needs to inform about scanty baggage to the reception.

- Arrange for paging service for the guests within the property whenever required and maintain the paging board stock.

- Maintain and supervise wake-up call procedures.
- Postage stock is checked and maintained at the bell desk and is provided to the guest on behalf of the hotel.

Bell Boy

Bell boys do multitasks like paging, luggage boys, lift operators, etc. A bell boy is expected to work for eight hour shift and on times to do broken shifts. He has to report to the bell captain and comes under uniform staff. The main duties and responsibilities of bell captain are:

- Carry luggage of the guest at the time of check-in and check-out.
- Carry the luggage of the guest after registration to guest room and escort the guest.
- Supposed to market hotels other products to guests while escorting to room.
- Delivery of newspapers, magazines, mails and messages, parcels to the guest rooms.
- Page guests in hotel public areas like restaurants, pool side, bar, banquets, health clubs, etc.
- Keep left luggage of the guest and issue luggage tags and request the same at the time of delivery.
- Keep track of scanty baggage guests and maintain register for same.
- Issue loan items to the guests like wheel chair, torch, tracking sticks, etc.
- Makes errands for each day and every arrival.
- Shifting of guest from one room to another.
- Check guest belongings in a check-out room.
- Check check-out room for any damaged property or a stolen item and inform the same to front desk personnel.
- Prepare and hand over departure errand to the bell captain.

Role and Function of Bell Desk

Bell desk is one of the important sections of front office. Being the first section to come in direct touch of guests makes its role significant. Efficiency and effectiveness are the basic requirements for the employees on this desk. The desk staff is engaged in performing various functions related directly or indirectly to the guests. The main roles and functions of bell desk are:

- Carry luggage at the time of arrival for both FIT's and Walk-in guests: The bell desk staff performs important function of greeting the guests at the time of arrival and helping them in unloading luggage from the vehicles. The bell boys further escort the guest to the room after registration and transport the luggage from lobby to the guest room. While escorting the guest, it is expected that the bell boy will inform the guest about various other facilities the hotel offers as an approach of suggestive selling. Once the guest reaches the room, the bell boy makes guest comfortable and gives details about different facilities in the room and the usage of various electronic/electrical gadgets.

- Carry luggage at the time of guest departure for FIT's and Walk-in guests: The bell desk is responsible to transport luggage of the guests from rooms to vehicles at the time of departure. Care needs to be taken while transporting luggage looking at the nature of luggage being carried as could be fragile.

- Luggage handling for groups at the time of arrival and departure: Handling luggage of groups becomes little complicated as the number of luggage could be high. And the important part is transporting luggage to different rooms allotted to group members after identifying the correct luggage of every individual guest. In this process, a rooming list is handed over by the front desk staff to the bell desk clearly indicating the guest name and room numbers allotted. Further the bell boy puts luggage tags on all the luggage items and makes a note of that separately. It becomes easy as the group members are informed to attach name tags on every luggage which is otherwise also recommended by tour operators for travel purposes. And then the bell desk transports the luggage to every guest room. The process of carrying luggage from porch/lobby area to guest room is called as Up-bell. On the other hand, at the time of group departure the luggage is collected from each dedicated room to a group and is brought down and loaded to the vehicle of the groups. The bell boys need to be careful for the same because on times a two or more groups may be checking-out at same time. The process of transporting luggage of group from rooms to porch/lobby is termed as Down-bell.

- Paging service for the guests: Another important function of bell desk is to provide paging services to guests in order to locate them for any message and mails delivered looking at the urgency of the message received on behalf of the guest by the hotel. A paging board is used for the purpose which shows the name and company of the guest.

- Newspaper/Magazine delivery in guest rooms: The bell desk staff is also responsible to deliver complimentary and requested newspapers and magazines in guest rooms. The process starts early in the morning as hotel receives them from the assigned vendor. The bell boys check from the register for the newspapers and magazines to be distributed in the guest rooms. The newspapers/magazines are packed in newspaper bags and are then distributed by bell boys' floor wise for speedy distribution. The bags are hung on guest room door knobs.

- Postal services to guests: The bell desk even acts as mini post office and provides various types of postal services like postal stamps, postcards, envelopes on guest requests. The bell desk also arranges for courier services for the guests for any urgent mails.

- Helping in housekeeping services: The bell desk staff also assists housekeeping staff in conducting light housekeeping services in lobby and reception area. The services may be light dusting and wiping of entrance door. The bell boys sometimes even help housekeeping staff in making rooms in case of urgent check-ins or due to lack of staff on times.

- Others: Bell staff even purchases various items requested by guests like cigarettes, drinks or may be some eatables if not available in hotel and asks reception to prepare visitors paid outs in case guests does not pay for the same at that moment of time.

Left Luggage Procedure

Left luggage term is given to a guest who has left their luggage at the hotel premises at the time of departure and wish to collect the same later. It generally happens when guests feel inconvenient and expensive to carry luggage to a place they are moving forward and would come back later. Moreover, if a guests flight/train is in the evening it becomes expensive to retain the room for that day and guest keeps the luggage in the left luggage room and goes out for a city tour and collects the luggage later. This facility indeed may bring back a prospective guest to the hotel on his/her next visit to the city. The hotel management takes guarantee of the safety and security of the luggage left by the guest.

Procedure for Receiving Luggage

- Before accepting the luggage from the guest, it is ensured whether the guest had settled all the bills.

- Bell boy needs to check the luggage properly for its locked or not. And in case of some damage on the baggage, same needs to be informed to the guest at the time of receiving only.

- A luggage tag needs to be prepared and the one part of tag needs to be pasted or tied to the guest luggage and the other part may be given to guest for the collection of the same.

- Bell boys need to check if luggage contains any fragile item and a suitable sticker for the same is pasted for the indication to other members on different shifts.

- Keep the luggage in the left luggage room safely under key and lock.

- The bell boys maintain and update the left luggage register.

Procedure at the Time of Luggage Delivery

- The guest is requested to produce the receipt/part of luggage tag and if the guest has lost the same, he/she may be requested to sign on the left luggage register.

- Check the luggage tag and bring out the luggage from the room safely.

- Bell boys then need to make entry in left luggage register mentioning the date, time and number of items delivered to the guest.

- The luggage is further transported to the guests' vehicle.

Left Luggage Register

Hotel ABC

Date	Room No.	Name of the Guest	Name of the Bell Boy	`Luggage Tag No.	Description of the Luggage	Date of Delivery of Luggage	Remarks

Scanty Baggage Procedure

Scanty baggage register is one of the important record to be maintained by bell desk staff for those guests who come to the hotel with few baggage or without any baggage. The scanty baggage record need to be prepared at all shifts of the hotel and to be verified by the lobby manager who signs the same and provides instructions for billing of scanty baggage guests. The list of such guests needs to be circulated among all the point of sales to keep a watch on such guests who may leave the hotel premises without intimation. These guests are even termed as Skippers in hotels. It becomes important for the hotel to take advance from such guests to be on safer side. The procedure adopted by bell desk for guests with scanty baggage is:

• Lobby manager and the reception are notified immediately for any arrival of a guest with scanty baggage.

• The arrival errand card prepared is indicated with scanty baggage.

• The registration cards at the reception are even stamped with 'scanty baggage.

• The registration card and the scanty baggage register needs to be signed by the lobby manager.

SCANTY BAGGAGE REGISTER

HOTEL ABC

DATE_____

DATE	ROOM NO.	NAME OF THE GUEST	NAME OF THE BELL BOY	`LUGGAGE TAG NO.	DESCRIPTION OF THE LUGGAGE	DATE OF DELIVERY OF LUGGAGE	REMARKS

Formats and Records Maintained At Bell Desk

Bell Desk Log Book

A log book has to be maintained by bell boys for all the shifts to keep a record of all activities and instructions that are performed during a particular shift and need to be shared with next shift.

LOG BOOK

HOTEL ABC

DATE:_____

DAY:_____

SHIFT:_____

LOBBY MGR./GRE:_____

S. NO.	DETAILS	REMARKS

Bell Boy Errand Card

The bell card is an important format maintained by the bell captain during the shift timings of individual bell boys to control the activities when they leave desk for any purpose like luggage delivery, newspaper distribution, message delivery, etc. The bell boy errand card is printed on both the sides, front side used at the time of arrival and the back side used at the time of departure.

BELL BOY ERRAND CARD									
FRONT SIDE FOR ARRIVAL									
GUEST NAME _____									
BELL BOY'S NAME _____									
ROOM NO_____ DATE _____									
MISCELLENOUS _____									
SERVICE CALL WAKE CALL ERRAND OTHER									

BAGS	BRIEFCASE	COAT	GOLF BAGS	TRUNK	PACKAGE	LAUNDRY	VALET	S/C	OTHERS

BELL BOY ERRAND CARD

BACK SIDE FOR DEPARTURE/SHIFT

SHIFT FROM ROOM NO. _____ TO ROOM NO. _____

B.N.P/B-IN HOLD

AMOUNT_____ HOLD TILL _____ ROOM NO _____

BELL BOY   CASHIER   LOBBY MANAGER

DEPARTURE: BAGS DOWN _____ ROOM NO. _____ DATE _____

INFORMATION   RECEPTION

CASHIER

Lobby Control Sheet

This sheet is maintained by bell captain during a particular shift in the hotel. The sheet is summary of all the activities performed by bell boys during shifts. It even helps in preparation of individual errand cards of the bell boys. This format is further used by lobby manager to counter check the moment of bell boys for better performance.

LOBBY CONTROL SHEET								
HOTEL ABC								
CAPTAIN _____					SHEET NO. _____			
DATE _____					SHIFT-FROM_____ TO _____			

ROOM NO.	ATTENDANT NO.	ARRIVAL	DEPARTURE	ROOM CHANGE TO	SERVICE CALL	TIME		COMMENT
						FROM	TO	

Guest Location Form

This form is used to know the location of the guest when they leave the room and inform the location which is kept in key/mail rack. When a guest is expecting any message, he usually informs whether he will be in hotel or outside and accordingly gives his location in hotel or provides a phone number in case goes out of hotel premises. And intimates to reception once returning back to room. In case of a visitor, only after his instructions by the guest about his where about.

GUEST LOCATION FORM		
HOTEL ABC		
DATE: _____		
TIME: _____		
NAME OF THE GUEST MR./MS _____		
ROOM NO. _____		
I WILL BE AT		
PLACE	FROM	TO
Swimming Pool		
Health Club		
Bar		
Beauty Parlour		
Business Centre		

Inventory Register

The inventory register keeps record of all inventory items of the bell desk such as: bell trolley, torch, formats, wheelchair, metal detector, paging board, stationery.

INVENTORY REGISTER				
HOTEL ABC				
S. NO.	ITEM	ISSUED TO: TIME:	RECEIVED FROM: TIME	REMARKS

Message Form

Message form is used to deliver any received message for an in-house guest in their absence from the hotel. The message is delivered immediately on the arrival in the hotel. Two copies of message are prepared, one copy is taken by bell boy and slotted through under the door of guest room and the other is kept as a record in key/mail rack. It is done to make the delivery/communication of message to the guest.

MESSAGE FORM

HOTEL ABC

DATE_____

TIME_____

NAME OF THE GUEST MR./MS. _____

ROOM NO. _____

A MESSAGE WAS RECEIVED WHILE YOU WERE AWAY

FROM:

MR./MS. _____

ADDRESS _____

TEL. NO. _____

MESSAGE

_____ _____

_____

MESSAGE TYPE	REMARKS
CALLED	
PARCEL	
WILL CALL AGAIN	
PACKET	
IN PERSON	

Wake-up Call Sheet

Wake-up call sheet is used to wake guests who wish for the same. It is generally requested by guests who want to be waked up early in the morning or want to get reminder about some important work. This sheet is prepared by the telephone operator or is done by the bell captain.

WAKE UP CALL SHEET

HOTEL ABC

DATE: _____

TIME: _____

Please wake up the following guests:

TIME	ROOM NUMBERS
3.00 AM TO 3.15 AM	
3.15 AM TO 3.30 AM	
3.30 AM TO 3.45 AM	
3.4 AM TO 4.00 AM	
4.00 AM TO 4.15 AM	
4.15 AM TO 4.30 AM	
4.30 AM TO 4.45 AM	
8.30 AM TO 8.45 AM	
TELEPHONE OPERATOR	BELL CAPTAIN

Room Shifting Slip

In case a room of a guest has to be changed, in that case room shifting sheet is used to maintain records of the same. It is done with the approval of front office manager/lobby manager.

ROOM SHIFTING SLIP HOTEL XYZ S. NO. _____ DATE _____ TIME _____		
SHIFTED THE GUEST	FROM	TO
NUMBER OF PAX	FROM	TO
RATE CHANGED	FROM	TO
NAME OF THE GUEST _____		
REASONS FOR CHANGE_____		
ROOM SHIFTED BY_____		
SHIFTING AUTHORISED BY _____		
RECEPTIONIST SIGNATURE		
C.C. BILLS, H.K., TEL DEPT., ROOM SERVICE, BELL DESK		

Check Out Procedure

Departure is one of the important phases of guest cycle. The last contact the guest has with the hotel is the check-out procedure and is most probably the last chance for a guest to interact face-to-face with the hotel staff. The standard operating procedures followed and the quality of service a guest will receive at the departure will influence their final impression of the hotel, even after a bad experience during the stay. Any dissatisfied experience of the guest can be corrected with the hotel. The check-out staff can improve their opinion of it by being friendly, courteous and efficient. It is of great significance that guest financial transactions with the hotel are settled before they leave. After departure, guest room will be available for re-sale to other guest, hence, room status information has to be updated immediately and the front office records must also be amended. At the time of departure, the guest receives an accurate statement of account and is requested to pay any outstanding balance. The guest is requested to return the guestroom key before leaving the hotel. The departure activities for front office staff involves account settlement and the updating of front office records. Accounts settlement includes both guest account and non-guest account reconciliation and receipt of payment. Guest accounts are settled at checkout in the presence of the guest. Guest account payments which are deferred to a credit card or an approved billing party are transferred to the back office accounting system to the accounting division for collection.

Functions of Checkout and Settlement

The checkout and settlement process is designed to three important functions:

- Settlement of guest account.

- Updating room status information.

- Create guest history records and create good lasting impression.

Settlement of Guest Account

Guest account settlement is one of the important functions of front office section and settlement of guest accounts is most effectively achieved only when the guest is staying in the hotel. A guest can settle an account through various modes like by paying cash, credit card, direct billing, and bill to company or using some combination of these payment methods. In case of credit card or direct billing information should be known in advance of checkout to obtain verification and authorization of a credit card account or confirmation by a direct billing party. Verification activities tend to reduce the guest's actual checkout time while enhancing the hotel's ability to collect outstanding account balances.

Updating Room Status Information

Front office records need to be updated after guest departure. Accurate room status information is essential to effective front office operations, as well as for overall hotel operations. The cashier needs to notify about guest departure to the front office staff so that suitable changes in the guest's room status are made. The information of the same is further notified to the housekeeping department about the departure. A housekeeping section cleans and keeps the room ready for inspection and resale for any point of the day. In order to maximize room sales, the front office must maintain 2 current occupancy and housekeeping status on all rooms, and communicate status information in an accurate and quick way to all concerned sections of hotel. Any miscommunication may lead to flaws in operations and moreover would raise complaints on times.

Guest History Records

Hotels industry being sensitive in nature, it becomes significant for hotel management to have updated information of the guest once stayed in the property. Hence on of the other important function of front office at the departure is maintaining guest history. The information required to be collected for maintain guest history has to be done during all phases of guest cycle for in-depth understanding of the guest. A guest history is a file containing guest personal and financial data who have stayed in the hotel. An individual record within the file normally contains personal and transactional information relevant to the guest's stay. This helps the hotel to better understand its guest and determine guest trends, and provides a powerful base for strategic marketing. Guest history files may be created from expired registration cards or created through sophisticated computer based systems which automatically direct checkouts into a guest history database file and may be gathered during the stay by observing guest. Proper analysis of guest history data may provide the hotel with a valuable competitive edge.

Individual Departure

Basic procedure at checkout includes:

- Greet guest with a smile and greet according to the time of the day. Always try to remember and use their names.

- The front desk staff needs to confirm guest details like name and room number against the guest's account. Simultaneously the staff needs to inquire about the guest's stay at the hotel.

- The guest departure date needs to be checked. In case guest is departing earlier than expected, then the other departments will need to be informed.

- The front desk staff needs to check if any late checkout charges have to be applied. If the guest is leaving after 12 noon check out time and is not a frequent guest, relevant charges are to be added to the guest account.

- Check for late charges: All current entries on a guest's folio need to be examined and check for any mini-bar, breakfast or telephone charges, so that the same may be added to guest account.

- The guest is handed over guest folio and/or master folio for verification of charges made. The receptionist determines whether one or two folios are to be produced. All queries at this time must be handled without fuss and in a pleasant helpful manner.

- Complete guest settlement of accounts. The settlement is done by appropriate means of mode of payment and the same has to be done while taking the guest in confidence by detailing the settlement.

- Front office services need to be provided upon guest departure such as receiving the guest's key and checking if they have used a safe deposit box which is required to be emptied or if they have returned any housekeeping items such as hairdryer, hand iron, etc.

- Once the settlement is completed and other services provided, bell staff is offered for the collection of luggage.

- Lastly the guest is inquired for making any future reservation, or an onward reservation in another hotel within the chain. Referral hotels may be even suggested at other locations.

- Update front office records. The most important records to update are the room status list in order that other departments can accurately know the room and guest status.

Group Departure

The group departure is quite same as individual checkout, but some note needs to be taken by various sections of front office involved at the time of checkout.

At the Bell desk

- Sufficient number of bell boys are required and arranged to handle luggage of the group, since the size of group may be more than 30 guests.

- Baggage down bell and wake up calls times are important and must be checked and followed strictly for better guest experience.

- Bell boys are allocated floors and rooms to bring down the luggage down to the lobby.

- If on the day of departure the guests are not in the room the bell boys go to each group member's rooms and "pull" each group members baggage out of the room and bring it down to the lobby until the group is ready to leave. This process is called as "down bell".

- Baggage is brought down to the lobby and counted. Bell captain obtains a baggage out pass.

- After the clearance from the cashier and room keys are handed to reception.

- Finally the baggage is loaded onto the respected vehicle by the bell boys.

At the Reception

- Departure notification slips are issued half an hour prior to actual departure by the receptionist to telephones, housekeeping, room service, and food and beverage etc. to avoid any late charges. The same is done telephonically for immediate action.

At the Cashier

- Cashier prints out the master folio and individual folios.

- Makes a room-wise summary is made for easy collection.

- Master folio is given to the tour leader and the individual bills are collected with the assistance of tour leader.

Problems at Check Out

Long Queues at Check Out

The standard operating procedure followed by hotels at the checkout requires observation at every step and most often guest may experience delays at checkout. Hotels may employ some speedy ways of reducing time and queues at the checkout are:

- Express checkout (ECO): Some hotels perform pre-departure activities that help reduce waiting time and delays. Most of the departures are experienced between 7:00 and 10 a.m. Hotels providing express checkout facility, communicate about the services provided at the time of check-in. A common pre-departure activity involves the production and early morning distribution of guest folio for guests expected to checkout that morning. The folio may be quietly slipped under the guestroom doors early in the morning before the departure of the guest. Moreover, the front office normally distributes an Express Checkout Option/Form (ECO) which approves transferring the outstanding account balance to an already imprinted credit card voucher. The guest then leaves the express checkout form at the front desk on his way out while departing form the hotel. It is important to include a note with the express checkout form requesting the guest to notify the front desk if there has been a change in departure plans: otherwise the front office will assume the guest is departing by the hotel's posted checkout time. It usually encourages guests who have changed their departure plans to quickly notify the front desk before checkout time. Although the guest leaves the hotel after depositing the express checkout form, the front office must complete the guest's check-out by transferring the outstanding folio balance to a previously accepted method of settlement-credit card. An express checkout system is effective only if the front office is well organized and obtains appropriate guest settlement information at the time of registration. The front office must also take extra care to update room status as soon as the guest departs and the express checkout form is received. The system is useful for both the guest and the front office section.

- Self-checkout: One of the latest way out for speedy checkout is to have self-checkout lobby terminals and in-room computer interfaces with a front office computer system that can reduce the time it takes to process guest checkout and significantly reduce front office traffic. The self-checkout terminals are similar to self-registration terminals and may vary in design. Some terminals resemble an automatic bank teller machine, while others may possess both video and audio capability. To use a self-checkout system, the guest accesses the proper folio and reviews its contents. Settlement can be automatically assigned to a credit card so long as the guest presented one at registration. The checkout procedure in this system is completed once the guest's balance is posted to a credit card and an itemized statement of accounts is printed and dispensed to the guest. The system then automatically updates room status and creates a guest history file.

- In-room folio review and checkout functions generally rely on in room computer terminals or guestroom telephone to access and display guest folio data on the guestroom television screen. An interface to a front office accounting system allows the guest to access folio data and approve a method of settlement for his account. Newer technology may provide computer- synthesized voice responses through the guestroom telephone. Each method provides guests with folio totals and details and directs a self-checkout procedure. Printed folio copies are typically available to guests to pick up at the front desk. Similar to other self-checkout technologies, in-room computer applications automatically updates room status and creates a guest history file.

Late Checkouts

The standard time of checkout for hotels is 12 noon, but hotels may encounter guests who do not checkout by the hotel's posted checkout time. It becomes important for hotels to communicate checkout timings at the time of registration or through notices in places like back of guest room, etc. A reminder of the same may even be given while distributing express checkout forms. Most of the hotels charge late checkout fees in case a guest departs after the stated checkout time. When guest requests permission for a late checkout, the front office should inform him if any additional charges will be applied and in case of regular guests charges may be levied depending on the checkout time not exceeding 3 pm. Checkout time is established by management to provide housekeeping department with sufficient time to prepare the rooms for newly arriving guests. Rooms must be cleaned and readied for arriving guests before the housekeeping staffs completes its shift.

Late Charges

Late charges are a major problem faced in guest account settlement. A late charge is a transaction requiring posting to a guest folio that does not reach the front office until the guest has checked out and left the hotel. Point of sales like restaurant, telephone and room service charges are common examples. If payment for these charges is not collected before the guest leaves, it may be difficult to ever collect. Reducing late charges is essential to maximizing profitability. There are several steps that front office cashiers can take to help reduce costly late charges:

- Post transactional vouchers form any point of sale as soon as they arrive at the front desk to minimize unposted charges during a busy checkout period.

- Before checking a guest out, survey front office equipment and area for unposted charges or vouchers.

- It's important to ask departing guests whether they have incurred any recent charges or recently placed telephone calls from their room telephones or had tea or a meal just before reaching the desk.

While guests tend to respond honestly to direct questions, many guests feel no obligation to voluntarily inform the front office cashier of charges not posted to the folio. Some guests will simply pay the outstanding balance on the folio and disregard unposted charges. Hotel management may consider establishing a system to ensure that revenue outlet charges are delivered quickly to the front desk for posting, especially during peak morning checkout periods. The front desk may employ runners to pick up transaction vouchers, telephone relays, or computer interfacing. A property management system like Opera/Fidellio that interfaces with revenue centre outlets is often the most effective means of reducing or eliminating late charges. With a POS interface, various charge vouchers can be verified for room account validity, checked for credit authorization, and posted to the guest's folio. Similarly, an interface with call accounting equipment reduces telephone late charges. Guests who make in room telephone calls and then go directly to the front desk to check out should find all telephone charges automatically posted. Most of the hotels are using property management system and the chances of late charges have been reduced.

Front Office Records

The front office usually makes at least two copies of each guest account folio. One serves as a receipt for the guest and the other is kept as the hotel's permanent record. Hotels that use a three – part folio usually file the third copy with the guest's credit card voucher or direct billing statement for reference in case of guest disputes or refusal of payment by a credit card or sponsoring company. In non-automated and semi-automated operations, registration cards and folio copies are often maintained in physical storage files. Registration cards are filed alphabetically, while folios are filed numerically by serial number. In a fully automated operation, computer system records may be stored on disks or in printed form. These records back up the original billing.

Promotional Materials

Nowadays, hotels are adopting various promotional activities to meet cut throat competition. A number of marketing programs may depend on the front office's performance and follow through at checkout. For e.g., if the hotel offers a promotion which rewards guests with a free stay after a certain number of visits, the front desk agent may have to validate a coupon that records the number of stays for the guest. Marriott Rewards is an example for the same. If the guest needs a reservation for the next stop on his trip, the front office may be able to perform this service. A reservation for a return stay at the hotel can be made at this time as well. Front desk agents should keep in mind that this is their last opportunity to sell on behalf of the hotel. The offer to make reservations for guests in transit, or to makes reservations for their next trip to the hotel will often pay off in repeat business regardless of whether the guest makes a reservation at this time or not. The guest is even requested for any further assistance.

Guest Histories

The last step in the settlement process is the creation of a guest history record. Many hotels simply use expired registration cards as the basis for their guest history files. Some hotels in particular often have extensive forms requesting specific information to help them cater to their guests needs. Names of spouses and children, birthdays, hotel room preferences, favourite foods, and so on may be placed on file for guests. A guest history record can be used by the hotel's sales and marketing division as a source for mailing lists or, in combination with other guest history records, can help identify guest characteristics important for strategic marketing. This information may be helpful for the placement of advertisements, indicate the need for supplementary services, or identify potential guest service enhancements. Software for a computerized guest history system may allow the hotel to except data for use in its marketing efforts, and to measure the effects of past efforts. For instance, a computerized guest history package may enable the hotel to determine the geographic distribution of its guest's home and business addresses. Hotel advertising may be placed more effectively with the help of such data. Front desk staff should know that guest history files are confidential and proprietary hotel records.

GUEST HISTORY CARD HOTEL XYZ NAME...POSITION...						
OFFICIAL ADDRESS:				NATIONALITY: PASSPORT NO.:		
RESIDENTIAL ADDRESS:				DATE OF BIRTH:		
VISIT NO.	ROOM NO.	ROOM RATE	DATES OF AR-RIVAL DEPAR-TURE	EXPRESSION	BILLING	REMARKS
1						
2						
3						

Modes of Bill Payment

The mode of payment refers to the various methods of payment by which the guest can settle or pay his/her bills in the hotel. Whenever guest checks in a hotel, he/she has to make clear about the modes of payment at the time of registration so that, it will greatly reduce the problem while settling the bills. When the guests check out of the hotel usually they pay the bills by cash or credit card, but in some cases, the charges are billed to the company account, by traveller cheque, and through travel agent/airlines voucher. The different modes of payment through which guest can settle or pay their bills are as follows:

- Cash.

- Cheques.

- Credit card.

- Company account.

- Travellers cheque.

- Voucher.

Cash

It is the simplest and common method of payment which is done in local currencies as well as foreign currencies. It is the most simple and instant mode of payment used by the guests. While doing the payment the bill is presented by front office cashier to the guest and payment is done on hand through cash. The cashier must know the current rate of exchange details and skill to evaluate the rates. Different countries have a different restriction to hotel regarding foreign currencies. Mostly in many of the hotels, there are a lot of tourists guest than the guest of same countries and many of the tourists pay with their own country currency so it is very important for the front office cashier to handle foreign exchange carefully because we cannot upset the guests. There is some procedure for foreign exchange transactions which must be adopted by the front office cashier while handling foreign exchange receipts. The procedures are:

- Collect the foreign exchange to be in crashed for the customer along with the passport.

- Ask the guest for his room number, verify the details with registration card.

- In most of the cases, hotels do not encash foreign exchange in case of non-resident. But it allows only up to 500 US$ against conversion.

- In most cases, the non-resident will be referred to lobby manager and their exchange will be encashed only after receiving authorization from him.

- Check the currency given for its acceptability with the list of currency.

- Check the currency note against fake, fraud, stolen and out of circulation from the respective current circulars issued by NRB.

- Fill up the encashment certificate with full details as required.

- Ask the guest to sign on encashment certificate.

- Calculate the total amount and remit in Nepalese currency after deducting the bill amount if any.

- Provide guest with the original copy of encashment certificate.

- Attach the foreign exchange to the second copy of encashment and deposit along with cash.

- Enter all the require details in the front office cashier report and record of foreign currency summary.

Cheque

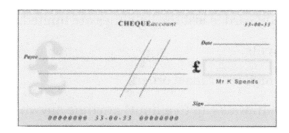

Every hotel has its bank account to facilitates business. Hotel accepts both company cheque and personal cheque up to a certain limit accompanied by the bank guarantee card. It is another form of cash. Payment through the cheque is the safer and convenient. So most of the customers prefer to the payment through the cheque.

Credit Card

A credit card is a wallet-size small card issued and guaranteed by the bank to its valuable customer that authorizes the person named on it to charge goods and services to his or her account. It differs from a debit card with which money is automatically deducted from a bank account of the cardholder to pay for the goods and services. Use of credit card was originated in the U.S. in the 1920s. Early credit cards were issued by various firms (for example, oil companies and hotel chains) for the use of their outlets only. Credit cards are issued by banks and financial corporations after scrutinizing the customer creditability and repayment power. While considering an application for credit card, following details are called for:

- To ascertain that the applicant is receiving a regular income above a minimum required the limit. Salary/income proof.

- To proof of residence. This is required for the safety of repayment. Under local laws, only a resident citizen is allowed credit card.

- For proof of saving and assets. To assess the creditability and repayment power of a client, it is required to find out the total savings in different schemes and assets in the name of the applicant.

Benefits for Credit Card

- Reduces the need to carry cash.

- Credit card can be only used by the card holder.

- Risk is lowered; if credit card is lost the liabilities are limited.

- Helps in urgent payments.

- Allows easy payment modes for male orders.

- Allows easy cash withdrawals (up to a limit) anytime anywhere from any ATM or branch of a bank.

- Allows the flexibility of the payment plan on an interest payment basis as per the convenience of the cardholder.

Benefits of Accepting the Card for the Merchant

- The merchant is assured for the payment by this mode.

- Risk of bad debt arising out of personal credit is not with credit card.

- Easy accepting and accounting system.

- No need to know the client personally.

- The service charge is cheaper than the interest lost in collecting credit payment.

- Provides more publicity through different schemes of the credit card companies from time to time.

There are also procedures for accepting credit cards which must be followed by the cashier and they are:

- Check the warning bulletins provided by the credit card companies. If the card is not in the bulletin the card cannot be accepted. In case it is listed in the bulletin then the card must be apprehended without offending the customer and inform the credit card company.

- Take imprint of the card on a charge slip provided by the bank.

- Now fill up the amount and bill details on the charge slip, give the charge slip to the guest to sign in the specific place.

Company Account

If the guest uses the hotel facilities and billing is instructed as per company account it means that the bill will be paid by the allied company. The big business organization makes an agreement with the hotel to provide services to their staff and customer of the company. Credit section of hotel sends a letter with the bill attached, to the respective company for payment. The bill should be signed by the guest who was sent by the company. The company may pay the bill through cash or by cheques.

Travel Cheque

As the name suggests it is a cheque which is issued by a bank to the travellers in exchange for cash. When a traveller visits a long distance, they exchange their currency into traveller's cheque. The bank which issues the travellers cheque takes the signature of the travellers in the cheque undersigned. Traveller cheque is also another form of cash. It brings down the trouble of carrying a huge amount of cash which does not seem to be safe for long distance traveller. Traveller check is encashed only when the cashier receives the specimen of the cheque holder signature and tallies it with the passport details. All uncashed traveller cheque are sent to the local bank for payment

Voucher

The special document which is printed form and issued by travel agencies and airlines stating the required services to be provided by the hotel to the guest. The hotel sends a bill to a guest to respective travel agencies or airlines who issued the voucher for payment.

Handling Guest Complaints

Complaints are inevitable in every business. As customers have become aware of their rights than ever before. A large segment of customers is tech savvy and they are aware of the platform available to express their discontentment. Therefore, companies spend millions to provide services to customers. However, no matter how hard you try but you can never satisfy 100% customers 100% times. A company's reputation is decided from the way it addresses its customer's problems. Clearly, failing to address or intentionally ignoring customer's complaints can cause bad consequences such as losing customers, negative reputation. Therefore, a company should never neglect their customer service segment and set up an efficient customer care unit. There are various ways through which a company can provide a platform for customers to reach them and get the solution for the problems they face.

If the customer's issues are addressed properly and they are provided with proper solutions and they feel satisfied and happy with your service there are up to 99% chances that they will do business with you again. With the internet becoming omnipotent, people prefer to complain about their issues publicly. They don't give a second thought to write ill words about to company who fails to provide service to them. However, there are many customers who complain and switch to another similar business because of the lack of good customer service. Therefore, it is advisable for companies to pay proper attention to the customers' complaints. To do this, it is important to understand different types of customers' complaints and how to address them to not lose business.

Public Multimedia Complaint

However, all the complaints have to be dealt with as fast as possible but public media complaint should be addressed fastest and provided solutions as soon as possible. Public multimedia has the reach of millions of people. If your customer takes his/her complaint to say Facebook, Twitter these platforms have the reachability to all those who are following your social media accounts. Failure to address such complaints put a negative impression on the current as well as on the potential customers of the company. Therefore, this kind of complaints must be addressed quickly (mostly within seconds) and with utmost care. A company should have enough trained people to handle their social media accounts and complaints should be sent to the related departments. To do so, first of all, the customer should be asked to provide contact information and contacted to get more details about the problem. Secondly, the customer should be asked politely to take down the complaint after solving it. Public media has given the power in the hands of customers, now, the management has to, listen to the complaints and solve them quickly to run a successful business.

Serial Complaint

There is something wrong if a customer complains about something again and gain or many customers complain about the same thing. Management should take effective actions to address such complaints before they go out of hand. A customer loses his trust in the company if his complaint is not addressed when asked repeatedly. Therefore, serial complaints must be handled quickly. Fixing such problems reduces the work for the future altogether. However, working on such complaints is good for the company because these complaints help to make the service better and also gives room to the management for introspection and improvement. On the other hand, a company should narrow down customers who complaints frequently about every other thing and find smart ways to deal with them, because there are always some mischievous people who just want to create a nuisance.

First-Time Complaint

Usually, customer care providers tend to ignore the complaints of a new customer or a customer who is complaining for the first time. If they do so, they make a big mistake and increase the chances of losing a loyal customer. On the contrary, such customers such be paid extra attention and helped to fix their problem instantly. In the scenarios where there is actually a fault in the product or service, management should offer something such as a discount or a free service to please him. This kind of gestures increases the chances of turning a customer into a loyal customer.

Good Customer Complaint

Good customers also are known as loyal customers are the segment of customers who bring maximum revenue for the company. No company can ever afford to lose good customers. Good customers have given you a lot of business in the past and are mostly satisfied with your services. But there are times when such customers also feel dissatisfied. Addressing the complaints of such customers should be the priority of every company. These customers had good experiences with you in the past and you can still retain them by providing the right solution when they are cross with the services of the company. Customer care executives should make a list of priority customers as per the business brought by them and see to the complaints made by them immediately.

Personnel Complaint

These types of complaints made by the customers when executives behave rudely or inappropriately with them. Few of the most common personnel complaints made by customers are "you don't seem to care." Or "Nobody bothers to solve my issue." These complaints should be dealt with utmost care because customers who have made such complaint already feel offended and we are well-versed with human nature. A human takes an extreme decision when angry or hurt. These customers can make a resolution to never buy anything from you which is very bad for the company. It is advisable to deal with these types of customers with empathy and provide them with better services.

Product Specific Complaint

Product specific complaints are made when a product or a service is faulty. When a customer makes such a complaint, he should be asked to hand over the faulty product or provide a detailed description of the faulty service. The faulty product must to replace with a similar new product and he should be given some compensation for the poor service. If you take such actions a customer will think that you give importance to his association with you and there are chances that they will bring more business to the company along with advocating it.

Wait–Times Complaint

These types of customer complaints are common and recurring on phone calls or in lengthy queues at a store or delay for food delivery at a restaurant or waiting too long to get the delivery of a product. Long waiting time irritates people and gives an impression of the inefficiency of the service. Time is precious to everyone and they prefer instant services. These complaints can be solved by confronting the customer and apologizing for the delay. However, it is a short time solution. To reduce wait times complaints, a company should plan and use the various methods by consulting with their team and management.

Complaints because of Misunderstanding

Misunderstanding takes place because of miscommunication. Miscommunication is inevitable when dealing with people. A customer can misunderstand or misinterpret what you say. Sometimes they can get annoyed also and accuse you of lying. However, in such a scenario, one should not lose temper and take the matter to the experienced executive and settle the matter. It is suggested that you should treat the customer with respect even when he is clearly misunderstood. To avoid such complaints requires knowledgeable and experienced staff and precise advertising material.

Delivery-Related Complaint

This is a common example of customers' complaint about online business. As the growth in the trend of online shopping, chances of delivery-related blunder increase. Customers lose patience when delivery get delayed by the expected date and complains about it. Such problems can be dealt with by discussing the issues with the shippers and providing online tracking details of the product. So that if there is a real issue with the delivery of the product, it can be resolved.

Quality of Service-Related Complaint

Quality of service-related complaints are types of complaint that no business would want to have. Great investments in the quality of products and service do not guarantee zero quality of service related complaint. Sometimes such complaints occur due to unrealistic expectations of a customer. such complaints play an important role to improve the quality of the product and service, which has long term benefits. Information from such complaints should be collected, processed and analyzed, so that the company can take information-based decisions in the future. This type of data is useful for the continuous improvement of the product and service. These types of customer complaint should be given the highest priority and great investment should be made to resolve such complaints.

Way of Handling

Handling guest complaint in hospitality industry is such an art which needs to be adopted by all hoteliers. There are some basic principles you need to know and use while handling any complaints raised by guests. These are some basic rules for the successful handling of complaints. If you ignore or forget any of these, a simple complaint can turn into a major issue. So, never dare to ignore. These are all basic but most powerful must follow principles of handling complaints.

- Mind Set Up: Setting up your mind is important. Keep good faith to help customer. It has been said that "Customer is the boss" or "Customer is always right". So, never take any complaint personally. Try to be professional and handle each complaint with professionally. Generally people don't complaint. If anyone complaint then try to understand his or her feelings. A complaint indicates that there must be loopholes in your service and this is the chance to solve your problem. Even world's greatest hotel can never fulfill all the gusts. Do you know why? It is because every guest has different thinking, different expectation, and different reasons to come in your hotel or restaurant. You are providing general standard service and facilities which will be suitable for most of your guests but not necessarily "EVERYONE" and for this reason you should always be ready to provide demanded service and facilities to each and every guest.

- Using polite Language: Use of language is the most important aspect of handling any verbal or written complaint. While you are handling any written complaint then you need to be sure enough about what you are writing, careful about each word and make sure any of the word does not give wrong meaning. When you are answering written then it is a document so proper structure should be followed. On the other hand, handling verbal complaint demands skills and tricks. Your experience and pressure handling power will be tested. Talk in polite language with proper volume, speed and tone.

Proper expressions should be made. Be professional and try to explain your point of view about the problem.

- Proper Listening: Proper listening is necessary for two reasons. First of all, if you don't listen complaints properly then you cannot explain properly. So, to give logical replies on guest complaints listen fully. Another big reason is that if you start replying on each point guest makes while complaints then there will not be any solution. Guest will become more aggressive. Let your guest express his feelings first then take your time, make your points and after finishing his part, start explaining.

- Remaining Calm: You may often find it difficult to remain calm to handle complaints but you have to be that. Just think in a logical way. Why guest become frustrated? Is it because of you? No. He is mad at the situation not at you. There is no personal clash. He is paying for having good services and as he is not satisfied so he has the logical point to complaint. It is your duty to react professionally. But yes, if guest becomes so aggressive that security measures need to be taken then don't hesitate.

- Showing Sympathy: Start with sympathetic words and expressions are the most advisable way to handle any complaints. If you show sympathy then you will get a psychological advantage. Guest will start feeling that you understand his feelings and you are very careful about him. Some catchy words and phrases can easily turn the hot and aggressive situation into cool and friendly atmosphere.

- Apology: Often some hoteliers come to a solution that why should I apology to guest whereas I have no fault? Don't think in that way. Whoever does the mistake, apology first. This does not mean that you agree on the complaint makes by the guest. It means that you feel sorry only for the reason that guest is not satisfied with your service. After apology you can easily defend yourself. In fact you should but at the beginning, seek apology.

- Never Blame Others: Never blame others or other department. All are your colleagues who are working as your team member and blaming each other will violet your team goal. In spite of blaming others take responsibility on your shoulder if possible to handle the complaint or call the proper person to deal with the situation but do not finish your job by just blaming others.

- No Excuse: Never excuse, No guest will love to pay to listen at your excuses. There are some common excuses like "today we are short of staffs", "we are very busy" etc. Each of the guests wants full attention to him. So for any reasons, even if it is logical, you should not try to get sympathy for that. Excusing is not the proper approach rather try to explain. If you are short of staffs explain it and show possible ways to solve it. From when you are selling your service from then it is your responsibility to be prepared for everything.

- Not try to make your Guest Wrong: It is told that guest is always right. Yes it is indeed. Even if your guest is wrong then do not directly make him wrong. Logically explain why you cannot fulfill his demand. This will represent that you are really caring about your guest as a person and this will make your guest comfortable and be friendly to you.

- Be Honest: Be honest within yourself. Never give any promise which you cannot maintain. Also, do take follow up steps. Whenever a guest comes to you with any complaint then responsibility puts on your shoulder. Even you are not engaged with the complaint but you have to take regular follow up to finish the circle. Here circle means from where the complaint has been started, finishes at that point.

Night Audit

Auditing is nothing but conducting financial inspection of the organization. For a hotel business, the finance management starts at the front office. Accurate posting of transactions on the guest folios start at the front office, which is further carried to the back-office accounting department. The guest accounts are counterchecked on a daily basis during auditing. Experts recommend the hotel management team to go through the night audit reports daily to get an insight of the hotel occupancy and finances. It is the process of auditing where the night auditor reviews all financial activities of the hotel that has taken place in one day.

The auditing process for the day is generally conducted at the end of the day during the following night, hence the name 'Night Audit'. It can be performed by the conventional method of using papers, receipts, vouchers, coupons, and files. But performing audit using modern PMS systems is easy, fast, and efficient.

Basic Activities during Night Audit

The night auditor performs the following steps during night audit activity:

- Posting accommodation and tax charge.
- Accumulating guest service charges and payments.
- Settling financial activities of various departments.
- Settling the account receivables.
- Running the trial balance for the day.
- Preparing the night audit report.

The Need for Night Audit

The objective of night audit is to evaluate the hotel's financial activities. Night audit not only reviews guest accounts by checking credits and debits but also tracks the credit limits of the guests and tallies projected and actual sales from various departments. Night audit reviews daily cash flow into and out of the hotel's account. Night audit has a large significance in hotel business operations. The management body refers night audit report to plan future goals and control the expenses. The managers can react immediately on the acquired information.

Responsibilities of a Night Auditor

Apart from the basic audit activities listed above, the night auditor carries out the following responsibilities:

- Taking over from the last shift.

- Checking-in or checking-out the guests after 11:00 pm at night.

- Registering the guests.

- Allocating accommodations to the newly checked-in guests.

- Settling transactions in the newly created guest accounts.

- Verifying guest folios.

- Verifying room status report.

- Balancing all paperwork with the accounts in the PMS.

- Remaining liable for security of the premises.

- Handling guest accommodation keys.

- Taking backup of the PMS generated reports.

- Preparing lists of expected guest arrivals for the next day.

- Closing financial activities for a day.

- Starting financial activities for the next day.

- Receiving and recording bank deposits.

Types of Night Audit Reports

Today, the PMS helps night auditors to a great extent in auditing and generating accurate reports. Here are some typical reports generated during night audit:

- Night Audit Accommodation Report: It gives a snapshot of the days when accommodations are occupied, the days when the accommodations are available, check-ins, check-outs, no-shows, and cancellations. This report can show further details for any of the items listed above.

- Night Audit Counter Report: It gives details on cash and credit card receipts and withdrawals.

- Night Audit Revenue Report: It delivers information on accommodation revenue, cancellation and no show revenue, and other POS revenue. Revenue generated through various agencies and bodies such as travel agents, corporate organizations, internet booking. etc., is also listed in this report.

- Night Audit Tax Report: Contains all the tax information on reservation revenue and other POS revenues such as VAT, luxury tax, and service tax.

- Cashier's report: It is the detailed list of cashier activity of cash influx and out flux, credit cards, and PMS totals. Cashier's report is very important part of the financial control system of a hotel. The front office manager reviews the night audit and looks for any divergences between the actual amount received and the PMS total.

- Manager's Report: It is a statistical list of previous day's occupancy. It includes details about available accommodations, occupied accommodations, sold and vacated accommodations, rack-rate, number of guests in the hotel, number of no-shows, and so on.

- General Manager's Report: Each department in the hotel is required to send daily sales report to the front office. Using their information, a departmental total report is generated for the general manager's assessment. The General Manager determines the profit-generating departments and evaluates the success of sales and marketing.

- High Balance Report: This is a detailed report about the guests who have exceeded the credit limit set by the hotel management.

- Ledger Balance Summary Report: It displays the opening and closing balances for the Advance Deposit Ledger, Guest Ledger, and City Ledger.

- Room Rate Audit Report: It lists all rates that are applied to each guest and the difference from the rack rate with the predetermined rack code.

Balancing Night Reports

Here are some formulae used to balance night audit:

1. Formula for Balancing Bank Deposit: The formula for balancing bank deposit is:

```
Total Bank Deposits

    - Total Cash Sales

    - Credit card received A/R

    - Cash received A/R

= 0
```

2. Formula for Balancing Guest Ledger: The formula for balancing guest ledger is:

```
Total Revenue
```

```
    - Paid-outs and non-collect sales
= Daily revenue
    - Total cash income
    - Today's outstanding A/R income
= 0
```

3. Formula for Balancing City Ledger: The formula for balancing city ledger is:

```
Yesterday's outstanding A/R
    + Today's outstanding A/R income
= Total outstanding A/R
    - Credit card received and applied to A/R
    - Cash received and applied to A/R
= balance of A/R
```

Telecommunication Services

Telephone communication is a verbal mode of communication which allows two or more users to communicate with each other. Telephone was the first device which facilitated people to talk directly when they are far away to be heard directly. Telecommunication is one of the widely used forms of communication for the exchange of information in day to day life and in different sectors such as agriculture, science, culture, public health, personal service, hospitality industry etc. It is a simple and fast method of communication. Telephone Exchange/Desk is a necessity in hotel to handle incoming and outgoing calls of a hotel. Operations of Telephone Exchange and telephone operators depend on the size of the hotel. A small hotel may satisfy its need by placing a telephone switchboard at reception counter. A larger hotel will have a dedicated room with telephone switch-boards and telephone operators for handling telephone calls. This section of Hotel maintains the communication network of the hotel which is usually situated near reception area to coordinate for providing better guest services. Telephone exchange maintains temperature for the room through air conditioning to keep the equipment of telecommunication in working condition for smooth operations. Telephone Exchange works on 24*7 hours basis. Now days, the use of mobile phones have reduced the work of telephone exchange in hotels.

Types of Equipment used in Telephone Communication in a Hotel

EPABX (Electronic Private Automatic Branch Exchange)

- Electronic Private Automatic Branch Exchange may be defined as a switching system which enables internal and external calls of an organization. It works as virtual telephone operators and responds to all the needs of a guest. The EPABX is based on satellite connections. EPABX enables call transferring, forwarding, auto conferencing, automatic redialling, direct dialling of internal extensions, call waiting facility, speed dialling, hold button, call blocking, caller identification, charge monitoring facility, wake-up call facility, Do-not-disturb service, voice message service, hands free speaker etc.

- Information Board: Information Board is used in telephone exchange to keep important information such as Room number and name of the guest, group detail, Events and functions of the hotel, Emergency Telephone Numbers etc.

- Others:
  - Walkie-talkies: Hotels use two way walkie-talkies preferably used by security staff of hotel to communicate with each other in big functions for better coordination.
  - Mobile Phones: Mobile phones which are purchased and maintained by telephone communication section in hotel. Mobile phone can be given to senior executives, and chauffeurs for better coordination in providing better guest services.

Organization Structure of Telephone Exchange/Desk

General Manager
↓
Front Office Manager
↓
Telecommunication Supervisor
↓
Telephone Operators
↓
Trainees

Job Description of Telephone Operator

Job Title: Telephone Operator.

Reports To: Telecommunication Supervisor/Front Office Manager.

Job Summary: To speak clear with a friendly and pleasant tone of voice. Use listening skills and provide prompt telephone services to guests and hotel employees as per hotel standards.

Duties and Responsibilities

- Maintain telephone exchange and telephone equipment's.

- Direct calls to guest rooms, staff, departments etc. as per request.

- Answer incoming calls.

- Receive guest messages and deliver to the concerned guest.

- Organise wake-up call service and perform wake-up call services.

- Provide information about hotel services to guests.

- Provide paging service for hotel guests and employees.

- Maintain information about the room numbers and name of VIPs and Groups.

- Use telephone etiquettes during telephone handling.

- Maintain caller privacy at all times.

- Know what action to be taken when an emergency call is required.

- Train new telephone operator in performance of duties.

- Take over shift log book and special instructions for the shift.

Minimum Educational Qualification: High School with certificate of telephone operation or Graduate or equivalent. Must speak, read and write and understand the language used in workplace and by the guest in hotel.

Experience: Six months training or knowledge of centralized telephone system.

Functions of Telephone Exchange

- To answer calls regarding the enquiries about hotel services, facilities and events.

- To coordinate emergency situation through telecommunication.

- To protect guest privacy.

- To process guest wake-up calls as per guest request.

- To direct calls through the switchboard as requested by the guest.

- To handle incoming and outgoing calls of the hotel.

- To handle computerized call accounting system.

- To give wake-up calls as per guest instruction.

- To monitor call accounting system.

- To provide guest paging services over the public address system.

Duties and Responsibilities of a Telephone Operator

- Log Book: Telephone operator maintains log book during their shift in hotel which keeps important information about happenings, instructions etc. which may include duty roaster, VIP list, wake up calls, new procedures, group detail, charges posting etc.

- Complaint Register: Telephone operator maintains complaint register which includes complaints of guests to be resolved which may be of different types related to technical fault, wake-up call, rude behaviour of staff etc.

- Wake-Up Calls: Telephone operator also keeps the record of wake up calls on wakeup call sheet with the detail of the guest such as Guest Name, Room No, Time of Wake-Up Call and give wakeup call as per scheduled time.

Qualities of a Telephone Operator

- Telephone Etiquettes: A telephone operator should know dos and don'ts of telephone handling. He should use telephone etiquettes and manners while handling a telephone call.

- Good Memory: Telephone operator should have a good memory which will help him/her to remember guest names, hotel extensions and important phone numbers to take quick action and provide personalized services to the guests.

- Good Communicator: Telephone Exchange works as a first contact of a guest with a hotel. So, it is very important for telephone operator to attend calls of guests with a clear and friendly voice with a pleasant tone of voice.

- Team Player: He must coordinate and help others departments for better communication. He should communicate with other departments as per guest requirements and requests. It is mandatory to coordinate with other on time for providing services on time.

- Secrecy: Telephone operator should be aware about the rule and regulations of the hotel about keeping privacy of the guest. It is an offence to disclose the private conversation of the guest. He is also not allowed to listen guest conversation. So, it is mandatory to maintain the secrecy of the guest.

- Pleasant Tone of Voice: It is very important for Telephone operator to have a pleasant tone of voice as guest can't see face expressions. It is only voice which creates first impression on the guest.

- Good Listener: Telephone operator should be a good listener as this is the first quality of a good communicator. He should listen first and then provide information as asked by the guest.

- Clear Speech: Telephone operator communicates verbally. So, it is very important to have a very clear speech for accuracy in message.

- Accuracy: Telephone operator must be accurate the information which is provided by him. Because, Guest expect accurate information of the hotel facilities and services. He should also maintain accuracy in connecting extensions, responding to guest queries and questions and also maintain charges of the guest calls.

Repeat your message and instructions so that the caller understands the message and also note if it is needed. Have a pen, pencil and a notepad.

- Confidence: Have correct information prior to call handling which will enable to speak with confidence about your property and other information.

- Intelligence: Because every caller is an individual who has different backgrounds and level of understanding. Meet the caller's level of understanding and language intelligently.

- Positive Attitude: Find out the positive points about your property and services and Provide information with positive attitude.

- Integrity: Be Honest, admit and apologize if you don't know about anything and come up with a solution. Don't mislead the caller.

- Tactfulness: Be tactful and convince the guest without hurting his/her feelings without promising the services which you can't fulfil.

Basic Etiquette and Manners for Telephone Handling

- Greetings: Telephone Operator must greet the caller according to the time of the day as it creates good first impression.

- Answer Call Promptly: Telephone operator should pick up the phone before three rings and answer promptly. Identify: Telephone Operator identify his organization and himself quickly i.e. "Good morning sir/madam, Hotel name....., Your Name .....Speaking, how may I assist you?" and don't use "Hello".

- Speak Clearly: Practice smile you speak which will make your voice pleasant and cheerful. Don't be loud and don't whisper during conversation.

- Listen with alertness: Listen attentively and patiently to hear actual words and meaning for better understanding the request or instruction of the guest.

- Sense the mood: Have a sense to detect the mood of the caller and handle accordingly.

- Be tactful and diplomatic: Avoid irrelevant conversation and don't promise which can't be fulfilled.

- Personalize the Call: By remembering guest name and calling guest name with courtesy and correctly makes the caller happy.

- Apologize for hold ups, delays and mistakes: Keep your caller informed and after returning on call after holding, apologize for hold ups. Don't let the caller leave without correct information. If you make mistake in giving information, then apologize immediately and correct the error.

- End all calls with Thank You: End a call after ensuring the satisfaction of the caller with the given information and say "Thank you for calling".

- Repeat your message and instructions so that the caller understands the message and also note if it is needed. Have a pen, pencil and a notepad.

- Use Magic Words: Always use magical words such as please/sorry/thank you in conversation with the guest.

- Ready with Telephone Directory: Telephone operator should have handy information about important phone numbers and directory for quick response and handling calls.

- Answer before three Rings: answer calls before three rings of the call as it represents the alertness, attentiveness about calls in hotel which give positive impression on the caller's mind.

- Use Friendly Language: During the call, observe the caller's comfort ability in language.

- Speak the language in which guest is comfortable which will make better understanding of message.

- Don't use Telephone personally: Don't use hotel phone for personal call.

- Be accurate in what you say: The caller wants accurate information. So don't 'Think' or 'Suppose' if you don't know the answer; find out and call back.

- Be courteous in explaining the hotel rules: Never argue with the caller, the guest is always right. Do not use the phrase" you have to" and be courteous in explaining the hotel policies.

- Take the correct name and contact number of the caller: By taking correct detail of the caller, telephone operator will be able to get back to the caller whenever it is required.

- Avoid the Five Forbidden Phrases: Avoid saying "I don't know", "I/we can't do that", "You'll have to", "Just a second" and "No". Use "LEAPS" with emotional caller: L-Listen, E-Empathize, A-Apologize, P-Positive and S-Solve the problem.

- Never Eat during Call: Never eat, drink or chew gum while on the phone. At the end Telephone Operator should not forget that he/she is representing the hotel or the organization so he/she should be knowledgeable, informative and confident about the call handing and the hotel property facilities and services.

Phrases used during Telecommunication in Hotel

- Phrases used in Internal Communication: During handling of internal call phrases can be used such as "Good Morning (or the appropriate time of the day), operator speaking, how I may help/assist you?"

- Phrases used in External Communication: During handling external calls phrases can be used such as "Good Morning (or the appropriate time of the day), Hotel XYZ, how may I help/assist you?"

- Putting the Call on Hold: If the caller asks for something for which you have no answer: "Let me check on that sir/madam, would you please allow me to put on hold for a moment?"

- Getting back to the hold call: After putting the caller on hold and getting back to the call, apologize for the same: "sorry to have kept you waiting sir/madam"

- Calling the guest back: If you call the guest back, make sure you introduce yourself: "(Greeting as per the time of the Day) Good Morning, Mr. Kumar (Guest Name), this is (You name) you had asked for information regarding"

Situation Handling in Telecommunication

- Fire Emergency: In the case of Fire Emergency, Telephone Operator plays an important role by identifying the origin of fire through display panel and immediately notifications to The Chief Security Officer, Chief Engineer, The City Fire Brigade, The General Manager, The Lobby Manager and The Guests in their rooms. He is supposed to evacuate at last as being hub of communication in emergency situation.

- Bomb Threat: As bomb threats are often received by phone, the telephone operator should be well prepared for this kind of emergency. Telephone Operator must follow the instructions and procedure for the Bomb threat call and will keep the record of the call such as:

  ○ The time of call and the extension on which it was received.

  ○ The exact conversation between the caller and telephone operator.

  ○ Caller telephone number (through the display of switchboard).

  ○ Listen to the background noises such as music, traffic, railway station, loud speaker etc.

  ○ Note down the gender of the caller and the approximate age.

  ○ Accent and language of the caller.

  ○ Telephone operator will try to keep the call long as long as possible.

  ○ During the call, Telephone operator will try to ask the location of the bomb in hotel, when it is going to explode, what type of bomb, what is the motivate behind this, what is the name of the caller.

- ○ After the disconnection of the call, Telephone operator will follow the hotel Standard Operating Procedure to handle the situation and to take appropriate action.

- Complaint Handling:

  - ○ Empathize with the caller means try to understand how the person is feeling.

  - ○ Apologize and acknowledge the problem means you don't have to agree with the caller, but express regret that there is a problem.

  - ○ Accept responsibility means make sure something is done. Take it upon yourself to so something.

Do's and Don'ts of Telephone Handling

- Have a clear message which you want to convey by ensuring proper use of language with clarity in pronunciation of words.

- Identify your organization, department and yourself to the caller.

- Use the other person's name often. People like to hear they name.

- Be prepared with the pen, pencil, paper etc. before connecting or receiving a call.

- Repeat the message to confirm understanding of the message.

- Do speak in a friendly, pleasant tone of voice with medium voice during conversation on telephone.

- Have a smiling face while you are talking on telephone which will improve your tone of voice automatically.

- Do use polite and professional language and don't ask about the caller's personal issues.

- Always follow up if you need to call someone then don't forget to call back.

- Do apologize for the interruption during call and ask permission before placing the caller on hold.

- Pick up the phone before three rings.

- Answer the phone call with a greeting as per the time of the day.

- Put the telephone two fingers away from the mouth for clear communication.

- Listen carefully without interrupting the caller when the caller is speaking.

- Do follow the "Golden Rule" – treat the caller the way you would like to be treated when you call.

- Sit straight during answering the phone call.

- Speak with confidence which comes after knowing your property well.

- Don't multitask during the phone call which may be cause of disturbance in communication.

- Don't give more importance to the telephone than the caller and don't play with the telephone and listen carefully to the caller.

- Don't use hotel terms a lot during conversation with the caller and use simple language to make the message clear.

- Don't get emotional or panic during the telephone call handling, because it will not help you to think properly and will also not help to provide a solution to the caller about the situation.

- Don't answer the phone call when eating, chewing, or drinking something.

- Don't say the words, "I don't know" when talking with someone on the phone.

- Never argue with a caller.

- Don't use slang words or short words during phone conversation which is considered as unprofessional.

- Don't say "Hello" after picking up the phone call.

- Don't use a speakerphone during the conversation on telephone.

- Don't guess about anything, if you don't know. Accept, apologize and get back with a solution.

- Don't end the call without a positive note (i.e., "Thank You for calling").

- Don't say, "No problem", say "You're welcome".

- Don't use Hotel Telephone for personal calling.

Globally used Common Telephony Spelling Codes

This table indicates the International Spelling Codes for letters of the alphabets which are used during telephonic or radio communication.

Letter	Code	Letter	Code
A	Alpha	N	November
B	Bravo	O	Oscar
C	Charlie	P	Papa
D	Delta	Q	Quebec
E	Echo	R	Romeo
F	Foxtrot	S	Sierra

G	Golf	T	Tango
H	Hotel	U	Uniform
I	India	V	Victor
J	Juliet	W	Whisky
K	Kilo	X	X-ray
L	Lima	Y	Yankee
M	Mike	Z	Zulu

References

- Source-of-hotel-reservation, front-office-training, train-my-hotel-staff: setupmyhotel.com, Retrieved 10, January 2020

- Modes-of-hotel-reservations, front-office-training, train-my-hotel-staff: setupmyhotel.com, Retrieved 21, July 2020

- How-to-cancel-reservations, front-office-training, train-my-hotel-staff: setupmyhotel.com, Retrieved 31, March 2020

- 10-types-of-customer-complaints: marketing91.com, Retrieved 11, August 2020

- Handling-guest-complaint-you-must-know: hospitality-school.com, Retrieved 25, April 2020

4

Front Office Coordination and Communication

Front office coordination and communication is an important area of front office operations and management. This chapter explains the role of the front office in interdepartmental communication, and coordination with housekeeping, food & beverage, sales & marketing, engineering & maintenance and safety & security departments. The topics discussed in this chapter will help in gaining a better perspective about front office coordination and communication.

To achieve the overall objective of front office operation that is sale of rooms and maintaining brand image of the property, the front office need to communicate and coordination tend to be important. The coordination for sale of rooms includes housekeeping which cleans and keeps rooms ready for sale and even helps in day to day services provided to the guests. In case of any maintenance problems in the room is handled by the engineering and maintenance department. Security department coordinates in keeping the hotel premises secure for hotel guests. All such departments that are a part of guest services need to have smooth coordination with front office.

Role of the Front Office in Interdepartmental Communication

The front office plays a pivotal role in delivering hospitality to guests. It sets the stage for a pleasant or an unpleasant visit. Guests, often in an unfamiliar setting and wanting to proceed with their business or vacation plans, are eager to learn the who, what, when, where, and how of their new environment. Requests for information often begin with the bellhop, switchboard operator, front desk clerk, cashier, or concierge, because these employees are the most visible to the guest and are perceived to be the most knowledgeable. These employees are believed to have their finger on the pulse of the organization and the community. Their responses to guests' requests for information on public transportation, location of hotel facilities, special events in the community, and the like indicate how well the hotel has prepared them for this important role. Front office managers must take an active part in gathering information of interest to guests. They must also be active in developing procedures for the front office to disburse this information.

The relationships the front office manager develops with the other department directors and their employees are vital to gathering information for guests. Developing positive personal relationships is part of the communication process, but it cannot be relied on to ensure accurate and current information is relayed. How does the front office manager encourage effective interdepartmental communication (communication between departments)? Figure below shows the departments in a hotel that interact with the front office.

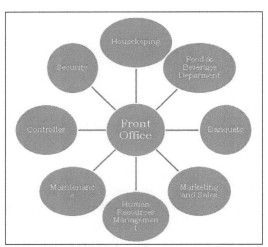

The front office serves as a clearinghouse for communication activities.

The front office is at the center of the diagram to illustrate the many interdepartmental lines of communication. These lines are based on the direction each department is given to provide hospitality in the form of clean rooms, properly operating equipment, safe environment, well-prepared food and beverages, efficient table service, and professional organization and delivery of service for a scheduled function as well as accurate accounting of guest charges and the like. These general objectives help department directors organize their operations and meet the overall goal of delivering professional hospitality. However, in reality, constant effort is required to manage the details of employees, materials, procedures, and communication skills to produce acceptable products and services.

Front Office Interaction with other Departments in the Hotel

The front office staffs interacts with all departments of the hotel, including marketing and sales, housekeeping, food and beverage, banquet, controller, maintenance, security, and human resources. These departments view the front office as a communication liaison in providing guest services. Each of the departments has a unique communication link with the front office staff. The front office in any type of lodging property provides the face and voice of hospitality for the organization around the clock. Guests are most likely to approach the front office staff for connections to staff in other departments. As you review the following lodging facility departments, try to grasp the role of the front office in communication with each. The front office is a clearinghouse for communication activities. The members of the front office team must know to whom they can direct guest inquiries for assistance. They learn this by means of a thorough training program in in-house policy and procedures and a constant concern for providing hospitality to the guest.

Front Office Coordination with Housekeeping Department

The most important and essential co-ordination can be established and recognized between front office and housekeeping department. Co-ordination with the housekeeping is one of the critical features of front office operations. The perfects co-ordination and efficiency of housekeeping and front office department results in the better sales of the rooms. Particularly in peak season co-ordination is most vital and helps in attaining 100% or more room occupancy if the housekeeping cleans and clears the rooms instantly as information is received from front office department.

Coordination between front office and housekeeping is required for following process:

1. As soon as there are guest departures the Front Office rings the Housekeeping Desk and reports the room numbers of rooms vacated so that Housekeeping can take them over to clean and prepare for sale. Once a room is clean, the Housekeeping Floor Supervisor rings the Front Office directly or through the Housekeeping Desk and hands over the room to front office for sale. Rooms received by Housekeeping for cleaning are called "departure room" while cleaned rooms handed to the Front Office for sale are called "clear rooms". The precision with which the above duty is done enables the Front Office to have rooms to sell to a waiting customer. This is especially critical in hotels with high occupancies.

2. The automated systems in this world of technology have made the communication as well as work faster and easier these days. However the employees ought to be trained to ensure that it acts as a supporting tool. The cycle of communication between the two is at each stage when the front desk provides the housekeeping department with a report called the Night Clerk's Room Report. The Purpose of the report is to inform housekeeping department very early in the morning the status of all rooms in the property as it appears in the front desk records. The nomenclature used varies from property to property but most common used abbreviations are SO – Occupied stay over; OOO – Out of order; V – Vacant; C/O – Guest has/Will Check out.

3. Front office department must forward arrival and departure list to housekeeping department so that rooms could be getting ready for expected guest on time. On the basis of arrival and departure of groups and VIP's list housekeeping make the duty roaster of its staff accordingly. The room sales projections - a weekly report is shared by the front office manager that indicates the number of departures, arrivals, walk-ins, stay overs, and no-shows-to schedule employees. Executive housekeeper plans the employee leaves on the basis of room sales projections.

Available Clean, or Ready	Room is ready to be occupied
Occupied	Guest or guests are already occupying a room.
Stay over	Guest will not be checking out of a room on the current day.
Dirty or On-Change	Guest has checked out of the room, but the housekeeping staffs has not released the room for occupancy.
Out-of -Order	Room is not available for occupancy because of a mechanical malfunction.

4. For small hotel arrival notification slips and departure intimation is sent to housekeeping department manually where as in large hotel or chain hotels these slips and intimation of departure are undated through property management system (PMS), but physical records are still maintained for future reference. This helps the housekeeping in knowing that who all have checked in or checked out from the hotel.

5. Housekeeping and front office communicates about the status of all rooms of the hotel. Housekeeping prepares room status report during each shift. Room status report is prepared on the basis of physical verification of each room. On the basis of physical verification, status of each room is indicated in front of the room number. Floor supervisor signs this report and sends to front office.

After these reports are made they are tallied i.e. the status as per front office and the status as per housekeeping in case of any discrepancy, the discrepancy Report is made and front office is informed about that so as to solve the discrepancies if any.

Housekeeping Room Status Report

Floor _____ Date _____ □ AM □ PM

Room Number	*	Code	Room Number	*	Code
01					
03					
05					
07					
09					
11					
13					
15					
17					
19					
21					
23					
Remarks :					

CODE **

OOO - Out of order   O - Occupied   V – Vacant

CO - Check out   SO - Sleep out   DL - Double locked

Maid's Signature

_____

Maid's Room Status Report:

```
HOUSE KEEPING DISCREPANCY REPORT
            TIME:     HRS.     DATE:
DND:#
12 Hrs. DND:#
Refused Service:#
12 Hrs. DND:#
Occupied No Luggage:#
Scanty Baggage:#
Double Lock:#
Extra Bed:#
HOUSEKEEPING:
```

6. Guests may request for extra amenities and guest room supplies and May sent request to front desk. Front office needs to inform the housekeeping department about the request so that housekeeping can promptly relay of requests for extra blankets, towels, soap and shampoo. A VIP is a very important person to the hotel and is welcomed by the front manager on his arrival. The House Keeping is informed so as to do his room in a better way and to the room service information is given about the various additional amenities that are to be placed in his room.

Front Office Coordination with Food and Beverage Department

Communication between the food and beverage department and the front office is also essential. Some of this communication is conveyed by relaying messages and providing accurate information on transfers, which are forms used to communicate a charge to a guest's account. Communication activities also include reporting predicted house counts, an estimate of the number of guests expected to register based on previous occupancy activities, and processing requests for paid-outs, forms used to indicate the amounts of monies paid out of the cashier's drawer on behalf of a guest or an employee of the hotel. These vital services help an overworked food and beverage manager, restaurant manager, or banquet captain meet the demands of the public. Incoming messages for the food and beverage manager and executive chef from vendors and other industry representatives are important to the business operation of the food and beverage department. If the switchboard operator is given instructions on screening callers (such as times when the executive chef cannot be disturbed because of a busy workload or staff meetings, or vendors in whom the chef is not interested), the important messages will receive top priority.

In a hotel that has point-of-sale terminals, computerized cash registers that interface with a property management system, information on guest charges is automatically posted to a guest's folio, his or her record of charges and payments. When a hotel does not have point-of-sale terminals that interface with PMS point-of-sale terminals, the desk clerk is responsible for posting accurate charges on the guest folio and relies on transfer slips. Also, the night auditor's job is made easier if the transfer slip is accurately prepared and posted. The front office manager should work with the food and beverage director in developing standard operating procedures and methods to complete the transfer of charges.

The supervisors in the food and beverage department rely on the predicted house count prepared by the front office manager to schedule employees and predict sales. For example, the restaurant supervisor working the breakfast shift will want to know how many guests will be in the hotel so he or she can determine how many servers to schedule for breakfast service. Timely and accurate preparation of this communication tool assists in staffing control and sales predictions.

Authorized members of the food and beverage department will occasionally ask the front office for cash, in the form of a paid-out, to purchase last-minute items for a banquet, the lounge, or the restaurant or to take advantage of other unplanned opportunities to promote hospitality. Specific guidelines concerning cash limits, turnaround time, prior approval, authorized signatures, and the general manager and front office manager develop purchase receipts. These guidelines help to maintain control of paid-outs. The banquet department, which often combines the functions of a marketing and sales department and a food and beverage department, requires the front office to relay information to guests about scheduled events and bill payment.

The front desk staff may also provide labour to prepare the daily announcement board, an inside listing of the daily activities of the hotel (time, group, and room assignment), and marquee, the curb-side message board, which includes the logo of the hotel and space for a message. Since the majority of banquet guests may not be registered guests in the hotel, the front office provides a logical communications centre. The daily posting of scheduled events on a felt board or an electronic bulletin board provides all guests and employees with information on group events. The preparation of the marquee may include congratulatory, welcome, sales promotion, or other important messages. In some hotels, an employee in the front office contacts the marketing and sales department for the message.

The banquet guest who is unfamiliar with the hotel property will ask at the front office for directions. This service might seem minor in the overall delivery of service, but it is essential to the lost or confused guest. The front office staff must know both how to direct guests to particular meeting rooms or reception areas and which functions are being held in which rooms. Front desk clerks, must be ready to provide information for all departmental activities in the hotel. The person responsible for paying the bills for a special event will also find his or her way to the front office to settle the city ledger accounts. If the banquet captain is not able to present the bill for the function, the front desk clerk should be informed about the specifics of food and beverage charges, gratuities, rental charges, method of payment, and the like.

- The occupancy of the hotel so that the FandB department is ready with its resources- manpower, catering equipments, finished food products, raw materials, etc.

- Arrival departure of groups and VIPs, so that the special and extra services like welcome drink, dessert and miscellaneous services pertaining to such guests can be given in the rooms like in case of VIPs special drinks liked by them or withdrawal of mini bar service from the rooms occupied by the groups.

- Arrival departure notification of guests staying in rooms.

- The processing of signed food and beverage restaurant and bar checks of the guests staying in rooms.

- Appraisal of customer requirement and satisfaction, meal experiences, etc. in the outlets through the GRE.

Front Office Coordination with Sales and Marketing Department

The marketing and sales department relies on the front office to provide data on guest histories, details concerning each guest's visit. Some of the information gathered is based on zip code, frequency of visits, corporate affiliation, special needs, and reservations for sleeping rooms. It is also the front office's job to make a good first impression on the public, to relay messages, and to meet the requests of guests who are using the hotel for meetings, seminars, and banquets.

The guest history is a valuable resource for marketing and sales, which use the guest registration information to target marketing campaigns, develop promotions, prepare mailing labels, and select appropriate advertising media. The front office staff must make every effort to keep this database current and accurate. The process of completing the booking of a special function (such as a wedding reception, convention, or seminar) depends on the availability of sleeping rooms for guests. The marketing and sales executives may have to check the lists of available rooms three, six, or even twelve months in the future to be sure the hotel can accommodate the expected number of guests. A database of available rooms is maintained in the property management system by the front office.

Messages for the marketing and sales department must be relayed completely, accurately, and quickly. The switchboard operator is a vital link in the communication between the prospective client and a salesperson in the marketing and sales department. The front office manager should instruct all new personnel in the front office about the staff in the marketing and sales department and what each person's job. In Short, these two departments' co-ordinates with the each other for the following information:

- Guest histories.

- Room Reservation Records.

- Current Room Availability Status.

- Group, corporate and travel bookings.

- Setting the transient and bulk room sales.

- The front office must take every effort to keep the room information on Room Availability Status and Guest Histories current and accurate.

- The Sales and Marketing executive needs information on room availability as to which rooms to sell in future to design marketing strategy for off season.

- Sales and Marketing needs information on guest types and slogans to develop marketing strategy and target key guest segments. The SandM department needs Front Office support in selling room facilities and service.

- Front office needs information on special promotion. For example: Special rates, Inclusion campaign etc.

Front Office Coordination with Engineering and Maintenance

Engineering and maintenance department is responsible for maintenance of equipment's and tools used in the operations. For following operations coordination is must between front office and maintenance department:

- Front office department keep its track on the status of room under maintenance. Front office department must update the out of order room as it got clearance from maintenance and housekeeping department.

- Before attending the plumbing, air conditioning, heating problem maintenance department confirms the room status from the front office department. Maintenance employees should know the room status before attending any maintenance problems.

- Sometime guest places the complaint at front desk regarding the issues such as heating, ventilating, and air conditioning, leaking, poor signal in LED and other room furnishing. These complaints should be communicated to the maintenance department immediately. The front desk clerk must work on the repair schedule as per guest order for maintenance department.

- Front office department must inform the guest that their complaint had been resolved by engineering and maintenance department.

Front Office Coordination with Safety and Security Department

Although the role of the Front Office is the responsibility of every guest, yet Front Desk staff plays an important role as they have the opportunity to observe all persons entering or departing the premis-es. The main security functions of the front office is protecting the guests and property. They are:

- People: Guests health, comfort or wellbeing. Employees and others.
- Property: Hotel Equipment, machinery, Hotel Room Supplies, fixtures and fittings, software, revenue, reputation etc.

Front Office Functions for Guest Security

- The Front Desk staff should never disclose the information about the guest to anyone.

- Front office staff should prohibit the staff to provide any information about the guests to any caller or visitors.

- Should never give room number, room keys and messages or mail of the guest to anyone else.

- Screening of caller before connecting the call to the guest/no connection of the call without the permission of the guest.

- Should also inform the guests of personal precautions they may take.

- The bell boy should give instructions to the guest of equipment use.

- Flyers/pamphlets of safety tips should be placed in the rooms.

- Front Office Staff also help protect guests' personal property.

- Front Office staff also important to asset protection (charging guests for breakages etc.).

Front Office Functions for Property Security

- The building should be enclosed with a Fencing-High rise concrete wall, wired etc.
- Adequate lighting on all side of the property.
- Security guards/manning of all entries/exits.
- CCTV placed at all strategic locations inside and outside the buildings.
- X-ray machines for luggage scanning.
- Inverted Mirrors for scanning of the lower side of cars/vehicles.
- Underground scanners for cars/vehicles.
- Underground Tyre-cutters for cars/vehicles.
- Door framed Metal detectors.
- Handheld scanners.
- Frisking of all guests/visitors.
- Multi-purpose room keys (for the use of lift/entry for adjacent mall etc.).
- Use of Sensors or Fire alarms.

Key areas for which coordination is required between these two departments:

- For routine check of guest security cooperation between both the departments is crucial.
- Front office should alert the security department regarding any suspicious person or activity.
- Coordination is required to deal with the problems such as guest locked out rooms.
- Both the departments handle the lost property.
- Security department communicates and gives instructions to the front office department about warning or emergency kind of situations.

Services of Front Desk

A front desk usually refers to a space in the lobby area of a hotel. Services of front desk include making direct contact with guests, attending and making calls, foreign exchange, room assignment, etc. The aim of this chapter is to explore the significant services of front desk.

Hospitality Service

Service in the hospitality industry is the level of assistance provided by a hotel staff to facilitate the purchase by the client.

It also encompasses a raft of efforts hotels makes to achieve pleasant customer experience for guests.

Of more importance, however, is the fact that customer experience goes hand in hand with customer service.

In principle, customer experience can be negative, indifferent or positive. Needless to say, everyone in the hospitality industry is gunning for a positive one.

In this topic, we have tried to define the purpose of service in hotel industry together with providing tips to ensure the purpose is met.

The Role of Service in the Hospitality Industry and the Purpose

Measure Customer Mood:

A recent study by industry's bigwigs shows that the clients aren't impressed by what you can offer or even what you know until they see that you actually care.

So, personable service is a sure way to improve your client's mood.

Judging the Customer's Needs:

This is similar to point one or a subset of point one but deserves a special mention.

It is very important to judge the needs of your customers without their asking.

For instance, if a family staying at your hotel has children then you should provide them children supplies without a need of them chasing you for everything.

It is important to ask yourself the question as well. What is service in the hospitality industry?

"Service is an act of respect, kindness and love. Service is the heart of hospitality industry".

This will help them get comfortable as they will feel more respected.

Improve Customer Loyalty:

An excellent customer service goes the extra mile to ensure that customers are happy and well taken care of.

Remember that a satisfied customer is a loyal customer. And, customers are a vital part of the business in the hospitality industry.

So, make them your centre of attention – at all times – and they will certainly be happy.

Feedback as a Crucial Part of Customer Service in the Hospitality Industry:

Sure you business model is water-tight. Sure your staff is top-notch. But, without general feedback from the customers, you wouldn't know if your business approach is actually working.

A famous Quote of Bill Gates would set things up here.

"Your Most unhappy customers are your greatest source of learning".

Customer Service, however, offers you an opportunity to measure how you are performing. It allows customers to communicate their experience – both bad and good. With this feedback, you will know what to fix.

Maintaining an updated information book helps you improve the quality of customer service in the hospitality industry. You should know about the time of their stay, so you could help them plan their stay in a better way.

You should recommend them good restaurants and guide them about other entertainment options.

On Time Services are Crucial in Hotels and in overall Hospitality Industry:

Time is the key to success when you're running a hospitality business. If you aren't able to provide on-time services to your valued customers then this will hurt your business.

Give individual priority to each customer. If you set customer satisfaction as your basic priority then you will be able to develop a loyal customer base.

Resultantly, your customers will not only come back again but will suggest your services to their friends and family members as well.

Following the Etiquette of Service in the Hospitality Industry:

Apart from ensuring that every service is being supplied on time, it is important to make sure that etiquettes of the service sector are also met. This includes both on-call and in-person services.

While conversing with customers it is important to maintain a level of respect.

Moreover, provide proper follow-up to make sure they are enjoying their stay at the hotel. If they have any complaints, get them sorted out at the earliest.

Meeting Customer Expectations:

Hotel customers are always seeking an energetic service and memorable experience. And, excellent service will enable you to do exactly that.

"On the whole, service in the hospitality industry allows hoteliers to meet – and possibly surpass – customer expectations."

Positive endings are extremely important in the hospitality industry as they are like fresh beginning that ensures patronage of a lifetime.

Always end things on a positive note. Always smile and greet when you see them. Call them by their name and maintain a good sense of humour when talking to them.

These are some of the things which must be ensured to understand and improve customer service in your hospitality business. If you don't pay much-needed heed to the improvement of customer service then levels of customer satisfaction will fall as well.

In contemporary times, the hospitality industry has emerged as one of the largest business domains in the world.

With more people travelling around the globe, this industry is expected to grow in future as well.

To succeed in hospitality industry customer service is the key and thus focus should be on the customers.

The Hospitality industry in future would be more inclined towards technology but service would still hold the key to success within the hospitality industry.

While all customers are not the same it is one thing that makes them all happy, superior service. So if they get something without asking, it makes them feel special.

When properly ensured, these services help businesses maintain a good environment. As a result, they are able to develop a loyal customer base which is essential for the growth and expansion of the business.

The Main Hospitality Services Include:

- Restaurant service.
- Food service.

- Coffee service.
- Valet parking.
- Laundry service.
- Room service.
- Customer service.

Customer Service

Customer service is the act of taking care of the customer's needs by providing and delivering professional, helpful, high quality service and assistance before, during, and after the customer's requirements are met. Customer service is meeting the needs and desires of any customer. Some characteristics of good customer service include:

- Promptness: Promises for delivery of products must be on time. Delays and cancellations of products should be avoided.

- Politeness: Politeness is almost a lost art. Saying 'hello,' 'good afternoon,' 'sir,' and 'thank you very much' are a part of good customer service. For any business, using good manners is appropriate whether the customer makes a purchase or not.

- Professionalism: All customers should be treated professionally, which means the use of competence or skill expected of the professional. Professionalism shows the customer they're cared for.

- Personalization: Using the customer's name is very effective in producing loyalty. Customers like the idea that whom they do business with knows them on a personal level.

Room service delivers food from the onsite restaurant to a guest's room. Unlike other delivery services, the staff provides all dishes, cutlery and trays. This allows guests to enjoy their meals in bed or at the table. Room service also extends to alcoholic drinks. However, many hotels stock such beverages in the mini-fridge.

Room Service

Room service delivers food from the onsite restaurant to a guest's room. Unlike other delivery services, the staff provides all dishes, cutlery and trays. This allows guests to enjoy their meals in bed or at the table. Room service also extends to alcoholic drinks. However, many hotels stock such beverages in the mini-fridge.

Room service is a convenience. It allows guests to eat in privacy or outside of regular restaurant hours. Most hotels take food orders throughout the day, accommodating late comers and early risers.

In many respects, room service also saves time. Guests can get ready in the morning while their food is prepared. This avoids restaurant waits and reduces the time between eating and starting the day.

Interestingly, despite its advantages, research posits that room service is nowadays less popular. PKF Hospitality Research reports that room-service related revenue fell 20% between 2007 and 2012. Consequently, many hotels have reduced room service resources and/or hours of operation. That said, some technology allows hotels to automate much of the service.

In the early 2000s, hotels used doorknob menus to fulfill orders. Such a system relied on an active staff member scanning floors for filled-out menus. Today, technology is smarter. Guests can submit food tickets from their personal devices or through the Smart TV. This is one example how hotels offset the cost of running room service programs.

Another way hotels have scaled back is through simplified menus. Most hotels serve both breakfast and all-day menus. They see no need to maintain lunch and dinner menus separately. Doing so lets the restaurant provide more variety on each menu, too.

Not every hotel offers room service. In particular, motels and inns typically do not find such programs feasible. Often, if the hotel includes a restaurant, there will be a dine-in menu of some sort available.

Coffee Service

Coffee service refers to the provision of coffee to people in restaurants and hotels, or to employees in a business or a workplace. Some establishments install coffee dispensers or vending machines for their coffee service, when they have high traffic of customers and employees. This allows the visitors some choice regarding beverage such as types of coffee, tea or hot chocolate. The instant coffee dispensed by these machines is generally considered of a low quality. An alternative to the ordinary coffee vending machine is the electric coffee maker, in which the coffee beans are crushed and the coffee prepared. The increasing use of frac pack is a modern phenomenon, which offers a simplified way of coffee preparation. It is a self-contained packet of ground coffee, surrounded by a filter. The downside to this is the reduced quality of coffee owing to the fact that coffee has to be brewed within a week of roasting, unless it is canned. It is a trend of the modern world, where companies have full espresso bars for employees and contractors free of charge or at highly subsidized rates.

Vending

Some companies, with high traffic of visitors and employees, opt to install a coffee dispenser (vending machine) as their coffee service. Typically these machines give the user the choice of various types of coffee, tea and hot chocolate. Money collected is usually kept by the employer to offset the cost of the maintenance contract and for the purchase of the instant coffee used by the machine. However, sometimes companies make the coffee from such machines free. Unfortunately, the coffee dispensed by these machines may be of low quality.

A coffee dispenser machine next to a water dispenser.

Electric Coffee Maker

Another option is to use an automatic espresso or drip coffee maker which grinds the coffee beans and dispenses the coffee into a cup. These machines do not charge per cup, but often provide a bypass slot where the employee can add their own coffee beans. By providing low quality beans, employees can be encouraged to provide their own beans. The cost of the maintenance contract still falls on the employer, however it is about the same as the cost of the machine per year.

Frac Pacs

An increasingly popular preparation offered by coffee service providers is known as a *frac pac*. This is ground coffee in a self-contained packet, enveloped by a filter. This allows a conventional drip coffee maker to be used, but without the mess of cleaning out the old grounds and without the requirement to measure out the right amount of coffee. The user only needs remove the old pack and to place the new pack into their coffee machine.

The downside of such a service is quality of the coffee. Unless canned, coffee needs to be brewed within the first week of roasting and within four hours of grinding for the best quality. Since local roasters will generally not have a filter enveloping machine, these packs are shipped great distances and may be weeks old before they even arrive at the office.

Onsite Espresso Bars

Some companies now provide on their premises full espresso bars where employees or contractors provide a full range of espresso drinks, free of charge or at company-subsidized prices.

Restaurant Service

The restaurant service practitioner provides high quality food and drink service to guests. A food service practitioner generally works in the commercial sector, offering a range of services to customers. There is a direct relationship between the nature and quality of the service required, and the payment made by the guest. Therefore the practitioner has a continuing responsibility to work professionally and interactively with the guest in order to give satisfaction and thus maintain and grow the business.

The practitioner is likely to work in a hotel or restaurant. However, the size, nature and quality of these establishments can vary enormously from internationally renowned hotel chains to smaller, privately-owned, more intimate restaurants. The quality and level of service provided and expected by guests will also vary. The styles of service will be dependent on the targeted customer and can range from simple self-service operations to elaborate service styles where dishes can be prepared at the guests' table. In its more elaborate form, food and drink service can be likened to a form of theatre.

High quality food and drink service requires the practitioner to have extensive knowledge of international cuisine, beverages and wines. They must have a complete command of accepted serving rules and must know the preparation of speciality dishes and drinks at the guests' table or in the bar. The food server is the most important person in attending to the guests and providing the meal experience. Skill and resourcefulness, good manners, excellent interaction with guests, aplomb, excellent personal and food hygiene practices, smart appearance and practical ability are all essential.

A wide range of specialist tools and materials will be used for the service of specialist dishes, drinks and wines. The practitioner will be familiar with their use in addition to the more usual pieces of equipment that are found in most dining situations.

Irrespective of the working environment, excellent communication and customer care skills are universal attributes of the outstanding practitioner. Food service personnel will work as part of a team and with other teams in the hotel or restaurant. Whatever the structure of the work, the trained and experienced practitioner takes on a high level of personal responsibility and autonomy.

This ranges from safeguarding the health and wellbeing of the guests and colleagues through scrupulous attention to safe and hygienic working practices, to achieving exceptional experiences for special occasions.

With the globalization of gastronomy, the expansion of travel for pleasure and business, and the international mobility of people, staff in the hospitality industry enjoy rapidly expanding opportunities and challenges. For the talented restaurateur there are many commercial and international opportunities; however, these carry with them the need to understand and work with diverse cultures, trends and environments. The diversity of skills associated with restaurant service is therefore likely to keep expanding.

Front Office Accounting

Accounting functions play a crucial role in front office operations. This includes maintaining guest folios, employee folios, visitors ledger, weekly bills, etc. This chapter closely examines all these functions along with budgeting for front desk operations.

Front Office Accounting

A front office accounting system is an essential process designed to monitor and chart the financial transactions of guests and non-guest at the hotel during each stage of the guest cycle. An effective guest accounting system includes tasks performed during each stage of the guest cycle:

- During the pre-arrival stage of the guest cycle: A guest accounting system captures data related to the form of guarantee for a reservation, and tracks pre- payment and advance deposits.

- When the guest arrives at the hotel: A guest accounting system documents the application of room rate and tax at registration.

- During occupancy: A guest accounting system is responsible for tracking guest charge purchase.

- During guest checkout: A guest accounting system ensures payment for goods and services provided.

- After guest check out: If a guest's bill is not fully paid at checkout, the balance is transferred from guest to non-guest records. When this occurs, collection becomes the responsibility of the back office accounting division.

The financial transactions of non-guests may also be processed within the parameters of front office accounting. A hotel may allow transactions involving non-guests in order to promote the hotel to local businesses; to track the unsettled bills of former guests; or to track transactions related to conference business at the hotel. So, the specific functions of a front office accounting system (FOAS) are to:

- Create and maintain an accurate accounting file for each guest or non-guest account.

- Track financial transactions throughout the guest cycle.

- Ensure internal control over cash and non-cash transaction.

- Obtain settlement for all goods and services provided.

The front office's ability to monitor and chart guest and non-guest transaction will directly affect its ability to collect outstanding balances. Incomplete of inaccurate monitoring may lead to difficulties in settlement.

Importance of Accounting for Front Office

- Being familiar with company procedures and accounting needs and being able to identify customer needs facilitates efficient work practices and promotes guest satisfaction.

- When proper, clear information is provided to guests, it prevents the occurrence of unpleasant surprises to guests in the form of unexpected charges, etc. that are sure to disturb them and cause unnecessary arguments and delays, especially at check out.

- Also guest accounts must be updated regularly with charges and adjustments because this impacts on company profits in the following ways:

  - Accounts are kept up to date with the minimum of effort. This impact positively on productivity and efficiency. Less time will be spent trying to find outstanding documents and dealing with discrepancies.

  - To minimise the chances of the guest departing before all charges have been posted. This would save on costs of contacting the guest and losing out on payments especially with foreign guests.

  - To reassure guests that their accounts are being managed accurately and efficiently. A satisfied guest implies repeat business.

- Security purposes: To prevent unauthorized access and the tampering of accounts, such as, the creation of false revenue and fraudulent charges and adjustments to guest accounts.

- Inaccurate transactions: The presence of unauthorised persons in one's work area increases the risk of inaccurate transactions. Not only will the company suffer from account imbalances and profit losses, but the guest may be upset at having incorrect charges etc. This affects guest satisfaction, which in turn affects repeat business.

- Personal accountability: Front desk staffs that handle and process guest accounts are responsible and accountable for computer transactions and for the filing and storage of account documentation while on duty.

- All guest information is confidential: This includes account information, and unauthorised persons must not be allowed access to such information.

Basic Accounting Terminology

The design of a front office accounting system is unique to hotel operations. Both, terminology and report formats, often differ from those of other accounting systems.

Account

An account is a form on which financial data are accumulated and summarized:

- An account may be imagined as a bin or container in which the results of various business transactions are stored.

- The increases and decreases in an account are summarized and the resulting monetary amount is the account balance.

- All financial transactions that occur in a hotel affect some account.

- Front office accounts are record keeping devices to store information about guest and non-guest financial transactions.

In its simplest written form, an account resembles the letter T:

Account Name	
Charge	Payment

For a front office account, charges are increases in the account balance and are entered on the left side of the T, while payments are decreases in the account balance and are entered on the right side of the T.

- The account balance is the difference between the totals of the entries on the left side and the right side of the T-account.

- A journal form is typically used for front office accounting documents. In a non-automated or semi- automated recordkeeping system, the journal form might look like this:

Description of Account	Charge	Payment	Balance

- In a journal, similar to a T-account, increases in the account balance are entered under charges, while decreases in the account balance are entered under payments.

- In a fully automated system, charges and payments may be listed in a single column with the amounts of payment placed within parentheses (brackets) to indicate their effect (a decrease) on the account balance or a positive amount depicting a debit charge and a negative amount indicating a payment made by the guest- usually this can be seen in automated or computerised guest folios.

- In accounting terminology, the left side of an account is called the debit side and the right side is called the credit side.

- In double entry bookkeeping, every transaction creates entries that affect at least two accounts. The sum of the debit entries created by a transaction must equal the sum of the credit entries created by that transaction. This fact forms the basis of the night audit.

There are three main types of accounts maintained by the front office cashier that record a hotel's transaction with three different types of customers: Resident guest accounts, City accounts or non-guest accounts and Management accounts.

Resident Accounts or Guest Accounts

Most of the accounts held by the front office cashier are the resident guest accounts, which show the financial transactions with guests who have registered and who are currently staying at the hotel.

- A guest account is a record of financial transactions, which occur between the in-house guest and the hotel.

- Guest accounts are created when guests guarantee their reservations or at the time of their registration.

- During occupancy, the front office records all transactions affecting the balance of a guest account.

- The hotel usually receives payment for any outstanding guest account balance during the settlement stage of the guest cycle, although circumstances may require partial or full payment at other times during the guest cycle.

- Some of the resident guests may have their accommodation charges settled by their company, while they settle incidentals themselves. In these situations, the resident guest has to have two folios:

  - The master folio or account for the room charges, which will be sent to the company for settlement. A copy of this account is sent to the city ledger.

  - The incidentals folio, which the guest will settle personally at check out.

City Accounts or Non-guest Accounts

City accounts are records of financial transactions between the hotel and non-resident guests. These accounts may also be called house accounts or city accounts. These could include accounts held by:

- Local business people who are not resident in the hotel but who use the hotel facilities and services for entertainment or business meetings agencies as a means of promotion.

- Guests who walk out of the hotel without settling the outstanding balance on their account (skippers). Walk-outs are no longer residents so their account is transferred to the city ledger, to either await eventual payment, or to be written off as a bad debt.

- Guests who have sent pre-payments to guarantee their bookings but have not yet arrived or checked in. These amounts are normally recorded in the accounts payable ledger till check in of the guest.

- Non-guest accounts also include accounts of former guests, which were not satisfactorily settled at the time of their departure- e.g. DNCO guests.

- Unlike guest accounts, non-guest accounts are normally billed on a monthly basis by the hotel's back office accounting division.

Management Accounts

These are expense accounts or allowances given by some hotels to the hotel managers to entertain guests or potential clients. For example, if a guest has a complaint about the hotel, the assistant manager may invite them to have a drink with him after the problem is resolved and this charge will be debited to management expense accounts.

Table: Distinguish between Guest Account and Non guest Account.

	Guest Account	Non Guest Account
1	Record of all financial transactions that occur between the guest and the hotel when they guarantee a reservation or they are registered at the Front Office.	Refers to all in-house charge privileges extended to local businesses or agencies eg. Banquets and conferencing facilities. These are also created when a former guest fails to settle his bill at the time of departure and the responsibility of recovering the balance amount shifts from Front Office to Accounts Dept. Or back office accounting.
2	These are compiled on a daily basis.	Billed on a monthly basis.
3	Front Office is responsible for its maintenance.	Back office or Accounts Dept takes the responsibility of account settlement.

Folios

Front office transactions are typically charted on account statement called folios. A folio is a statement of all transactions (debits and credits) affecting the balance of a single account. When an account is created, it is assigned a folio with a starting balance of zero. All transactions which increase (debits) or decrease (credits) the balances of the account are recorded on the folio. At settlement, a guest folio should be returned to a zero balance by cash payment or by transfer to an approved credit card or direct billing account.

The process of recording transactions on a folio is called posting. A transaction is posted when it has been recorded on the proper folio in the proper location and a new balance has been determined. When posting transactions, the front office may rely on hand written folios (if it is using a non-automated system), a machine-posted folios (with a semi-automated system), or computer-based electronic folios (with a fully automated system) Regardless of the posting technique used, the basic accounting information recorded on a folio remains the same. In a non-automated or semi-automated record keeping system, guest folios are maintained at the front desk. In a fully automated record keeping system, electronic folios are stored in a computer and can be retrieved, displayed, or printed on request.

Guest Folio

Guest Folio is considered as the master bill in the hotel which is also known as Guest Account Card. A guest folio contain all transactions of both cash and credit occurred by each resident guests. In manual system Folios are maintained manually and kept in the folio rack at the front office cash. In computerized system the folios are kept in the computer and only printed out at the time of a guest check-out.

Guest folio records each entry of guest transaction and the recording process is called posting. In the folio the posting is done consecutively in the order of transactions on a given date. The amount of money that is payable by the guest to hotel is recorded on the debit column and the amount of money that is collected from the guest through setting his/her bill as well as advance deposits is recorded in the credit column. The balance column of the guest folio shows a progressive balance between debit and credit column which is determined by subtracting the credit amount from the debit amount. It also includes previous balance.

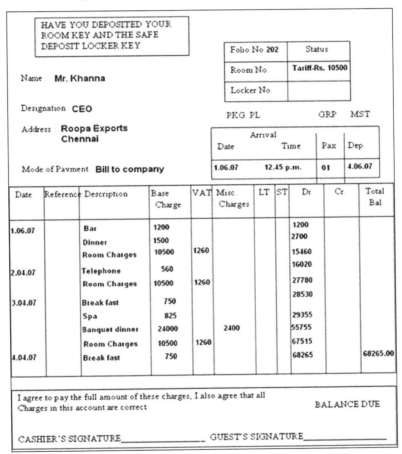

Just after the guest entry the front desk clerk create a guest folio with the inclusion of:

- Guest name,
- Room number,
- Date of arrival,
- Date of departure,
- Room rate,

- Guest address,

- Billing instruction to the cashier.

In order to perform the audit process the folios need to be maintained chronologically. Thus each folio contains a serial reference number for maintaining the chronological order. Till the guest departs from the hotel the cashier is in charge for the guest folio. During a guest's stay, his/her stay is on a credit. For example the goods or services that are provided to the guests are required to pay only upon his or her departure. However, forgetting this credit facility, a guest has to provide proof of his credit worthiness (especially for the new guests) by showing credit card, credit deposit, MCO and so on. Before offering a line of credit to a guest there are two checks is required, one by reservation agent who receives a booking and the other by the receptionists who registers a guest into the hotel. If there is any doubt, both staff can refer the issue to the lobby manager or front office manager who makes final decision. The receptionist of any is generally fully responsible for reconciling the guest's bills.

The hotel sets house credit limit in order to discourage the guests to overspend. If the guest's bill reaches or exceed the house credit limit, then the guest must clear up his or her bills. If the guest fails to pay, the hotel has the authority to seal the room for guest entry. The house credit limits are supervised closely by the front office cashier and later the night auditor who produces a daily statement of house guests exceeding the house credit limit. Guests basically go after the following procedure to settle the bills:

- Cash payments, in which a guest receive cash voucher from the cashier as an evidence of such payments.

- Guests sign their bills to be recovered by the city ledger by prearrangement with their organization.

- Paid bills through an acceptable credit card.

- Debit cards.

- Guests sign their bills to be adjusted against advances and deposits.

- Traveller's check which is considered as the check in the hotel.

The guest can settle his or her bill from any outlet of the hotel. If a guest wants to sign the bill in the guest folio at any of the post, the cashier will ask the guest for his/her room number. After verifying the room number the cashier will then make a charge voucher like the restaurant voucher in where the guest will sign and then the voucher will be forwarded to front office cashier to post the amount into the guest folio.

If a guest wishes to buy anything from the hotel shopping arcades, the guests are required to settle their bill or accounts directly with them (each shop has independent account system) as the shopping arcades are leased by the hotel. Some hotels also provide arrangements to shopping arcade to sign the guest bill. After providing the authentic documentation of the guest bill, the hotel will repay the amount to the shop owner. To sum up here are some key points about Hotel Guest Folio:

- Right after successful guest registration, a guest folio is created automatically in hotel's computerized Property Management System or manually.

- Every guest folio is opened with zero (0) outstanding balance in hotel.

- All kinds of information related to guest expenditure or loss made by guest has been recorded to handle future legal actions from any party.

- It is expected that all guest are trustworthy. So generally guest folios are presented and paid in check out period.

- Strict advanced payment procedures need to be taken for special guests like walk in guest, scanty baggage etc.

- For long term guest it is advisable to accept payment for few days and bill them weekly and try to collect payment and update the folio on weekly basis.

Master Folios

Master Folio is a collection of sub-folios and can be associated with a single guest or group of guests. For a master folio with a single guest, is it composed of all guest folios registered for a single guest. For master folio with groups, is collection of guest folios registered to multiple guests.

Non-guest (or Semi-permanent) Folios

A Hotel folio used to assign to non-guest businesses or agencies with charge purchase privileges. Accounts assigned to non-guest businesses or agencies with charge privileges at the hotel called a folio, taxes are posted. Refer to the set of guest accounts that correspond to registered guests or guests who have sent advance deposits. Any advance received from the guest is considered as the opening balance of the folio.

Employee Folios

Employee Folio is accounts assigned to employees with charge purchase privileges. Apart from the above mentioned common folios, front office department get use of some other types of folios such as A-type, B-type, C-type, D-type, and E-type folios.

Additional types of folios are frequently created by front office management to accommodate special circumstances or requests. For example: A business guest may request that his or her charges and payments be split between two personal folios: one to record expenses to be paid by the sponsoring business, and one to record personal expenses to be paid by the guest. This is referred to as a split folio. In this situation, two folios are created for one guest. If the room and tax portion are to be separated from other charges, the room and tax is posted to the room folio. This is sometimes called the A folio. Food, beverage, telephone, and other charges are posted to the incidental folio or B folio.

Every folio should have a unique serial number. Folio serial numbers are needed for many reasons. First, they serve as identification numbers that help ensure that all folios are accounted for during an audit of front office transactions. Second, folio numbers may be used to index information in automated system. Automated systems frequently create folio numbers when reservations are made. Folio numbers are then transferred to the front desk for use during registration. Finally, folio numbers can provide a chain of documentation. In non-automated and semi-automated systems, folios have specific length and can hold only a limited number of postings. When a balance must be carried forward to a new folio, the old folio numbers should be shown as a reference of where the balance originated.

Vouchers

These are documents that have details of transactions made by guests from various point of sales in hotels like, room service, restaurant, etc. The voucher is sent to front office for posting in the guest's folio and record keeping. Vouchers acts as a supporting document of the transaction happened between the hotel and the guest. A voucher also acts as a proof that a transaction has taken place in the hotel. Charge vouchers, Correction vouchers, Allowance vouchers, Transfer vouchers and Paid Out vouchers are examples of vouchers. Most automated systems require only few vouchers, as the terminals interfaced with property management system are capable of electronically transmitting transaction information directly to electronic folios.

1. Charge vouchers: The guest receives goods and services from the hotel but does not pay for them immediately known as deferred payment transaction. Where ever the transaction occurs, same has to be communicated to front office for posting in folio and the same is recorded on a charge voucher duly signed by the guest. The charge voucher is also called as account receivable voucher.

2. Correction vouchers: If an error is found in a guest folio, an account correction transaction corrects the same. It has to be carefully done on the same date of the business day. An account correction can either increase or decrease an account balance. E.g. If a charge is wrongly posted as higher than the actual rate, it can be corrected on the same day after entering the details of correction in a correction voucher.

3. Allowance vouchers: Allowance vouchers require management approval. They are generally of two types. One type of allowance is a compensation given to a guest for poor services or dissatisfaction related to goods or services etc. The other type of allowance is a correction to a posting error on an existing account after the close of business. The allowances given must be documented with the use of an allowance voucher.

ALLOWANCE VOUCHER		
NO._____		
DATED_____		
NAME_____ ROOM		
A/C NO._____		
DETAILED EXPLANATION	AMOUNT	
	RS.	RS.
RUPEES IN WORDS		
TOTAL RS.		

4. Transfer vouchers: A transfer voucher is used when the account balance or account entry is transferred or shifted from one folio to another folio. An account transfer may also occur when a

guest checks out by paying through credit mode. The guest's outstanding account balance is transferred from a guest account to a non-guest account through the use of a transfer voucher.

5. Paid Out vouchers (Visitor's Paid Out): A guest may sometimes request services which are not available in hotels. In such cases the hotel will arrange those services from outside organisations. The staff will arrange and pay for these services and notify reception or cashier of the charges to be added to the guest folio. It is cash paid out by the hotel on behalf of the guest. Petty payments like taxi fare, cinema tickets, purchase from outside hotel, postage etc. are made by the front desk, a Visitor's Paid Out Voucher is issued on guest's name and his signature is collected and the amount is debited in guest's folio.

```
HOTEL XYZ

PAID OUT VOUCHER

DATE_____          TIME_____

Guests Name_____

Room no._____ Account Folio No._____

Detailed explanation_____

_____

_____

Rs. _____ (In words_____)

Prepared by_____

Authorised by_____

Audited by_____

                              Signature of the guest_____
```

Point of Sale

Point of sale (POS) refers to a critical piece of an critical piece of a point of purchase, refers to the place where a customer executes the payment for goods or services and where sales taxes may become payable. It can be in a physical store, where POS terminals and systems are used to process card payments or a virtual sales point such as a computer or mobile electronic device.

Points of sale (POSs) are an important focus for marketers because consumers tend to make purchasing decisions on high-margin products or services at these strategic locations. Traditionally, businesses set up POSs near store exits to increase the rate of impulse purchases as customers leave. However, varying POS locations can give retailers more opportunities to micro-market specific product categories and influence consumers at earlier points in the sales funnel.

For example, department stores often have POSs for individual product groups, such as appliances, electronics, and apparel. The designated staff can actively promote products and guide consumers through purchase decisions rather than simply processing transactions. Similarly, the format of a POS can affect profit or buying behavior, as this gives consumers flexible options for making a purchase.

POS and its Importance

Nowadays, having an effective Point Of Sale System for hotels is very important. Some of the Major importance of an effective POS system within the hotel are:

- It helps to increase the operational efficiency of the hotel.

- Improves customer service.

- Inventory and tracking management.

- Accuracy in accounting.

- It provides a fast check out experience to the customers.

- Helps in managing customer data.

By seeing the requirements of the customer nowadays, it's clear that shortly, we will see enormous growth in adaption the POS system for the businesses. Point of Sale system business has proved to be a long-term initiative and has the potential to grow faster than other businesses.

Booking Methods for Hotel

In today's era hotel booking is just a matter of a few clicks or few calls. Mainly there are two distinct sources for the hotel booking and they are through:

- Online Booking: Any booking which are done through online sources such as through various media sources or through the hotel websites is stated as online booking. Online bookings are also done directly to the hotels or through the agents. When the booking is done through the agents it states as indirect booking.

- Offline Booking: Many people do hotel booking through the phone call or by visiting the hotel. In the offline booking, the toughest part is to manage the inventory as it creates the real-time syncing issue. So having an effective hotel POS system can solve this issue. It helps to update the inventories in real-time.

Transaction and Inventories

These days, the hotels are having their own Food and Beverage outlets. Since most of the people stay in the hotel for a long duration, they prefer to have their meals from the hotel FandB outlets only. Apart from the FandB outlets, nowadays the hotel has an option of room service and mini-bars as well.

So there are many places where a guest can spend and it means a greater number of places to keep track of and account for at the time of final bill generation. So the hotel POS must be capable to keep the record of all the transactions and inventories for each room and it will include all the ordered food and the extra charges which are charged on every customer.

Fast and Effective

Nobody these days want to wait for a long time, neither do the customers. So having a fast POS system for the hotels is very important. If the hoteliers are having the manual billing system, then it could cause inconvenience to the customers, when they want the early checkout from the hotel. The POS system for the hotels must be fast and effective in such a way that it computes and calculates all the expenses of the customers more effectively and accurately. It allows the staff to make the most of the checkout experience to engage customers and make sure they leave with a good impression.

A point of sale system is one of the best ways to improve your hotel. In fact, these are all the benefits of using POS systems in hotels:

- Seamless Management: Hotels are unique in that they often run several kinds of operations at once. Hoteliers obviously manage guests and rooms, but many buildings also boast a bar or restaurant inside. Hotels can even be a part of local resorts and tourist attractions, thus increasing the management needs of front desk staff. This means people should be able to book a room, retrieve their key, make a reservation, find a local tour guide, and order a drink all at the same place. That is a lot to handle. Luckily, our team at Business Software Solutions hand-crafted a point of sale system for hotels. Our system can help you manage your property, guests, gift cards, restaurant, and more all in one place.

- Unified Analytics: As the name implies, point of sale systems manage the transactions and reporting for your business. With a hotel-specific POS system, you can easily see how you are doing and what services are most sought after. An unintegrated approach would leave you grappling with several sources of information. But with a POS system that handles both your guests and your food operations, you can see the totality of your business all in one. These reporting statistics are then essential for your accounting and planning purposes.

- Improved Food Scene: The restaurant or bar that you run alongside your hotel is essential to the overall success of your business. Between serving breakfast to your customers and giving them a mid- or upper-level dining experience, your food scene is critical to the atmosphere of your establishment. However, properly running these two businesses can be challenging. Quality POS software for small business owners can make this headache into a dream. Many customers want to add their tab to their room. Instead of denying this request or jumping through a whole host of hoops on the back end, a POS system can simply charge their food and drinks to their room directly. This will not only help your staff as they perform their duties, but it will also improve the customer's overall experience.

Ledgers

A ledger is a grouping of accounts. A hotel uses two main types of ledgers: A Back Office Accounts Receivable ledger (A/R) and A Back Office Accounts Payable ledger.

Transfer of Guest Accounts to the Back Office Accounting

Some methods of payment require transferring folio balances to the back office for further processing:

- Credit card payments are processed and added to the master credit card account according to type of card - Visa, MasterCard, etc. The Controller maintains this account as an accounts receivable.

- Bill-To-Account/Direct Billing (for company/travel agent) charges must be transferred to the back office accounts receivable. The controller processes the account according to standard operating procedures, which are handled electronically in a PMS.

Back Office Accounts Receivable (A/R)

Once the guest has received the goods and enjoyed the services of the hotel, and settled the folio on a third party account, then this financial record must be transferred to the master accounts receivable for the hotel. Example: at checkout, if a guest folio shows a debit balance of Rs. 15,000/- and the guest wants to pay that off by charging it to his MasterCard, then the amount is transferred to the MasterCard Accounts Receivables. Front office accounting commonly separates accounts receivable into two subsidiary groups: The Guest ledger (for guest receivables) and a City ledger (for non- guest receivables).

Guest Ledger

- The guest ledger is the set of all guest accounts currently registered in the hotel.

- Guests who make appropriate credit arrangements at registration may be extended a privilege to charge purchases to their individual accounts folio.

- Guests may also pay on their accounts at any time during occupancy.

- Guest financial transactions are recorded onto guest ledger to track receivable balances.

- The guest ledger may also be called the transient ledger, front office ledger, or rooms' ledger.

City Ledger

- The city ledger, also called the non-guest ledger, is the collection of all non-guest accounts (house accounts and unsettled departed guest accounts).

- If a guest account is not settled in full by cash payment at check-out, the guest's folio balance is transferred from the guest ledger to the city ledger for collection.

- At the time of transfer, accounts collection becomes the responsibility of the back office accounting division.

Table: Distinguish between Guest Ledger and City Ledger.

	Guest Ledger	City Ledger
1	Is the set of guest accounts for registered guests or guests who have sent advance deposits.	Refers to the set of non-guest accounts. For e.g., if a guest account is not settled in full on check out, the balance is transferred to the back office accounting division for collection.
2	Corresponds to registered guests or guests reserved for future dates.	May or may not account to registered guests alone.

3	Records all financial transactions of an in-house guest.	Contains Credit Card payment accounts, Company accounts, direct billing accounts, outstanding accounts of guests stayed earlier and are due for collection.
4	Also referred to as transient ledger, front office ledger or rooms ledger.	It is also called Non-guest ledger.
5	Maintained at front office.	Maintained by accounting division (back office accounts).

Back Office Accounts Payable

These handle amounts of money prepaid on behalf of the guest to the hotel for future consumption of goods and services. Example: When a guest deposits a sum of money (cheque) for a future stay or reservation before arrival, the cheque, must be credited first to the hotel's back office accounts payable and then to the guests folio (at check in). This amount is held for the guest's arrival on March 10th, after which it is displayed as a credit (minus amount) entry in the guest folio which is activated upon registration.

This shows that activities in the guest ledger and city ledger are not isolated but reflected in the back office accounts. The guest and city ledger are temporary holding facilities for the guests' account the back office accounts are the permanent areas for financial processing.

Accounting System

The formats of guest and non-guest account folios may be different, depending upon the front office recordkeeping system. The process of guest accounting is operated either:

- Manually i.e., non-automated: In this operating mode all the phases involved in accounting process are carried out by the staff. Guest folios in a manual system contain a series of columns for listing individual debit and credit entries accumulated during occupancy. At the end of the business day, each column is totalled and the ending balance is carried forward as the opening folio balance of the following day. The entire system is prone to omission and computation errors. Another drawback is handling and re-handling of numbers data. This type of system is useful for small hotels only where the workload is not much.

- Mechanically i.e., semi-automated: This system is used by hotels which are medium-sized or large but yet don't have automatic machines like computers. Usually they use a combination of office machines, clerical equipment and manpower to operate these systems. Guest transactions are printed sequentially on a machine-posted folio. The information recorded for each transaction includes the date, department or reference number, amount of the transaction, and new balance of the account. The folios outstanding balance is the amount the guest owes to the hotel or the amount the hotel owes the guest in the event of credit balance at settlement. If the posting is done by mechanical equipment, it does not retain individual folio balances. This means that each accounts previous balance must be re-entered each time an account posting is made to the folio.

- Through Computer i.e., fully automated: This system comprises of computers and other electronic devices located at every point of sale and interfaced with the main cashier at the front desk. All task done manually is easily done by automatic machines whether it's posting, auditing, correction of errors, etc. The machines are fast and practically no possibility of late charges. Necessary steps such as sorting, of vouchers, identification, posting code and reference code, posting are automatically carried out. Since computers are machines operated by humans, it is obvious that the accuracy will depend upon the software developed and the efficiency of the staff operating.

Visitors Tabular Ledger

V.T.L is one of the important ledger maintained by front office cashier in order to keep the record of all the transaction of the guest during his/her stay in the hotel. V.T.L is generally made for each guest who check-in to the hotel and use the hotel facilities. This sheet is prepared daily basis by front office cashier. After the completion of billing procedure, each day transaction is carried out by a night auditors. The account of guest is calculated and carried down in a new ledger for the next date which is usually close when the guest checkout from the hotel.

Importance and Purpose of V.T.L

- It shows the total sales of each outlet in a hotel.

- It shows the overall sales of hotel in a particular day.

- It shows the types of service used by the guest.

- It shows the cash deposit made by the guest and also the credit balance.

- It shows the cash paid by the guest during their stay and also the discount offered to them.

- It shows the total balance of the guest transferred to a city ledger.

- It shows the total transaction of a particular guest in a particular day.

Posting Procedure of V.T.L

- Always use capital or block letter and use ink or ball pen for writing the name of the guest.

- Details about the guest information should be written legible after the registration of the guest such as pax, plan, tariff, etc.

- Use dashes where there is no transaction or figure.

- All the transactions should be entered as per the bills or voucher sent by the outlets.

- Enter total amount in the respective debit and credit column.

- Guest charges for different service are written in the respective columns as per the heading.

- Cash advance or deposit made by the guest is written in the guest account under cash deposit column.

- Guest amount or charges are written under the column "city ledger", if the guest do not settle bills during check-out. Generally these types of guests are from company or travel agency.

- If the guest's amount is paid by other party or guest, the amount is written under transfer column, which includes debit and credit.

- Calculate the sub-total from all the charges under individual after adding the tax and vat.

- Grand total is carried out after adding or reducing from balance brought forward in the daily total.

- In allowance column, amounts are written for those guest who are provided amount from the hotel.

- Last balance column in the V.T.L under the column balance b/d or c/d and respective debit and credit column.

Advantages of Visitors Tabular Ledger

- Easy: It is an easy system to understand and after a day's training cashier can be asked to prepare the visitors tabular ledger.

- Economical: The ledger is prepared in the ruled sheets so it does not cost much money.

- Fewer mistakes: Voucher is debited directly. The chances of making mistakes are minimized.

- Sale under various heads: Different heads columns are made and totalled horizontally. It helps in knowing the sale of various departments.

- Cross Checking: In case of any controversy cross-checking can be done through voucher.

- Arithmetical checking: All columns are totalled both horizontally and vertically It helps in cross checking the total and in case of error it can be rectified instantly by the cashier.

Disadvantages of Visitors Tabular Ledger

- Difficult to handle: Due to a big size it becomes discult to handle.

- Store: Since it is in loose paper form and it gets torn very fast so it becomes difficult to store for a longer period.

- Wrong Posting: The columns are usually very small and cashier might enter one room sentry to other room by mistake and this mistake cannot be rectified by checking the cross totalling.

VISITORS TABULAR LEDGER									
ROOM NO.	101	102	103	201	202	203	301	302	TOTAL
NAME									

NATIONALITY									
TYPE OF ROOM									
NUMBER OF PAX									
G.R. NO.									
DATE/TIME OF ARRIVAL									
DATE/TIME OF DEPARTURE									
PLAN	RS. P.	RS. P.	RS. P.	RS. P.	RS. P.	RS. P.	RS. P.	RS. P.	RS. P.
ROOM									
BREAKFAST									
LUNCH									
DINNER									
SNACKS									
LAUNDRY									
TELEPHONES									
V.P.O.									
FLOWRIEST									
DAILY TOTAL									
BALANCE DR CR									
G. TOTAL									
DR CR									
ALLOWANCES									
LEDGER									
TRANSFER									
BALANCE									

Guest Weekly Bill

Guest weekly bill is prepared for each guest and is presented on checkout for settlement. It is called a weekly bill as for one week one bill is prepared. There is no hard and fast rule that a bill has to be prepared for one week. In case majority of guests in a hotel stay for three days then one may adopt a three day bill. If a guest stays beyond three days then another bill is attached. The guest weekly bill is opened immediately on check in by receptionist. The copy of the guest registration card is stapled with the weekly bill/folio. The cashier can refer to guest's signature on guest registration card and compare his/her signature with the voucher. If signature tallies then the cashier debits the voucher to guest's account otherwise he/she sends the bill back to the outlet with a remark that signature does not tally. All the weekly bills are placed numerically in the vertical file and it helps in taking out a particular bill instantly. The vouchers after posting in the guest weekly bill should be kept in the bills rack.

GUEST WEEKLY BILL
HOTEL XYZ
T. NO.   SERIAL NO. 4546454
E. MAIL
ROOM NUMBER..........................
NAME OF THE GUEST MR./MS. ....
NATIONALITY...
DESIGNATION...
OFFICE ADDRESS.. E. MAIL .... T. NO. ....
PERMANENT ADDRESS.................................... E. MAIL .... T .NO. ....
DATE AND TIME OF ARRIVAL................................... DATE AND TIME OF DEPARTURE..............
TYPE OF ROOM.................................... NUMBER OF PAX...................................
RATE.................................. ROOM...................................... PLAN.......................................
BILLING INSTRUCTIONS...
CREDIT CARD... CARD NUMBER...................................
DATE OF EXPIRY..........................
BOOKED BY...............................

DATE									
DAY									
ROOM	RS. P.	RS. P.	RS. P.	RS. P.	RS. P.	RS. P.	RS. P.	RS. P.	RS. P.
BREAKFAST									
LUNCH									
DINNER									
SNACKS									
LAUNDRY									
TELEPHONES									
V.P.O.									
FLOWRIEST									
DAILY TOTAL									
BALANCE DR CR									
G. TOTAL DR CR									
ALLOWANCES									
LEDGER									
TRANSFER									
BALANCE									

Front Office Budgeting

Budgeting is a very significant tool for any organization irrespective of its size and nature, if they need to survive in the modern world economy. Budget helps not only in controlling but also in increasing profits and better coordination. There are several control techniques adapted to manage the business operations and budget is one such control technique. It is the most significant tool of profit planning and control and also acts as an instrument of coordination. Therefore, budget is a written paper which is useful for two most important functions of a firm i.e. managerial and accounting. There is no planning without policy. Thus policy is pre-requisite to planning and budget is the detailed coordinated plan-statement. In short, budget is an estimate facilitating planning and control of business.

Budget

The term is supposed to be derived from the French word 'bougettee,' meaning a leather pouch in which funds are appropriated for meeting the anticipated expenses. Budget is a statement of management policy expressed in physical and monetary terms. The term budgeting is used for preparing budget, planning, coordination and controlling functions of an organisation. These may be prepared for organization as a whole or in parts for different sections of an organization.

It is a plan or statement showing expected or estimated results for the definite future period expressed in numerical terms. It is an ad hoc or a single-use plan. It contains anticipated operating results over some future period of time. It provides a base for measuring, comparing, and controlling performance. And, hence, it is used for planning, coordination, and controlling purposes. It may be in terms of time, money, units, or otherwise. Budget is both a planning and a controlling technique. Budget concerns with 'how much' aspect of planning.

Front Office Budget

Front Office department of any hotel is responsible for sale of rooms and is a responsible around 70% of the total earning for a Hotel. That is why budget making is an important activity of the department. Front office has several sub-sections such as reservation, reception, lobby, information, business center etc. depending upon the needs of the establishment. Front office head has to prepare budgets for all sections and for their labour, materials, sales, costs, capital etc. These budgets are based on the previous figures in consultation with the section heads and controller to achieve organizational goals. Once approved, it is implemented and observations are recovered and matched with the set standards to identify any deviation and to be corrected.

Revenue forecasting and estimating expenses are another two functions of front office budgeting. For the purpose, a front office manager requires expected information, in term of room numbers, regarding followings:

- Arrivals,
- Walk-Ins,
- Stay over,

- No-Shows,

- Cancellation,

- Under stays,

- Check-outs,

- Overstays.

From the above mentioned data following daily operational ratios are calculated in percentage:

- No-Show (percentage) = (Number of NoShow Rooms ÷ Number of Rooms Reserved) × 100.

- Cancellation (percentage) = (Number of Cancellation Rooms ÷ Number of Rooms Reserved) × 100.

- Walk-ins (percentage) = (Number of Walk – in Rooms ÷ Total numbers of Room Arrivals) × 100.

- Overstays (percentage) = (Number of Overstayed Rooms ÷ Number of Check – out Expected) × 100.

- Understays (percentage) = (Number of Understay Rooms ÷ Number of Expected Check – outs) × 100.

Whereas, following formula can be used to predict number of rooms available for sale on a given date for future:

Expected Rooms Available for Sale for a date = Total Number of Guest Rooms – (Number of Out Of Order Rooms + Number of Stayovers Rooms + Number of Reserved Rooms + Number of Overstay Rooms)+ (Number of No-show Rooms + Number of Cancellation Rooms + Number of Check-Out Rooms + Number of Understay Rooms).

There are certain operational ratios which help in budgeting:

Occupancy Ratios

These ratios are used for measuring occupancy of the hotel and are calculated daily. This is one of the jobs of the Night Auditor to compute and convey these ratios to the top management. These ratios are used for comparison and auditing the hotel performance against the set benchmarks. These are often compared with ratios of:

- Previous same time period.

- Targeted ratios.

- Competitors' ratios.

- Industry's ratio.

Room Occupancy (percentage) = (Number of Occupied Rooms ÷ Total Number of Rooms Available) × 100.

Multiple Room Occupancy (percentage) = (Number of Rooms Occupied by more than one guest ÷ Total Number of Rooms Occupied) × 100.

Single Room Occupancy (percentage) = (Number of Single Rooms Occupied ÷ Total Number of Single Rooms Available for Sale) × 100.

Double Occupancy (percentage) = (Number of Double Rooms Occupied ÷ Total Number of Double Rooms for Sale) × 100.

Triple Occupancy (percentage) = (Number of Triple Occupied Rooms ÷ Total Number of Triple Rooms Available for Sale) × 100.

Other Operational Statistics

These are not occupancy ratios but are very significant:

- Average Guests per Rooms Sold = (Total Number of Guests) / (Total Number of Rooms Sold).

- Average Daily Rate = (Actual Room Revenue) / (Total Number of Rooms Sold).

- Average Rate per Guest = Revenue per Available Customer (RevPAC) = (Actual Room Revenue) / (Number of Guests).

- Revenue per Available Room (RevPAR) = (Actual Room Revenue) / (Number of Available Rooms).

Yield Statistic

These are prepared by the Night Auditor for the top management for evaluating the success of Front Office and Sales Department for selling hotel facilities and services at the prescribed price i.e hotel rooms. It is calculated by dividing actual room revenue by potential room revenue i.e. (Actual Room Revenue ÷ Potential Room Revenue).

Essentials of a Budget

A budget must have following essential elements:

- Prepared for a definite future period.

- Prepared earlier to the defined period of time.

- It is policy matter that is related to money and different quantities.

- It is a prearranged report and its main aim to achieve pre-defined objective.

Budget Preparation

The preparation of budget involves several steps or stages. They are as follows:

- Collection of Relevant Data: Budget formulation commences with the collection of relevant data (i.e., immediate past data) and analysis. This analysis sheds light on the trend of capital movement, profit growth, etc., which provide a strong base for the preparation of budget.

- Forecasting the Activities: Each functional department should be asked to forecast its activities and assess its resources. This helps in preparing functional budgets. The goal of the concern, the key factor of the function, and the way of overcoming the key factor, should also be considered while framing the functional budget.

- Establishing Organisation Chart, Budget Committee, etc: An organisation chart should be established to define the functional responsibilities of each member of the management team associated with the preparation of budget. Fixing the budget period and the establishment of budget committee and budget centre should also be taken care of at this stage.

- Preparing Accounting Records: Budget formulation requires several accounting records. A chart showing the requirement of accounting records of each functional area should be prepared. This helps in facilitating the analysis and interpretation of the accounting information required for the preparation of budget.

- Framing Guidelines: The guidelines required for the preparation of budget should be framed. Such guidelines are related to production, stock levels, channel choice, product promotion and general investment policies.

- Awareness of Task: For the smooth preparation of budget, everyone concerned with its preparation should be made known his task.

- Preparation of Budget Manual: The budget manual assigning the responsibility to each person engaged in the preparation of budget is to be prepared at this stage.

- Submission of Budget Prepared for Discussion: Every functional department is required to place the budget prepared as per the set guidelines before the budget committee for discussion and reformation. The budget approved by the budget committee in turn should be sent to the top management for approval.

- Implementation of Budget: The budget committee should send the approved budgets to the concerned departments for implementation. It should have the responsibility to conduct periodic reviews for assessing the performance of each functional area. It should also ascertain whether actual conform to the budget.

Classification and Types of Budgets

Budgets are usually classified according to various activities as given below:

- Functions:
  - Purchase budget.
  - Sales budget.
  - Production budget.

- ○ Production cost:
  - Materials budget.
  - Labour budget.
  - Factory overhead budget.
  - ○ Administrative overhead budget.
  - ○ Selling and distribution overheads budget.
  - ○ Plant utilization budget.
  - ○ Research and development budget.
  - ○ Capital budgeting.
  - ○ Cash budget.
- Nature of expenditure:
  - ○ Fixed budgets.
  - ○ Flexible budgets.
  - ○ Operating budgets.
- Time:
  - ○ Short-period budget.
  - ○ Long-period budget.
  - ○ Current budgets budget.
  - ○ Rolling budgets.
- Activity level:
  - ○ Fixed budget or single level budget.
  - ○ Flexible budget.

These budgets are what functions they perform. The various functional budgets are as follows:

- Purchase Budget: The budget which guides the management in making necessary purchases to be made during the budget period is known as purchase budget. Purchase budget is mainly concerned with the raw materials in the case of a manufacturing concern.

- Sales Budget: Sales budget is the basis of budgetary control. It is an estimate of expected sales during a budgeted period. It can be expressed either in monetary terms or in physical units.

- Production Budget: Production budget is a forecast of the production for the budget period. It determines the quantity of the products to be produced.

- Production Cost Budget: It fixes the target in terms of quantities to be produced. Once number is determined, then these are converted into monetary costs. Then it is refereed as production cost.

- Material Budget: The budget which is concerned with determining the quantity of raw materials required for production is called raw material budget.

- Labour Budget: Only direct labour budget is prepared from the costing point of view.

- Factory Overheads Budget: Under this budget, all the indirect costs are estimated i.e. materials, labour and factory expenses.

- Administrative Overheads Budget: The budget which covers the expenses of all administrative offices and of management salaries is called the administrative overhead budget.

- Selling and Distribution Overhead Budget: The budget which estimates the expenses involved in selling and distributing the product is known as selling and distribution overhead budget.

- Plant Utilisation Budget: The budget which estimates the extent of plant and machinery to be used in the production process is called the plant utilization budget.

- Research and Development Budget: The budget which is prepared to know the estimated cost on research and development comes under the category of research and development budget.

- Capital Budgeting: Capital project planning or capital budgeting is the process by which funds are allocated to various investment projects designed to ensure profitability and growth.

- Cash Budget: The budget which shows the cash requirements for a future period is called the cash budget.

Nature of Expenditure

According to nature of expenditure, budgets can be divided into following categories:

- Fixed Budgets: A budget prepared on the basis of standard or fixed level of activity is called the fixed budget or single level budget.

- Flexible Budgets: A budget which is designed to change in accordance with the level of activity actually attained is called the flexible budget or dynamic budget.

- Operating Budget: A firm may prepare operating budget on the basis of programmes or responsibility areas.

Classification According to Time

In terms of time, budget is classified into:

- Long-term Budget: A budget which is designed for a long period (i.e., a period of 5 to 10 years) is termed as a long-term budget. Such a budget is usually prepared in physical units for the planning of the operations of a concern.

- Short-term Budget: A budget designed for a short period (i.e., not exceeding 5 years) is termed as short-term budget.

- Current Budgets: Budgets which cover a very short period (i.e., a month or a quarter) are current budgets. These budgets are prepared for short period in accordance with the prevailing conditions.

- Rolling Budgets: Rolling budgets are also known as progressive budgets. Firms which follow such budgets will always be planned for a year ahead.

Approaches to Budgeting

In past, budgets are prepared on the basis of the past year budgets. But now days, new approaches to prepare budgets have been developed and practiced. These are as follows:

- Past Data-based Budgeting: In this approach, the current year or past year budget is taken as the base for preparing the budget for the future. Adopting some additions and deductions, the next year budget is prepared. It is a traditional way of preparing budget.

- Performance Budgeting: Performance budget is prepared for evaluation of an organisation's performance in terms of input and output or cost and result. This budget estimates the total cost of activities and the resulting performance.

- Zero-based Budgeting (ZBB): It is comparatively a newer concept in business and non-business fields. It was first time used by Texas Instruments of USA in 1971; later on, it was applied by Georgia in 1973. Now, it is used in several countries, including India. Here, each time, a new budget is prepared for any area of business operations. In this approach, all costs or expenditures are calculated afresh for the budget period instead of considering the past data. It offers a number of benefits over traditional budgeting.

- Strategic Budgeting: It is also a new concept. It is used as a tool for resource allocation to various strategic business units. It is based on the performance and results that an organisation expects, and key activities, tasks, and jobs that organisational units need to perform.

Importance of Budgeting

Budgeting is an important managing an organisation. Its benefits for a business are as follows:

- It helps an organisation in achieving its objectives and its long-term goals which are translated into specific plans and tasks, providing clear guidelines to-managers regarding current operations.

- It assists management in making comparison and selection between alternative courses of action and their evaluation.

- It provides a means of communicating organisational plans to all members of the organisation.

- Constraints upon production capability are highlighted (the limiting factors).

- Preparing budgets provides an opportunity to review operations and revise if necessary.

- Performance at all levels of the organisation can be measured and evaluated against an accepted yardstick of the budgeted plan.

Problems Associated with Budgeting

Despite large number of benefits, there are certain problems associated with budgeting. These are as follows:

- As a planning tool budgeting is only as good as the calculations made and limitations on managerial calculation affect this.

- The budgeting process can be viewed as a competitive bidding for funds rather than as a planning process.

- The existence of detailed budgets can cause inflexibility and a resistance to adapting to changed business circumstances.

- Variations require explanation and this may use managerial time ineffectively if these explanations do not help future performance.

- Control through budgets can only be exercised by an 'after the event' comparison of actuals with budgets and this may be of little help as a guide to current operations.

Budgetary Control

It refers to the principles, procedures and practices of accomplishing given objectives through budgets. It is an overall management tool for the business planning and control. Budgetary control is a control system adopted in an organisation through which every business operation has to be carried out as per the plan. The performance appraisal is made at the end and the whole control activity takes place with the objective of maximizing profit. The following steps are involved for the successful implementation of budgetary control system:

- Organisation for Budgetary Control: The chief executive is the overall in-charge of budgetary system. He constitutes a budget committee for the preparation of budgets. There is a budget officer who is the convenor of the budget committee. He has to coordinate the budgets of various departments. However, the managers of various departments are responsible for their departmental budgets.

- Budget Centre: A budget centre is that part of the organisation for which the budget is formed.

- Budget Manual: Budget manual is a written document for facilitating the formulation of budget. It spells out the duties and responsibilities of the various executives concerned with the budgets.

- Budget Officer: The budget officer is empowered to scrutinise the budgets prepared by various departmental heads and to bring changes if the need arises. He will see to the regular periodical budget reports from every department.

- Budget Committee: In a large concern, a committee known as budget committee comprising the heads of all the important departments is formed. It is responsible for the preparation and execution of budgets. The budget officer acts as the coordinator of budget committee.

- Budget Period: The length of time for which a budget is prepared is budget period.

- Determination of Key Factor: Key factor is mainly referred to as the 'limiting factor' in a functional area.

Advantages of Budgeting/Budget Control

- Eliminates uncertainty: It provides a planned approach to every activity. This eliminates uncertainty.

- Result of team effort/various brains: Since it is a collective effort by the top management, it is made by several heads keeping in mind organization objectives.

- Optimum use of capital resources: It guides the hotel to use its capital resources in the most profitable manner.

- Easy availability of working capital: The cash receipts and expenses budget ensures that sufficient working capital is available for efficient functioning of the hotel.

- Effective coordination: Budgeting results in effective coordination between departments as goals of each department are interlinked with each other.

- Responsibility can be pinpointed: It pinpoints the person on whom the responsibility can be fixed.

- Spotlight on deviation: Deviations can be seen and areas of improvement can be identified to take suitable corrective action.

- Serves as a guiding light: Budgeting provides a benchmark for actual performance and shows the path to achieve the standards.

- Optimum utilization of man, machine and material: Budgeting distributes work and provides clarity on using resources – man, machine and material.

- Good incentives for employees: Meeting budgets can be a good incentive for employees who get rewards and recognition on achieving targeted budgets.

Disadvantages of Budgeting

- Budgets are estimates hence can never be accurate. Inflation and rapidly changing business environment tend to distort budget data.

- Budget is simply a tool to efficient management not a substitute for it. Effective planning, implementation is crucial.

- Budgets cannot guide as to what action should be taken.

- Proper system of supervision and control is essential otherwise the budget will be ineffective.

- Budgeting can face the danger of inflexibility and everyone may think that without adherence to it, they will be called inefficient.

- Budgets may be misused by bosses to find faults in employees and restrict performance rather than improve it.

- The initiative and creativity of an employee may be hampered if budget is the only yardstick.

- Budgeting is a time consuming process and involves expenses.

- Budgeting goals may lead people to supersede organization goals.

- Success of budgeting depends on the motivation of people involved. It should be a gradual and cooperative exercise.

- Budgeting is just a pathway and does not guarantee successful implementation.

- Budgeting helps arrive at important management decisions however if used in isolation may lead to harmful consequences for the business.

References

- What-guest-folio-hotel: hospitality-school.com, Retrieved 19, May 2020

- Point-of-sale: investopedia.com, Retrieved 24, March 2020

- Hotel-booking-pos: webkul.com, Retrieved 17, January 2020

- Benefits-of-using-pos-systems-in-hotels: bpapos.com, Retrieved 09, July 2020

- Visitor-tabular-ledger-vtl: jrajeshac.blogspot.com, Retrieved 30, April 2020

Revenue Management in Hotels

The application of analytics to optimize price and maximize revenue growth is known as revenue management. This chapter delves into the purpose and importance of revenue management in the hospitality industry. It also discusses the relevant strategies for revenue management.

Hotel Revenue Management is defined as selling the right room to the right client at the right moment at the right price on the right distribution channel with the best commission efficiency.

Hotel Revenue Management is about becoming the architect of your own fortune. A hotel room is a perishable product, since the number of hotel rooms is limited. As a result, customer satisfaction and pricing remain the most important dynamic variables, which are subject to Hotel Revenue Management. It is all about balancing demand and capacity by forecasting prices for the purpose of maximizing the effectiveness of hotels' resources.

However, the rise of the Internet during the 21st century (and with it the rise of Online Travel Agencies and Review Portals) has added another dimension to this field. This development has made traditional Hotel Revenue Management much more complex, while providing new ways to cheaply and objectively measure both customer satisfaction and pricing.

Airlines' Yield Management

Originating from a mathematical sales model within the airline industry, the concept made its way into the hospitality industry as Hotel Revenue Management in the 1990s. Marriott International was one of the first major players to draw large earnings by introducing the concept into its business strategies. Hotel Revenue Management has grown in importance ever since.

Hotel Revenue Management in Practice

As there are many aspects that must be taken into consideration, it is impossible to effectively apply the concept of Hotel Revenue Management overnight. You need to carefully analyze and evaluate big data sets about your property and its business environment.

This Includes Information about Basic Factors Like:

- Past occupancy rates.
- General sales.
- Company target groups.
- Customer segmentation.

- Market (share) information.

- Customer satisfaction.

but also about external influences, such as:

- Past weather conditions.

- Holiday and event information.

- Closing of nearby hotels.

- Competitor price information.

- Similar circumstances that are likely to affect your business climate.

In earlier days, all these data were evaluated manually by the Hotel Revenue Management. Over the years, more and more elaborated Revenue Management Systems (RMS) were designed with the purpose of facilitating this process. However, the functioning of Hotel Revenue Management has fundamentally changed within the past decade. Demand patterns have become much more unpredictable, while increasingly dependent on user generated content, especially reviews.

This is why, next to Revenue Management Systems, also Review Management Systems, working complementary to each other, have grown in importance.

Purpose of Revenue Management

Revenue management is about attracting the right guest, at the right time to any given property. Every hotel, regardless of its location and the success of its destination, is subject to the seasonal ebbs and flows of the tourism industry. With an effective revenue management strategy in place, a hotel operator is able to drive bookings during the slow season while capitalizing on high demand during the busy season.

While the top priority of any revenue management strategy is to create competitive hotel pricing and increase hotel revenue, there also are other benefits to implementing a hotel revenue management strategy that works. For instance, effective hotel revenue management strategies can help hoteliers better manage their resources, ensuring that they are not paying too many staff members during a slow time of the year, while also verifying that they have adequate staff on hand during the busiest time periods.

The best hotel revenue management strategies recognize that hotel pricing is fluid, and can change from one day to the next. It's critical that any hotelier creates a revenue management strategy that is adaptable to the current conditions. With this in mind, it's pivotal that hotel operators, managers and owners utilize a software solution that can implement any revenue management strategy at any given time.

Types of Hotel Room Rates

There are various types of room rates that hotel operators will need to calculate as part of their revenue management strategies:

Rack Rate

The rack rate is the full price of the room prior to any discounts or promotions that may be available. In most cases, hotels will advertise their rack rates in hopes of securing guests who are willing to pay full price.

Commercial or Corporate Rate

Many hotels, particularly those that attract a lot of business travellers, will offer discount corporate rates to businesses who frequent their brand. The commercial or corporate rate is often calculated based on the assumption that this booking will continue to generate repeat business.

Group Rate

A group rate is often given to a large travel party who will be booking a significant number of rooms during a specific period of time. In many cases, groups are given a discounted group rate by hotel operators.

Reward Rate

Some hotel brands create a reward rate for their frequent customers, or those who purchase a membership with the hotel. This is a way to incentivize them to continue to book with that particular hotel brand, and to also encourage them to refer their family members and friends.

Package Rate

Hotels that offer packages that include extras, such as upgrades or activities, often offer a different rate for these deals. Package rates often vary based on the season and the demand for rooms at the hotel.

Hotel Pricing Strategies

There is not one correct pricing strategy for every hotel. Each hotelier must consider the pricing strategy or pricing strategies that work best for their particular brand.

Competitive Pricing Strategy

In a competitive pricing strategy, a hotelier must identify their top competition in the local area and price their rooms accordingly. This puts the hotel in direct competition with other top hotels in the area, and requires guests to recognize the superior options that your particular brand offers.

Middle Market Pricing Strategy

With this pricing strategy, a hotelier will price their high-end rooms around the same rate as basic rooms that are available at competing hotels. This allows the hotel to grab the attention of the middle market — the travellers who are looking for a good price as well as value in their next hotel.

Value-added Pricing Strategy

This pricing strategy offers a surprising twist. With this strategy, the hotelier should set their room rates higher than the local competition while also offering more extras in the basic package. This gives the illusion that the hotel offers a premier experience that focuses on value rather than just low rates.

Discount Pricing Strategy

This pricing strategy is an ideal option for the slow travel season, when it's more important to get low-paying bookings than to let a room sit empty. With a discount strategy, rooms are priced as low as possible for a very short period of time to drum up extra business.

How to Calculate an Average Room Rate

The Average Daily Rate, or ADR, is a metric that is used by hoteliers around the globe. It allows them to determine the average rate for their hotel rooms during a specific time period. It's critical to keep track of the ADR in order to evaluate the success of the hotel revenue management strategy. Hoteliers who need to calculate their ADR can do so by dividing their room revenue by the number of rooms sold over a specific time-period, for example 30 days.

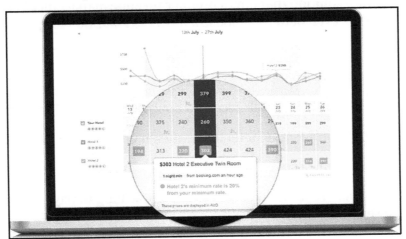

Features to Look for in Revenue Management Software

Revenue management software can assist in hotel revenue generation and in implementing the hotel revenue management strategies that a hotelier develops. There are several features that hotel operators must have in their revenue management software:

- Competitor rate monitoring:

  Keeping track of your competition and monitoring their rates is part of the job, but that doesn't mean that it should take up all of your time. With the right revenue management software in place, you can get access to your competitors' rates as well as monitor their pricing strategies. Receiving accurate and reliable data about your competitors in real time allows you to improve your own yield management techniques.

- Market alerts:

  Your hotel brand likely has different revenue management strategies and rules based on the conditions in your local market as well as tourism market conditions around the globe. An effective and innovative revenue management solution will allow you to set alerts so that you get first-hand information about market changes. This allows you to change your revenue management strategy and hotel pricing strategy accordingly, ultimately increasing your average daily rate as well as the amount of revenue that you generate per booking.

- Real-time revenue management metrics:

  To develop effective hotel revenue management strategies, you need to monitor and evaluate key metrics that allow you to make adjustments accordingly. With revenue management software, you have access to real-time revenue management metrics in one convenient location. This allows you to make quick evaluations and effective decisions regarding your hotel room rates, keeping you one step ahead of the competition. With these metrics on hand, you can generate a number of reports that allow you to study your progress and refine your hotel's revenue management strategies. Ultimately, you can use these metrics to improve your short-term and long-term business growth.

Opting for a hotel software solution that offers premier revenue management features is beneficial for any hotel brand, but it's even better to choose a business solution that provides every feature a hotelier could need.

How A Revenue Manager Fits In

First let's look at common problems hotels face and how the Revenue Manager fits into them.

What are the most common problems a hotel faces when it comes to managing booking?

1. As soon as the last room is sold, someone calls for a longer stay.

2. Or, as soon as the last room is sold, someone calls, willing to pay a higher price, or from a higher-priced segment.

3. No matter what public rate you set or price you charge, it never exactly meets the price expectation of the guest.

4. When you are completely sold out, someone cancels last minute or does a "no show."

Let's take a look at an example to explain these issues. Let's say you have a negotiated rate of 80 euros per night, but could sell the room for 100: no big deal. Yet, think about exchanging 1 night for 3 nights, both at 100 EUR. That equals 200 EUR more. So how can one guest be more valuable than another? If they pay a higher price or they stay longer.

If this is starting to get complex, don't worry. That's why we have Revenue Managers.

Put simply, a Revenue Manager's job is to optimize the revenue based on demand, and also to limit the risks for the management team, owners, and asset managers in the investment of their time and money.

The Revenue Management Actions and Process

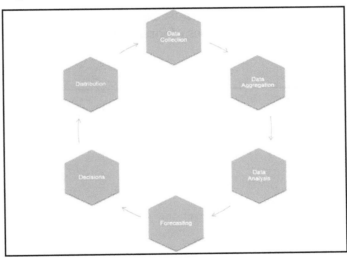

The first step for a revenue manager is to collect data, aggregate it, analyze it, and then forecast both the demand and performance. Once that is done, it is time to make informed decisions and put them in place through the various channels. In simplified terms what a Revenue Manager does is understand, anticipate, and react to market demand in order to maximize revenues.

Revenue Management Levers

There are three main controls or "levers" that the revenue manager can use to optimize revenue, and by working those "levers" the hotel can maximize its revenue. Of course that's the theory, but getting to know these levers of revenue management will help managers better understand the opportunities and limitations of maximizing revenue.

1. Price:

Raising or lowering the price is the most basic task of a revenue manager. By raising the price we increase revenue but potentially lower the number of bookings. If demand is high this is often the right strategy as there are enough potential guests willing to pay the high rates.

2. Yield:

    Yielding is often misunderstood as raising or lowering the public rates, but historically, it is about turning away less attractive guests. To do this, we open or restrict the rates (segments), room types or channels. Setting a minimum length of stay is one way to do it. Adding or removing inventory for a channel is another option.

3. Marketing:

    Marketing works a little differently than price or yield. That's because marketing doesn't run on the same clock as the other two- you can't simply "turn on" marketing in the morning and fix today's problem. Yet marketing can be an extremely effective tool. Imagine that you forecast the next month will be lower than usual. Once identifying the cause of the problem, you can request more marketing actions in that area or channel.

To properly manage these three levers, one must be able to forecast, and this is where the real science happens. There are two common types of forecasting and can mean very different things.

Forecasting is Step Zero

	Wednesday 20-02	Thursday 21-02	Friday 22-02	Saturday 23-02	Sunday 24-02	Monday 25-02
Min	15 °C	16 °C	15 °C	14 °C	14 °C	14 °C
Max	22 °C	22 °C	21 °C	21 °C	20 °C	19 °C
Sun ❶	60%	55%	60%	70%	65%	55%
Precipitation ❶	20%	30%	15%	5%	10%	15%
Wind direction	W	W	W	NE	E	SE
Wind force	3	3	2	2	2	2

The two types of forecasting are "constrained" performance forecasting and "unconstrained" demand forecasting. The difference may seem subtle but it isn't. Constrained performance forecast is simply the estimated or expected performance and is "constrained" or limited by the number of rooms available for sale. This is what General Managers, Banks, and investors generally mean when they use the term "forecast." The other type of forecasting is used by the revenue manager as a tool to help make availability controls and pricing decision. This is the "unconstrained" demand forecast and tells you how many rooms guest would like to book; even if there aren't enough rooms available.

1. Constrained Performance Forecast: A Performance forecast is an estimate of what revenues (rooms and rates) you will finally sell. It's what the rest of us usually think of when we hear the word "forecast." Many Revenue Managers as well as General Managers have, after

some experience, an intuitive feeling how a particular week or month will perform and this is usually supported by a review of historical data such as what happened last year, and adjusted based on current market conditions and the competitor position.

2. Unconstrained Demand Forecasting: Far more mysterious is the Revenue Manager's Unconstrained Demand Forecast. It is not an estimate of how many rooms you will sell, but instead an estimate of the demand for your rooms (how many rooms people would like to buy). The most important part of doing this forecast is to ignore the number of rooms you have.

Why do Revenue Managers create demand forecasts? Even the best performing hotels are rarely sold out more than 100 days or so in a year. That means most days you have rooms left to sell and the last thing you want to do is turn someone away before the hotel is absolutely full (or even oversold). However, on those days where there is more demand than number of rooms to sell, you want to make sure that you decide who doesn't get the room. The Unconstrained Demand Forecast helps you identify those days when you need to turn people away, and make sure you're turning away the lowest profit guests.

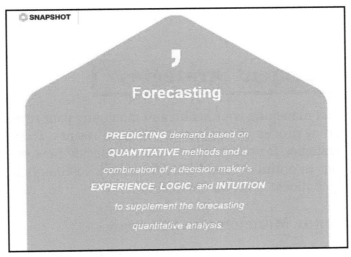

So how in the world do we estimate the number of guests that want to stay with us, when our historical performance data only tells us how many people already stayed? One way would be to religiously monitor all the guests that are turned away over different channels. This is however fraught with difficultly for a number of reasons:

1. Most channels do not freely provide this information to hotels.

2. Especially in the electronic world, one shopping request is not the same as demand for one room; it could be a rate shopping tool or even worse- a single guest could shop our website many times before making a booking.

Fortunately, there are some simple models that can help us out:

Model 1: Average Pickup

Let's say we already have a number of rooms on the books for a particular date in two weeks' time.

From our historical pickup pace we might know that for a typical Wednesday we normally pick up about 50 rooms during the last two weeks prior to arrival. Especially, if we do this for each market segment, we can then have ourselves a good estimate.

Model 2: Pace Based Pickup

Average Pickup, though, has the problem that it ignores if you have more rooms on the books today for that Wenesday in two weeks than you normally would two prior to arrival. If this is true, it is probably safe to say there will be more total demand for that Wednesday than an average Wednesday.

To be sure, both forecasting methods provide valuable insight. Both are, however, just a helpful tool for the Revenue Manager who must adjust these mathematically-based forecasts to reflect local knowledge. The key is to forecast consistently. Once you have a reliable forecast and understand your typical errors, you can start to leverage rate management, yield of segments, Lengths of stays or channels and help focus marketing strategies. Only by having a systematic approach to estimating demand will you be able to strategically increase your hotel's revenue and bottom-line.

Revenue Management Strategies

As odd as it may sound, but managing your health and managing your revenue has many things in common; both if followed by proven strategy, gets you great results. To start planning your hotel revenue management strategies for the year, you need to decide how much to spend on digital marketing, which channels to optimize, and where to make investments in new technology while keeping up with the budget allocated for the financial year.

Planning Hotel Revenue Management Strategies

Now, most businesses don't have an adequate budget to fully invest in all aspects of digital marketing. That's why in order to initiate planning the hotel revenue management strategies, there is an ongoing struggle to optimize the expense between the practical reality of running a business and a wide array of marketing options. Everything you do from a budgeting perspective must start with your business goals.

At the very outset, you must decide what is of most importance for you:

1. Are you trying to drive more revenue?

2. Do you care mostly about customer acquisitions?

3. Do you wish to maintain or grow your brand?

4. Are you interested in building brand loyalists?

Depending on your goals, the hotel revenue management strategies you implement and technology you deploy may differ.

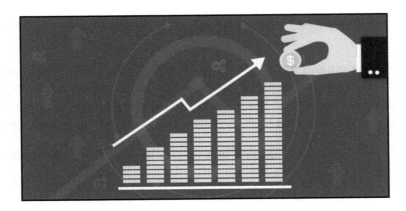

Knowledge yourself with Market Segments

The first step to hotel revenue management strategies is defining your hotel's relevant target audience. A crucial step towards more control over your business, it is the market mix of your hotel, which makes it worthwhile for you to spend time and understand this. Once you zero in on your market segment, it will let you set up appropriate rates for the right inventory in order to maximize revenue from various areas of business. Plus, you need to constantly ensure that your budget is used in the most logical method to track your business performance and success.

Begin by looking into which category of guests you mostly cater to, what is their buying behavior, why are they booking with you and how're they doing it. All of this will enable you to apply valid and targeted actions to your business and measure your profits from time to time.

Relevant market segments will differ for each hotel, but they will surely deliver the advantage of being able to drive more business and monitor your performance regardless of where your hotel is located and which type of hotel it is. This is where the actual hotel revenue management starts, which will gradually take your hotel business to new heights of recognition and success.

Analyze the Booking Behavior Patterns of your Guests

In most industries, the time and place where the business is conducted are of essence and hospitality is no different. From where your booking was made, when was it made, for which dates, you need to keep an eye on each of this parameter. Each of your target audience has their own preferences on when and how they'd like to book with you. Leisure groups usually book few months in advance, some few weeks in advance, some even at the last minute. Understanding this too will help in planning the revenue management strategies for your hotel to fill the holes.

Now, in the bookings made at your hotel, you can see a pattern which will indicate on your high and low occupancy seasons. And this can be immensely helpful when it comes to forecasting the rates you put up at such times and how much inventory you keep open. Understanding these kinds of patterns and taking appropriate action on the same should definitely be a part of your strategy.

Think about Supply and Demand

When it comes to hotel revenue management strategies, supply and demand is a principle that should be cleverly implemented. Measuring and monitoring the supply and demand of your hotel rooms is also one of the tactics you should employ when it comes to boosting your revenue growth.

Prices tend to rise when demand exceeds supply, which is why effective rate management is the most practical way to increase revenue. It's simple, you just need to focus on high-profit bookings instead of high volume bookings. As a result, by increasing bookings on low-demand days and by selling rooms at higher room rates on high-demand days, you can increase its profitability.

In short, your room rates should be higher when there's high guest influx at your hotel, and lower when the occupancy is low.

Analyze your Hotel's Past data

Data is important and spending a considerable amount of time in analyzing your past and present statistics can help you in channelizing your marketing efforts. The hotel software that you've invested in should give you detailed reports that include the revenue you earned, your best selling factors, your ADR, and everything else which can help you form important decisions for your business. This data will help you extract ideas and come up with better hotel revenue management strategies for increasing your hotel's revenue.

Upgrade your Online Inventory Distribution Strategies

The old school ways of your inventory distribution on OTAs and GDS doesn't work as expected these days. You need to gear up and put up appropriate and attractive content to describe your hotel, location, and services; offer different packages and run promotions regularly to get more bookings, and have more OTA connections for your hotel to witness your revenue rise.

Keep up with Mobile Trend

There's no denying that mobile is now one of the strongest marketplaces when it comes to booking travel. People have less time to sit at home and research so whether it's via mobile browsing or on an app, they love to use their smartphone to find deals and make purchases. Getting equipped with new mobile trends is one of the keys to productive hotel revenue management strategies. 51% of smartphone owners use their device for travel-related activities so a mobile presence is non-negotiable for your hotel.

With this tech-savvy world, it becomes important for you to be that 'A' grade hotel. This, in turn, will help you to analyze your hotel's data for increasing profits. Here's the bottom line: to grow revenue from mobile, you need either a responsive or adaptive website, and you need to follow conversion best practices on mobile.

Go for Direct Bookings

You can't ignore the fact that direct bookings also play a significant role in your hotel's revenue generation. In your hotel revenue management strategies, don't leave out direct bookings. A majority of your guests prefer to book direct with you.

Plus, you shouldn't let go a chance to gain unlimited commission-free bookings. You can let your guests book from your website easily, engage with them and know their preferences; which will make them feel valued.

Like hundreds of fellow hoteliers, start working on increasing direct bookings on your hotel website.

Test and Measure

Another trick to planning your hotel revenue management strategies is analyzing each of your promotions and pricing strategies. This will give you an idea of what worked, and what didn't.

As the travel market keeps on changing, it becomes impossible to answer or bring a solution to pricing. However, the Internet is perfect for testing, so keep experimenting. Continuously try new ideas and offers, but make sure you set up reporting and measure the results.

Successful hotel revenue management keys

- To sell the right product (guest room, banquets, ancillary services).
- To the right customer (business, leisure, government guest).
- On the right day (weekday, weekend).
- For the right price (rack rate, corporate rate, group rate, government rate, discount rate).

Without appropriate hotel revenue management strategies, you are simply leaving money on the table. Not only will your booking pace be slower than it should be, but you'll often be charging a lower price for your room than ideal rate, and lose many booking opportunities when you keep high rates than required. So, it's extremely important to start optimizing your pricing as much as possible.

Demand Calendar

So how can we make informed decisions about our pricing strategies? We mean decisions founded on solid data and statistics. A demand calendar is the answer for your revenue management operations.

A hotel needs an extensive revenue management demand calendar show multiple demand indicators to appropriately analyze market situations. Sounds nice, right? But what are we talking about?

The most basic version of a demand calendar contains the following information:

- RevPAR last year.
- Groups or events last year.
- Demand level indicator last year (High, Medium, Low, Distressed).
- Demand level indicator this year.
- Bank holidays.
- School holidays.
- Exceptional demand indicators.

Take a look at the example below:

HOTSTATS
Hospitality Intelligence

BRIEFING DATA
UK Chain Hotels - Market Review
Currency: £ Sterling

	The month of September 2014				The Calendar year to September 2014				The twelve months to September 2014			
	Sep'14	Sep'13	Var b/w		YTD'14	YTD'13	Var b/w		Rolling'14	Rolling'13	Var b/w	
SCOTLAND Occ %	96.6	96.8	-0.1		77.2	76.3	0.4		75.8	74.9	0.9	
ARR	113.07	93.60	21.7%		95.97	87.82	9.5%		93.19	86.25	8.0%	
RevPAR	93.56	81.09	21.6%		74.10	67.30	10.1%		70.81	64.56	9.4%	
TRevPAR	157.70	138.79	13.6%		126.54	117.04	7.3%		123.51	115.46	7.0%	
Payroll %	25.3	27.6	2.2		30.2	30.9	0.6		30.9	31.4	0.6	
GOP PAR	67.14	53.20	27.3%		41.71	37.05	12.6%		38.85	34.81	11.9%	
BRISTOL Occ %	84.6	79.2	5.8		78.5	72.6	3.0		74.5	71.8	2.7	
ARR	84.99	72.15	17.8%		75.68	70.58	7.3%		75.07	70.59	6.3%	
RevPAR	71.97	57.17	25.9%		57.12	51.16	11.7%		55.80	50.66	10.3%	
TRevPAR	113.47	94.69	19.8%		93.46	86.05	8.6%		94.22	87.09	8.2%	
Payroll %	27.0	29.4	2.4		31.0	31.6	0.6		30.7	31.4	0.7	
GOP PAR	42.05	29.33	43.4%		26.58	23.10	15.1%		27.15	23.93	13.5%	
MILTON KEYNES Occ %	82.1	79.4	2.6		78.2	79.3	0.9		75.5	75.2	0.3	
ARR	77.60	70.79	8.6%		75.18	68.77	9.3%		74.00	67.82	9.1%	
RevPAR	63.66	58.17	13.3%		57.78	51.79	10.6%		55.96	50.97	8.6%	
TRevPAR	91.13	84.30	8.1%		86.12	80.11	7.5%		86.57	81.73	5.9%	
Payroll %	28.6	27.3	0.7		29.1	29.5	0.4		28.4	28.6	0.2	
GOP PAR	41.64	29.03	43.1%		30.07	26.41	13.9%		29.81	27.42	8.7%	

So a lot of the information is easy to get. RevPAR last year, groups or events in the hotel etc, can be retrieved from internal PMS data. To determine if school holidays or bank holidays affect you, you should run arrival statistics of last years holidays per feeder market (country) against their holidays. This way you can see if any particular school or holiday from a particular country affects your hotel. It will allow you to target it intelligently with special offers and packages this year.

The data and information from your demand calendar can now be integrated into your OTB (on the books) and pick-up summaries. It will give you a much broader view of where your hotel is trending.

In the end informed decisions are better decisions, leading to better results.

Market Segmentation

Market segmentation is a technique that groups consumers with similar needs and common buying behaviors into segments. These segments become the basis for targeted marketing, which is a more efficient and effective method of marketing than advertising to the masses.

A marketing segmentation approach is essentially a customer-centered approach that matches products and offerings to consumer interests. These adjustments are designed to better match the distinctive attributes and behaviors of segments, or groups, of consumers.

A market segmentation approach is conducted by following certain fairly standard steps that are designed to understand the correlations patterns among large consumer groups. Segmentation begins by identifying a constellation of metrics that will be used as the basis for determining how to group consumers.

A feature of target market segmentation is the creation of consumer personas or profiles that are used to cluster or group consumers for more effective marketing.

Market Segments

Relevant market segments for your hotel are still the foundation for setting your pricing strategy correctly. They are mainly defined by the different booking behaviours and the price sensitivity of a hotels' customers. This allows you to uniquely price each segment according to the type of customer you are looking at. In addition, market segments allow you to specifically define and bundle sales and marketing efforts according to any trends and movements you can derive from the analysis of those segments. The ultimate goal with that is clearly to work towards an ideal market segmentation mix for your hotel.

Market segments can obviously be different depending on the type of hotel and the market it operates in, but quite generally a hotel sees "Transient" and "Groups" as main differentiators for customers booking habits. However, to make this more accurate and specific, there are market categories assigned to those indicators which then actually make up for the market segmentation.

Let's compare an inner-city business hotel and a coastal resort hotel to see how their segmentation could look like:

City Hotle	Description	Resort Hotel
Transient (Individual Travellers)		
Bar	Includes non-restricted rates that are available to all customers	Bar
Discount	Includes restricted rates (advance purchase. Length of stay cancellation. Guarantee or age restrictions e.g.)that come with a discount from the BAR level for you were selling	Discount
Corporate/Negotiated	This is referred to as "qualified business, as those rates are agreed between the hotel and the company or the partner for a certain period of time , and can only be booked by guest who qualify for that rate	
Fit	Include agreed and contracted wholesalers and tour operator rate	Fit
Groups		
Busniess Group	Usually includes bookings for more than 10 rooms nights and normally have a longer lead time as well as stricter cancellation policies than most others rates in the hotel. Pricing wise it's either a fixed rated or a discount of BAR	
	For group of 10 or more rooms booked by tour operator or wholesaler at a negotiated rate or ad-hoe quoted rate	Leisure Grpoup

Of course, there's the possibility to make these segments even more specific and relevant for any hotel. For e.g. you could break down the Corporate segment into high and low volume accounts or LRA (Last Room Availability) and NON-LRA accounts.

Also on the group side, you could make the differentiation between Business Groups with meetings and without meetings. The FIT segment also gives you space for more differentiation as you can divide the segment into "FIT contracted" and "FIT ad-hoc". All in all however, you should aim for not having more than 8-10 relevant market segments in place to keep it simple and effective. Each of the segments will then be subject to tailor-made sales and distribution efforts helping you to yield the best business you can for your hotel.

Source of Business

Each of your defined market segments will have various sources of business that come to different costs. So here we are looking at distribution channels like GDS, OTAs, Direct channels (email, phone, own website) for example. Your hotel's PMS and also business intelligence tools will help you dig deeper into your distribution mix as you would want to track which distribution path your customers actually used to book your hotel. Ultimately, this will not only help you optimize your distribution mix and manage your distribution costs rigorously, it will also help you spot movements from one channel to another at a very detailed level. Therefore, this information will be beneficial in setting your distribution strategies per market segment.

Examples of Two Consumer Profiles for Couples Traveling to Barcelona

- Ambassadors of Architecture: The consumers in this group are young, newly married, university graduates, traveling on their honeymoon. They are seeking romance and luxury on a budget. Their travel plans include spending time together, indulging in quality walking sightseeing tours and following their passion, which is the architecture of Antoni Gaudi.

- Gallery Gazers and Gourmet Grazers: The consumers in this group are keenly interested in visiting the art galleries in Barcelona and, are particularly fond of the work of Picasso. Since they enjoy regional foods, they are interested in the internationally renowned restaurants in the city. Because the couple in this profile is upper-middle age, they plan to avoid climbing stairs and walking long distances. They prefer public transport and taxicabs to travel to the sights of Barcelona. They are considering some guided tours to locations just outside of Barcelona.

Rationale for Selected Sites

When selecting the accommodations, sights, and destinations for the travelers' itinerary, components of the marketing mix were considered. For each choice of the excursions, one or more of the 7Ps of marketing was found to be more relevant than other components of the marketing mix. Note that not all of the following components can easily be linked to an excursion choice: Product, place and time, price, promotion and education, process, physical environment, people.

For the choice of hotel accommodations, the most relevant attributes were the physical environment, price, product, and people. Many travelers look for a relationship with their hoteliers and loyalty is highly rewarded in the hotel industry. The hotel booked for the customers was one of their favorite European hotel chains: Mandarin Oriental Hotel. Sights and destinations are typically selected by travel agents and travelers based on price, promotion, and education, with many of the choices free for viewing from the outside.

Forecasting

The revenue management position did not exist in most hotels prior to 1990, and even today does not show up in many property organization charts. Nevertheless, as hotel business survival demands more sophisticated management techniques, the revenue management job continues to expand in duties and responsibilities. The most critical chore that has fallen to the modern revenue manager is forecasting. Although, it is the most important and time consuming function of the revenue manager, it is the least appreciated and understood of his or her duties.

Some call forecasting a "no win black hole" where you are charged with setting the forecast and then charged with beating it. Then, when you beat it you are asked why your forecast was low in the first place. Unfortunately, these chase your tail discussions take place all too often in hotel properties around the world. If this dysfunctional conversation sounds remotely like your hotel, then read on for some tips that may be useful to get out of the forecasting fog.

First of all, many properties do not have a proper definition of what the forecast should be. We have witnessed all of the following:

1. The lowest revenue figure that the property owner will accept without firing the management company.

2. A reasonable number that we are 100 percent certain we can exceed for the period.

3. Any number as long as it is at least .0001 percent above the same period last year.

4. The revenue number for the period that is required for the annual plan.

5. A revenue or occupancy number that is at least as high as the previous forecast for this period. In other words, never lower a forecast.

All of these are counterproductive because they reduce forecasting to a mind game, where everybody in the process knows what is happening, but they continue it because it's difficult to change. It is like setting your watch ahead by 5 minutes so you won't be late.

The best place to start to transform your forecast from a mind game into a strategic tool is to come up with a set of common definitions for all stake holders including ownership groups and all levels of the management company. A good one might be: the forecast is the best current estimate of rate, revenue and occupancy for a future specific time period based on common assumptions, such as no change in the current rate strategies, booking pace and competitive marketing initiatives.

With this definition, it is easy for all parties to see that the forecast is loaded with uncertainty. Nonetheless, it is extremely important for the business to understand where the current strategies and competitive environment are leading. For example, it is essential to know if the property should be in a sales mode or an allocation mode of marketing. A sales mode is where all departments should be aggressively attempting to bring in business with all channels open and rate promotions at full speed. On the other hand, an allocation mode is where the property is doing well and will probably end up with full occupancy. Here, the property departments should be focusing only on high yield revenue sources, closing down some channels, and not be offering any rate discounts or promotions.

There are many forecasts needed for the economical and efficient running of a hotel, but they all need a point of departure that is provided by the primary forecast of occupancy, rate and revenue. For example, housekeeping needs to forecast rooms to be cleaned, sheets to be laundered, room attendants to bring in on a daily basis, etc. Similar forecasts are needed throughout all other departments. Finance needs to forecast the source and use of funds, F&B ordering needs a forecast of table covers, and sales needs a forecast of rooms available for group sales. All of these are secondary to the four primary forecasts that come from revenue management. These primary forecasts are the annual budget, the annual forecast, the annual outlook, the 30-60-90 day forecasts throughout the year. They all focus on occupancy, rate and revenue. As an important side note, although revPAR and revPAR index are essential measures of a hotel's performance, they are not inputs to the forecasts and budgets. Rather they are outcomes of the process and actual performance.

The annual budget: This is prepared in early fall each year and provides the basis for all other planning. It is usually prepared once for the year and is etched in stone so to speak, so it represents the thinking at the time of preparation. Usually there are several iterations of this plan before it is set. The most useful iterations are the top down approach (that looks at the overall market and seeks to set a plan on what should be able to be attained on a macro basis) and the bottom up approach (where each department estimates what results it can achieve). There are pitfalls in each effort if top management seeks to achieve record profits and individual departments seek an easy to achieve budget to preserve their job security. The proper approach calls for top management to provide a set of assumptions related to competition, market position, the local economy and the major initiatives to improve next year's results. This allows department to bake in some resources to achieve the budget. Although the budget is out of date the day after it is presented, it is an important document and should be used as a basis for understanding the mindset at the time of preparation if nothing more.

The annual forecast: Since very few assumptions remain intact from the time the budget is set until year end, an annual forecast should be done just once on December 31 to capture these updates and document where the thinking stood before any implementation plans were embarked. This forecast also provides a base line for future forecast updates throughout the year.

The annual outlook: Each month, as the year unfolds, requires an annual outlook forecast. This is a snapshot of what the yearend will look like based on current performance and future forecast estimate. It is prepared in the first few days of each month and represents the actual year-to-date performance through the previous whole month and the current forecast for the rest of the months of the year.

The 30-60-90 day forecast: Technically this is needed each week so that all the hotel strategies and operational efforts are on the same page and are consistent with what is in the near future. In some hotel markets, the 30-day and 60-day forecasts can be done weekly and the 90-day updated every two weeks to save time. The key use of this forecast is to set rate strategies for each day in the booking window and to allow tactical decisions at the department level.

Recipe for success in forecasting: Regardless of whether you are forecasting for the first time, continuing a legacy forecasting approach, or using an automated revenue management system, the rules for success are similar:

1. Recent history: If you have historical results, put them into your forecasting spreadsheet. If you have no history, then start immediately to keep daily records of occupancy, rate and

revenue by segment. Try for a minimum of three years, but keep all the results so when periodic events like floods or the Olympic Games occur you have historical benchmarks. This provides a basis for day of week and seasonal profiles of your property.

2. Use small bites: Unless your customers are monolithic, do not forecast at the property level. Although it is more time consuming, you must usually forecast at the market segment and sub-segment levels so you know right where the business is coming from and can check for reasonableness. Also, although you only forecast weekly, all your forecasts should be done by day because each day represents a new situation to optimize.

3. Market reference: As you move from the known (history) to the unknown (forecast) assess appropriate market data points like Smith Travel results and trends for your comp set and local market. Include an estimate of the actual impact these forces will have on percent changes in your occupancy, rate and revenues.

4. Competition: Assess new entrants, renovated properties and closures, and estimate their impact on your revenues.

5. Booking pace: Always keep your eye on your booking pace in each segment so you can adjust either your forecast or your marketing strategies.

6. Channels: Stay abreast of third-party channels and their sales opportunities. Even if you do not participate you need to know what your market place and competitors may do that will impact your results.

7. Communicate: Gain agreement on all assumptions and definitions. There is no such thing as a perfect forecast of an uncertain future. Just do the best estimate and move on so you have time for implementation.

8. Sanity check: Finally, when you are finished with your forecast, just before issuing it, perform a sanity check. Ask yourself if it would take a personal best or record breaking performance to achieve any of these numbers.

9. Honesty: Never try to make up for a revenue shortfall by trying to pick it up later in the year. This is a surefire way to turn a small mistake into a career ending event.

Booking Curves

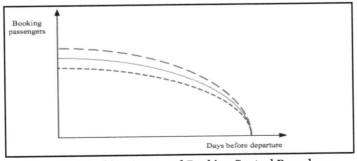

Expected Booking Curve and Booking Control Boundary .

Booking curve is an important tool for booking control policy in revenue management. The most basic data used here is $N_r^{w,d,t}$, the number of booked tickets for origin/destination pair w, departure date d, and train number t, at reservation date r. As the example shown in figure above, a booking curve is the cumulative booked tickets at every reservation date. For the specific market studied in the paper, booking curves of three trains are illustrated in figures below. Train 1005 only has service during weekend, that is Friday, Saturday, and Sunday; and its departure time is 7:30 A.M. and arrival time is 11:30 A.M. Train 1007 has service every day; and its departure and arrival time is 8:00 A.M. and arrival time is 12:41 A.M. Train 1009 has service every day; and its departure time is 8:36 and arrival time is 12:44. It is clear that these booking curves have different patterns, in terms of shape of the curve and the magnitude of booking level. In order to reduce the effect of magnitude, we standardized the data using booking rate, i.e. booking number/ booking limit. Figure below shows standardized booking curves for the three trains. The basic data or a point in a standardized booking curve is $X_r^{w,d,t}$, the cumulated booking rate for origin/destination pair w, departure date d, and train number t, at reservation date r. A booking curve is a vector of $X_r^{w,d,t}$, and is written as $X^{w,d,t}$. It is evident that some curves different in figure TRA's Booking Curves below, are similar in figure TRA's Standardized Booking Curves below.

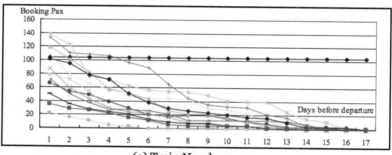

(a) Train Number 1005.

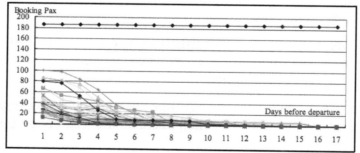

(b) Train Number 1007.

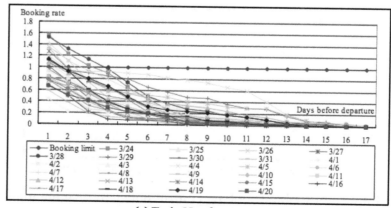

(c) Train Number 1009.

Figure TRA's Booking Curves

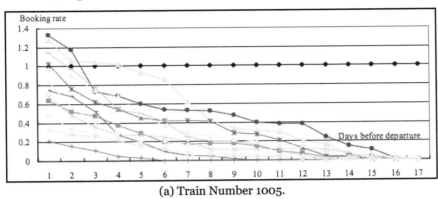

(a) Train Number 1005.

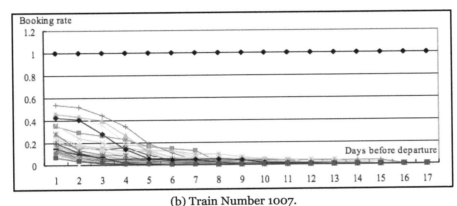

(b) Train Number 1007.

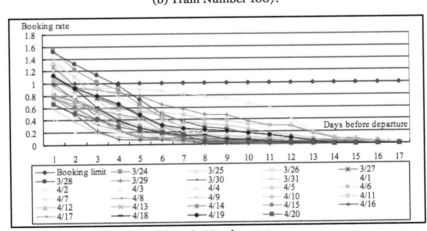

(c) Train Number 1009.

Figure TRA's Standardized Booking Curves

After examining the observed booking curves, we generate basic patterns of booking curve using two criteria: risk level and booking level. As illustrated in figure below, there are three types of booking curve due to risk level: risk-averse, risk-neutral, and risk-seeking. For the risk-averse booking curve, many passengers book tickets at early dates in the reservation period. On the contrary, for the risk-seeking booking curve, most passengers obtain tickets at dates close to the departure time. Moreover, comparing to booking limit, there are several magnitude levels for the booking curves: e.g. above expectation, about expectation, below expectation, and far below expectation. Therefore, as shown in figure below, there are many types of booking curve based on the combinations of risk preference and magnitude level.

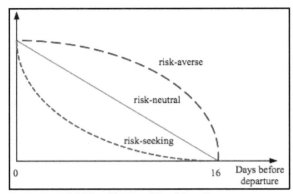

(a) The Shape of Booking Curve.

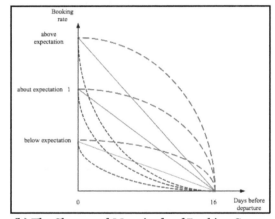

(b) The Shape and Magnitude of Booking Curve.

Figure Booking Curve Pattern

The Method

The proposed method of pattern analysis consists of three steps. They are cluster analysis, discriminant analysis, and prediction analysis. The first and second steps are very popular in multivariate data analysis in all fields for pattern analysis (Hair, Anderson, Tatham, and Black, 1998). Prediction analysis is in the proposed process, because the purpose of pattern analysis on booking curve is to estimate the expected booking curve, so as to implement booking control policy. Hence, the effect of prediction accuracy should be at least one criteria considered in cluster analysis and discriminant analysis.

Cluster Analysis

Cluster analysis is to partition the set of booking curves into several groups based on the pattern of curve. The objective of cluster analysis is booking curve, $X^{w,d,t}$. The similarity of the booking curves is focused on the proximity of objects, and it is measured by squared Euclidean distance. That is, the similarity of two booking curves is $\sum_r \left(X_r^{w,d,t} - X_r^{w,d',t'} \right)^2$. In other words, we measure the correspondence of booking rate across the reservation date. Cluster algorithm is used to maximize the difference between clusters relative to the variation within the clusters. The nonhierarchical or K-means clustering method contained in SAS is used in the study. Using the algorithm, the best cluster solution is to be found once the number of cluster is specified. In other words, the six-cluster solution is not a combination of two clusters from the seven-cluster solution. Selecting seed points $\left[Z^1, Z^2, ..., Z^g \right]$, is the first step in the clustering algorithm; where Z^j is the cluster centroid of the booking curves in the jth cluster. In the study, the initial seed points are the average points in the data set. Secondly, every booking curve is assigned to its nearest seed. That is, a booking curve $X^{w,d,t}$, is assign to group j if $\sum_r \left(X^{w,d,t} - Z_r^j \right)^2$ is the minimum of { $\sum_r \left(X_r^{w,d,t} - Z_r^j \right)^2$, for $j = l \sim g$ }. After that, the seed points are updated by $Z_{new}^j = Z_{old}^j + \eta (\overline{X^{w,d,t}} - Z_{old}^j)$ until the algorithm is converged, where η is a parameter of learning rate. In order to decide the number of clusters should be formed, we consider several stopping rules. First, we prefer to have low value of the average within cluster distance. Secondly, two statistics showing notable success in the literature, Pseudo F statistic and Cubic Clustering Criteria (CCC), are used to check the similarity improvement at each successive step. Pseudo F statistic is the ratio of the between-cluster variation to the average within-cluster variation, and it equals to $\left[R^2 / (g-1) \right] / \left[(1-R^2) / (n-g) \right]$, where R^2 is the coefficient of determination, g is the number of clusters, and n is the sample size. CCC is written as ln $[(1 - E(R^2)) / (1 - R^2)] * K$, where R is the coefficient of determination and K is the variance stabilizing transformation.

Discriminant Analysis

In cluster analysis, we classify booking curves into g groups. Then, discriminant analysis is used to explain how the groups differ on relevant dimensions. First, we have to identify dimensions of discrimination between groups and select independent variables. For a booking curve in origin/destination market w, $X^{w,d,t}$, characteristics associated with departure date d and train number t are the dimensions of discrimination between groups. Please refer to the table below for a list of the variables. With regard to departure date, there are 7 week variables, $W_1 \sim W_7$, and 5 festival holiday variables, $H_0 \sim H_4$. For example, H_1 is an index variable for the departure date just one day before a long holiday. With regard to departure time or arrival time, there are 4 time of day variables, $G_1 \sim G_4$ or $T_1 \sim T_4$. For example, D3 is an index variable for the departure time at afternoon period 15:00 to 19:00. Consequently, considering the joint effect of two independent variables, there are several hundreds of interaction variables. For example, $H_1 T_3$ is one, if the departure time is the afternoon just before a long holiday; otherwise, it is zero. With all single and interaction variables, the stepwise estimation method contained in SPSS is used to calibrate the discriminant functions for the g groups. After that, hit ratio and some statistics are used to assess overall fit of the discriminant model.

$W_i = 0$ or 1, $i = 1 \sim 7$	Wi represents the ith day of week.
	It is 1 if the train is in that day of week; otherwise, it is 0.
$H_j = 0$ or 1, $j = 0 \sim 4$	H_j represents the characteristics of festival holiday. H_0 represents normal time, H_1 represents one day before festival, H_2 represents the festival period, H_3 represents one day after festival, and H_4 represents the last day of festival.
	It is 1 if the train is in that day; otherwise, it is 0.

$G_k = 0$ or 1, $k = 1 \sim 4$	G_k represents the k_{th} period of day. Time periods are four: morning, noon, afternoon, and night.
	It is 1 if the departure time of the train is that period of day; otherwise, it is 0.
$T_l = 0$ or 1, $l = 1 \sim 4$	T_l represents the l_{th} period of day. Time periods are four: morning, noon, afternoon, and night.
	It is 1 if the arrival time of the train is that period of day; otherwise, it is 0.
$W_i H_j$, $W_i G_k$, $W_i T_l$, $H_j G_k$, $H_j T_l$, and $G_k T_l$	They represent "and" relationship between two variables.
	It is 1 if both variables are 1; otherwise, it is 0.

Definition of Clustering and Discriminating Variables.

Prediction Analysis

First, predication analysis is to check the capability of the above mentioned process, cluster analysis and discriminant analysis, for predicting the booking curve of a train service. For a future and unknown booking curve $X^{w,d,t}$, given the characteristics of origin/destination pair, a departure date, and a train number; we estimate its cluster number, j, using the discriminant functions. Then, with the cluster number, we have the cluster booking curve Z_r^j, which is the centroid of the historical booking curves in the cluster. We use the booking curve Z_r^j as the expected booking curve of $X^{w,d,t}$, . In the study, the corresponding values in the real booking curve $X^{w,d,t}$, and in the expected curve Z_r^j, are compared by mean absolute percentage error (MAPE). MAPE is written as follows, where $X^{w,d,t}$, is the real booking rate, Z_r^j is the estimated booking rate, and nr is the number of reservation dates. In general, the prediction capability is good, if MAPE is less than 20%. Moreover, we test the prediction oriented pattern analysis. That is, we choose the number of clusters and its associated discriminant functions, using the criteria of MAPE.

$$MAPE = [\frac{1}{n_r} \sum_r \frac{\left| X_r^{w,d,t} - Z_r^j \right|}{X_r^{w,d,t}}]100\%$$

Cluster Analysis Booking Curves Count

For the market of Taipei to Kaohsiung and the rapid train, we get 647 booking curves. Following the method discussed previously, we run the K-means method of cluster analysis by SAS, with standardized booking curves. In order to decide the number of clusters, we check several criteria. As the pseudo F statistic and Cubic Clustering Criteria shown in the figure below, there is a peak at 7 clusters. With 7 groups, the average booking curves, or cluster centroids, are illustrated in the figure below. It is evident that there are one booking curve of risk-averse, two booking curves of risk-neutral, and four booking curves of risk-seeking. Based on the basic patterns of booking curve described in the figure Booking Curve Pattern discussed previously, we interpret and name the clusters in the table below. Some people in Taiwan are not used to have activity plan, and prefer to deal with trouble when it happens. It is also the case for passengers' booking behavior, even for some hot trains with high load factors, e.g. cluster 4 and 5. However, with the development of advanced reservation system and dynamic pricing strategy, it is in a transition process.

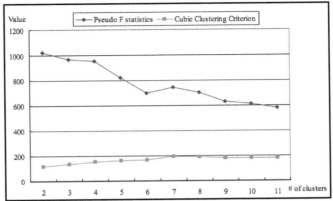

Figure: Pesudo F Statistic and Cubic Clustering Criteria in Cluster Analysis.

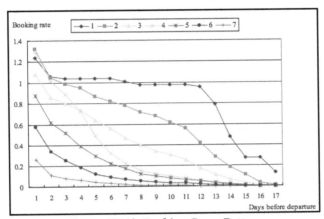

Figure: TRA's Booking Curve Pattern.

Cluster	Name of Cluster	# of booking curves	Percentage (%)
1	Risk-averse/ Above expectation (1.2)	3	0.46
2	Risk-neutral/ Above expectation (1.3)	18	2.78
3	Risk-neutral/ About expectation (1.1)	42	6.49
4	Risk-seeking/ About expectation (1.3)	42	6.49
5	Risk-seeking/ About expectation (0.9)	105	16.23
6	Risk-seeking/ Below expectation (0.6)	158	24.42
7	Risk-seeking/ Far below expectation (0.3)	279	43.12

(Final booking rate = passenger volume/ booking limit).

Discrimination Analysis Booking Curve Count

For the 7-cluster solution, we first identify variables of discrimination. Using the variables, described previously and listed in the table Definition of Clustering and Discriminating Variables, we describe the characteristics of each cluster in the table Clustering Variable Profiles for Seven-Cluster Solution. For example, passengers of cluster 1 have risk-averse booking behavior for the trains, running in Sunday or the end of festival holiday, departing Taipei at noon and/or arriving

Kaohsiung in the evening. In order to have a good explanation, we have to use several variables simultaneously. That is, we need to consider not only independent explanatory variables, but also interaction variables. As the list in the table Definition of Clustering and Discriminating Variables, there are 20 independent variables, and about 4-hundred interaction variables. With all these independent and interaction variables, we run the stepwise estimation method of discriminant analysis by SPSS. As the result illustrated in the table Discriminant Analysis Results Using the Stepwise Estimation Method, only interaction variables are selected, with significant statistical effect. The discriminant functions and classification functions are listed in the table Discriminant and Classification Functions. The importance of the variables can be identified by the absolute values of their coefficients. It is clear that H4G3 (the end of festival holiday and departing in the afternoon), H4G2 (the end of festival holiday and departing at noon), H1G2 (one day before festival holiday and departing in the afternoon), have high values of coefficients, and there are especially the situations for passengers to book tickets in risk-averse manner. Moreover, by several statistics, such as Wilks' Lambda value and Chi-square test for discriminant functions, the difference between clusters is in general significant. At last, the overall hit ratio is 58.9%; and the hit ratio for each cluster is respectively 100%, 77.28%, 45.24%, 54.76%, 24.26%, 35.44%, and 86.02%. Therefore, we have pretty good overall fit, although we need to understand more on cluster 3, 4, 5, and 6.

Table: Clustering Variable Profiles for Seven-Cluster Solution.

Cluster	Day of week	Holiday	Departure period	Arrival period
1	Sun	End of holiday	Noon	Evening
2	Fri	The day before holiday	Noon	Afternoon
3	Fri	The day before holiday	Afternoon	Evening
4	Fri ~ Sun	Not holiday	Noon	Afternoon and evening
5	Mon ~ Sun	Not holiday	Afternoon	Evening
6	Mon ~ Sun	Not holiday	Noon	Afternoon and evening
7	Mon ~ Sun	Not holiday	Morning and noon	Noon and evening

Table: Discriminant Analysis Results Using the Stepwise Estimation Method.

Cluster	Day of week	Holiday	Departure period	Arrival period
1	Sun	End of holiday	Noon	Evening
2	Fri	The day before holiday	Noon	Afternoon
3	Fri	The day before holiday	Afternoon	Evening
4	Fri ~ Sun	Not holiday	Noon	Afternoon and evening
5	Mon ~ Sun	Not holiday	Afternoon	Evening
6	Mon ~ Sun	Not holiday	Noon	Afternoon and evening
7	Mon ~ Sun	Not holiday	Morning and noon	Noon and evening

Table Discriminant Analysis Results Using the Stepwise Estimation Method.

Variables	Tolerance value	F statistic	Wilks' Lambda value
W5H1	0.56	11.23	0.08
H4T3	0.71	33.24	0.10
W7T4	0.67	32.38	0.10
W5G3	0.79	20.50	0.09
G2T3	0.71	11.52	0.08
W6G1	0.87	15.41	0.08
H1T3	0.54	4.95	0.08
H2T1	0.95	9.49	0.08
W5G4	0.89	10.08	0.08
W7T3	0.50	14.19	0.08
G1T3	0.65	4.66	0.08
H4T4	0.21	155.67	0.18
H4G3	0.29	85.00	0.13
H4G4	0.48	52.18	0.11
W5G2	0.53	5.59	0.08
H2G2	0.94	5.41	0.08
W1G1	0.95	4.39	0.08
H1G2	0.31	3.96	0.08

Table Discriminant and Classification Functions.

	Discriminant Functions						Fisher's Classification Functions						
	1	2	3	4	5	6	1	2	3	4	5	6	7
W5H1	0.36	0.62	1.02	1.45	-0.19	2.04	3.61	6.39	3.48	3.40	3.83	2.67	1.37
H4T3	0.52	0.86	1.34	1.77	-0.61	1.25	3.44	7.17	2.52	3.20	3.68	2.37	0.45
W7T4	1.80	1.99	1.66	-2.86	0.76	-0.44	11.71	4.50	2.19	14.22	9.20	6.23	0.37
W5G3	2.45	2.53	1.11	-1.77	-0.86	-0.46	15.78	7.59	2.12	15.68	15.89	6.00	0.42
G2T3	1.20	1.50	1.66	-0.51	1.27	1.80	8.55	6.25	3.96	9.63	7.47	5.40	0.86
W6G1	1.58	1.50	0.15	-0.53	-0.85	1.50	10.86	5.16	2.21	9.53	12.20	3.08	0.72
H1T3	1.34	1.72	1.79	2.05	-4.62	-0.30	7.30	11.77	0.77	7.17	7.42	1.78	-0.21
H2T1	1.42	2.03	2.60	1.27	0.22	-1.89	9.00	11.64	3.42	9.31	8.69	7.16	0.81
W5G4	-1.26	-1.22	-0.09	-1.21	6.29	1.37	-5.79	-6.70	2.87	-4.31	-7.27	2.23	1.36
W7T3	0.34	0.57	0.89	0.56	1.90	0.98	3.30	3.74	3.20	3.14	3.46	3.67	1.06
G1T3	1.08	0.61	-2.39	-0.05	3.79	-4.48	6.75	-3.20	-1.33	-0.35	13.85	2.35	-0.42

H4T4	0.76	1.10	1.43	0.88	-0.27	-1.04	4.77	6.75	1.76	4.89	4.65	3.67	0.45
H4G3	-13.34	12.63	0.10	-4.57	-0.77	-0.27	-339.02	-2.15	-0.42	-3.28	-34.77	1.29	-0.06
H4G4	-14.91	11.43	0.02	-0.86	5.37	-7.05	-349.57	-3.95	-0.91	-17.80	-41.34	3.55	-0.12
W5G2	1.41	0.56	-3.00	-0.92	-4.57	2.63	8.53	-2.16	-2.84	3.98	13.08	-5.08	-1.01
H2G2	4.46	4.05	-2.14	5.26	-2.07	-0.97	28.98	18.06	3.61	13.31	44.65	6.33	0.88
W1G1	4.63	2.78	-7.81	-0.20	3.60	-1.21	31.11	-3.06	-0.48	10.10	52.12	2.51	-0.15
H1G2	14.59	-11.78	-0.41	-0.75	0.21	2.11	347.48	-2.15	0.05	15.17	39.79	-0.25	-0.01
Const	-0.81	-0.72	-0.57	-0.23	-0.36	-0.28	-183.61	-7.96	-2.43	-10.56	-25.23	-4.00	-0.94

Prediction Analysis Booking Curve Count

Prediction of booking curve is important in revenue management, for implementing booking control policy. We use mean absolute percent error (MAPE) to test, if the cluster centroid is a good estimate for the expected booking curve or not. As testing results of MAPE illustrated in the table below, with 7-cluster solution, the error on predicting booking rate by cluster centroid is 56.7%. If the discriminant analysis in the process of pattern analysis has 100% hit ratio, every booking curve will be assign to the correct cluster, then MAPE is 31.5%. That is, the variation between clusters, or the possible improvement in discriminant analysis, is 25.2%; and 31.5% error is due to the variation in the cluster. Although there is a specific objective function in cluster analysis or discriminant analysis, the overall objective of the pattern analysis is to predict booking curve. The table below shows the result of a prediction oriented pattern analysis, that is, we choose the number of clusters and do discriminant analysis accordingly based on MAPE. As the number of clusters increases, the hit ratio of discriminant analysis decreases, MAPE due to the variation between clusters increases, and MAPE due to the variation in the cluster decreases. It is clear that the hit ratio of discriminant analysis is not a good overall fit index for the prediction purpose. Overall MAPE is dependent on both cluster analysis and discriminant analysis. Six-cluster solution gives the best value of MAPE, 55%. However, the overall MAPE is in general not good for most cases; in order to fulfill the prediction requirement, some forecasting techniques of growth curves have to be included in the pattern analysis in the future.

Table Prediction Oriented Cluster and Discriminant Analysis.

The number of clusters	2	3	4	5	6	7	8	9
The Hit ratio in discriminant analysis	87%	80%	72%	64%	63%	59%	57%	56%
Mean Absolute Percent Error	66%	65%	58%	58%	55%	57%	57%	57%
Variation in the cluster	59%	50%	42%	41%	36%	32%	30%	29%
Variation between clusters	7%	16%	17%	17%	20%	25%	27%	27%

Price Positioning

Reflect your positioning on a matrix. Does your positioning make sense? How often are you more or less expensive than your competitors? Do you take into account your positioning and value offer when deciding of your daily rates? One more element to consider in your hotel revenue management plan.

A Rate or Price Value Matrix looks like this. Again something we have looked at or might remember from back in the days during marketing class but probably never used again. It is vital though to understanding and communication your hotel pricing strategy and positioning.

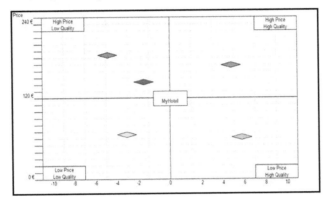

Choosing a clear price positioning strategy for your base rate will help strengthen your value perception to consumers. There are several strategies you can follow;

- penetration pricing strategy.
- equal pricing strategy.
- surrounding pricing strategy.
- skimming pricing strategy.

Penetration Pricing Strategy

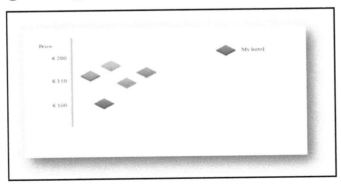

The market accepts and understands your positioning: among the cheapest in the market. That can work if that positioning does not drive the market rates down. Is there an opportunity to still sell more expensive on specific periods? How does your client value your hotel?

Equal Pricing Strategy

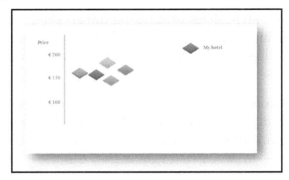

The hotel sells at comparable rates. Your hotel value proposition will make the difference in the clients' decisions.

Surrounding Pricing Strategy

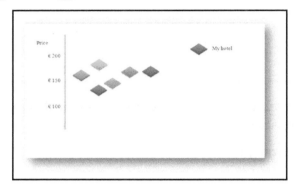

Your first room type will be the cheapest in the market or among the cheapest ones. Your superior room type will be sold at a rate close to the first available rates of your competition. The key success is to offer added value. Think in terms of roomtypes with better facilities or specific features, and additional amenities.

Skimming Pricing Strategy

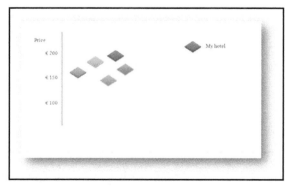

The skim strategy is to position clearly your hotel among the most expensive. Price leaders often achieve among the highest profitability.

Stay Controls

The Dos and don'ts of Length of Stay

How far in advance can you predict demand for your hotel? In hotel management, we continually stress the importance of creating demand, rather than simply responding to it. How to do it?

Well, proper use of length of stay controls during high-demand periods enables you to control customer demand, plan for the future, and maximize revenue.

Minimum Length of Stay

When to use

Minimum length of stay can be used at any hotel where there will be a period of high demand (a string of busy nights) followed by a period of low demand. Some example scenarios are: a resort hotel over a winter holiday or any hotel in the vicinity of a major national festival or conference.

What to do

Implement a rule to accept longer-duration reservations and reject shorter-duration reservations for arrival during a hot period. That way you can fine-tune demand during hot times to increase occupancy during the slow period that follows.

Potential Problems

You may not have anybody who wants to stay longer than the minimum you have in mind. Also, your guests may decide to leave early.

Requirements

Be sure you have sufficient demand for longer lengths of stay. Otherwise, use of this control could have a detrimental effect on RevPAR instead of improving it.

Maximum Length of Stay

When to use

This control is used when you are expecting to be able to sell out your rooms at higher rates. Using maximum length of stay, you can limit the number of rooms sold at large discounts during the high rate time period by limiting the (discounted) multi-night stays extending into that time period.

What to do

Do not accept reservations at specific discounted rates for multiple-night stays extending into the sold-out period. To do this, use the start of the sold-out period as a guide to determine the maximum length of stay allowable for discount customers. To accommodate guests who would like to stay at the hotel longer than the maximum length, it is possible to charge two rates: the discount rate for nights up to the maximum and the rack rate for subsequent nights.

Potential Problems

Your guests may decide to stay longer. By law, you can't force them out of their rooms.

Requirements

Be sure you have high demand. Otherwise, you could decrease RevPAR instead of improving it.

Closed to Arrival

When to use

This control can be used to restrict arrivals during a time when you expect to reach maximum occupancy through guests staying on at the hotel for multiple nights (through "stayovers" as opposed to through new arrivals). Using this control would only make sense if you believed you would achieve higher occupancy by selecting a particular set of guests (i.e. those arriving before the closed-to-arrival date).

What to do

Do not accept reservations for arrivals on the day in question. Allow guests staying through from previous nights only.

Potential Problems

Be very, very careful with this control, because using it will have an impact on the day you've closed to arrivals, and the day after, and the day after that. You may end up improving revenue on some days, but decreasing it on others.

Requirements

Be sure you have extremely high demand.

Rate Fences

Customer segmentation and the implementation of targeted price strategies for each segment are cornerstones of a good revenue management strategy.

To successfully differentiate pricing by customer segment, each price difference must be explainable and justifiable. Potential guests need to feel that they are buying different products when they pay different prices. Rate feces in hotel revenue management are the elements that create this product differentiation. Rate fences are characteristics, conditions or rules that apply to a rate. They are generally used to prevent customers who are willing to pay a higher amount, to have access to a discount.

The secret is to design and offer products that combine the hotel room with fences. These products must meet the needs of each segment and must be priced appropriately. For example, if business travelers are not so sensitive to price, value flexibility of cancellation and like to have breakfast included in the price, a hotel could offer a free-cancelation breakfast included plan to attract them.

For a holiday segment that is very price sensitive, the hotel may offer a non-refundable no-meals included plan at a lower rate. These are two products targeting different segments where the price difference is defendable and justifiable.

The most common types of fences are the following:

1. Physical fences: Physical fences are features such as the location of the room, the view, furniture, amenities, size, etc. For example, a resort hotel can offer an ocean view room priced higer than a garden view room. The ocean view is without a doubt a physical fence. Some segments will be willing and able to pay more for such rooms, while other segments will prefer to forgo that view in return for a lower price.

2. Fences related to the characteristics of the transaction: These fences involve time, place, quantity of purchase and flexibility of use. An example of the application can be non-refundable rates. It is very likely that non-refundable rates will not be attractive to a business customer. On the contrary, a more price-sensitive holiday traveler might prefer a non-refundable product over a refundable higher priced option.

3. Fences related to the characteristics of the buyer: These fences are related to attributes such as age, affiliation to an institution or group and frequency or volume of consumption. An example of these "fences" would be the specific products for a membership a frequent flyer program.

4. Controlled availability fences: In this case, availability and price points are assigned based on geographical criteria or distribution channels. For example, charging different prices according to the customer´s residence. In some beach destinations, the Canadian market price is lower than the US market price. These fences are less effective because today it is very easy to find what other customers are paying. It´s not easily justifiable and hard to accept for customers that they must pay more because they live in a different country.

Benchmarking

Benchmarking has become a widely accepted practice in different industries. But knowing that you should benchmark does not mean you know exactly what it is and how it should be done.

Benchmarking as A Method of Management

In the literature one can find numerous definitions of "benchmarking":

- External view of internal activities, functions or operations in order to achieve continuous improvement.

- The process by which entrepreneurs identify and are financed by the industry leaders, comparing their products, services and practices and implement procedures to improve their performance to become equal to or better than the competition.

- Continuous, systematic process of evaluation of products, services or business organizations that are recognized as best practice with the aim of organizing improvement.

- The art of determining how and why some individuals or companies do business better than others.

- Measuring your results with others and learning from others, most direct competitors. He begins by comparing their own strategies with the strategy competitors, continues to comparison of various business processes, products, technical solutions and functions of the competitors with their own solutions and functions, and therefore to know the current shortcomings and to assess opportunities to become better than your competitors.

- A systematic procedure for comparative measurements with the aim to realize a continuous improvement.

- Techniques and tools to improve performance and to establish quality process directed toward the best.

- The term benchmarking comes from the term benchmark. Benchmark is a norm or standard by which some phenomenon can be measured and assessed. Here comes to the fore the meaning of benchmarking as a method of quality evaluating. It is known that the quality of products and services is a market category that can be measured. So it is a comparison in relation to established standards that characterize the performance of products, services and processes. Benchmarking is a continuous process of identifying, understanding and adaptation of equipment, processes, products and services of organization with the best results in order to improve their own business.

There are many different types of benchmarking:

- Process benchmarking: the initiating firm focuses its observation and investigation of business processes with a goal of identifying and observing the best practices from one or more benchmark firms. Activity analysis will be required where the objective is to benchmark cost and efficiency; increasingly applied to back-office processes where outsourcing may be a consideration.

- Financial benchmarking: performing a financial analysis and comparing the results in an effort to assess your overall competitiveness and productivity.

- Benchmarking from an investor perspective: extending the benchmarking universe to also compare to peer companies that can be considered alternative investment opportunities from the perspective of an investor.

- Performance benchmarking: allows the initiator firm to assess their competitive position by comparing products and services with those of target firms.

- Product benchmarking: the process of designing new products or upgrades to current ones. This process can sometimes involve reverse engineering which is taking apart competitors products to find strengths and weaknesses.

- Strategic benchmarking: involves observing how others compete. This type is usually not industry specific, meaning it is best to look at other industries.

- Functional benchmarking: a company will focus its benchmarking on a single function to improve the operation of that particular function. Complex functions such as Human Resources, Finance and Accounting and Information and Communication Technology are unlikely to be directly comparable in cost and efficiency terms and may need to be disaggregated into processes to make valid comparison.

- Best-in-class benchmarking: involves studying the leading competitor or the company that best carries out a specific function.

- Operational benchmarking: embraces everything from staffing and productivity to office flow and analysis of procedures performed.

In business practice there are two basic types of benchmarking: internal and external. Internal benchmarking is carried out within the organization, to identify delay Strengths, Weaknesses, Opportunities and Threats (SWOT analysis). In this way, it made business insight, and conducts a kind of quality control of products, services and processes. External benchmarking is a process of comparison with other organizations. It appears in several forms: competitive, trans-industrial and sector benchmarking. When done in comparison with organizations within the same sector, then it is the competition benchmarking. When comparing the organization performs relative to the aggregate indicators concentrate on the level of sectors or industries, then it is the sector benchmarking. Sector benchmarking is territorially defined. When it comes to comparison with other organizations in the sector, thus non-competitors, then it is the trans-industrial benchmarking. Trans-industrial benchmarking can be conducted in relation to the activities of other organizations operating in the same socio-political conditions.

Benchmarking Application in Hotel Industry

Benchmarking is applied in hotel management. It is often used in order to achieve business strategies, and less as a method of quality evaluation. International consulting companies use benchmarking methods in their research, to analyze the situation and to project the future development of hotel industry in a certain area. The work of these companies can be considered a sector destination benchmarking. Destination benchmarking can have a very great deal of space. It can be seen in the tabular overview that follows:

Table: Word Regions - Main Hotel Industry Results.

August 2011 vs August 2010 (in Euros)									
Region	Occ %		ADR		RevPAR		% Change from 08 10		
	2011	2010	2011	2010	2011	2010	Occ	ADR	RevPAR
Asia Pacific	68,1	68,0	98,74	100,24	67,27	68,21	0,1	-1,5	-1,4
Central & South Asia	52,3	56,8	95,71	106,99	50,07	60,73	-7,8	-10,5	-17,6
Northeastern Asia	68,9	69,5	90,99	96,07	62,65	66,73	-0,9	-5,3	-6,1
Southeastern Asia	66,2	63,7	98,84	98,66	65,47	62,80	4,0	0,2	4,2
Australia & Oceania	74,6	72,6	122,19	111,98	91,12	81,31	2,7	9,1	12,1
Americas	66,3	64,1	72,28	79,34	47,93	50,84	3,5	-8,9	-5,7
North America	66,4	64,1	71,61	78,77	47,53	50,48	3,6	-9,1	-5,8
Caribbean	59,8	60,3	99,66	110,49	59,63	66,65	-0,8	-9,8	-10,5
Central America	58,4	60,9	72,93	83,03	42,57	50,55	-4,1	-12,2	-15,8

South America	68,4	67,4	99,00	93,88	67,76	63,26	1,6	5,5	7,1
Europe	71,0	69,2	94,96	96,53	67,37	66,80	2,5	-1,6	0,9
Eastern Europe	65,8	61,9	72,37	72,91	47,60	45,10	6,3	-0,7	5,5
Northern Europe	77,2	74,8	84,75	89,25	65,45	66,78	3,2	-5,0	-2,0
Southern Europe	68,5	66,2	111,29	110,90	76,29	73,46	3,5	0,4	3,8
Western Europe	66,3	66,3	102,26	101,05	67,83	67,04	0,0	1,2	1,2
Middle East/Africa	48,3	53,4	103,44	104,35	49,98	55,71	-9,5	-0,9	-10,3
Middle East	45,4	48,9	137,70	135,21	62,47	66,12	-7,2	1,8	-5,5
Northern Africa	44,1	61,6	48,38	64,41	21,36	39,70	-28,4	-24,9	-46,2
Southern Africa	56,3	53,8	90,21	97,64	50,78	52,50	4,7	-7,6	-3,3

Explanations of abbreviations:

ADR – Average Daily Rate (Room revenue divided by rooms sold).

OCC – Occupancy (Rooms sold divided by rooms available multiplied by 100).

RevPAR – Revenue Per Available Room (Room revenue divided by rooms available).

Based on data from the table above, achieved results can be compared toward regions. It is also possible to see the best relations between the presented indicators. This form of sector destination benchmarking is suitable for defining and implementing the development strategy of regional professional associations dealing with tourism and hotel industry.

The second example also applies to external, sector and destination benchmarking. This time the focus is on hotel chains which operate hotels with 4 and 5 stars in selected European cities that are famous tourist destinations. The benchmarking survey is undertaken by TRI Hospitality Consulting.

Table: Selected European cities - Main Hotel Industry Results (December 2010, in Euros).

City	Occ %	ARR	RevPAR	TrevPAR	Payroll %	GOPPAR
Amsterdam	58,4	151,75	88,63	136,57	35,7	41,54
Barcelona	45,1	109,01	49,20	75,81	50,1	4,30
Berlin	59,4	113,11	67,21	113,33	31,3	34,27
Budapest	47,4	82,61	39,15	70,47	39,6	5,62
Frankfurt	59,0	99,50	58,68	100,45	33,3	27,26
London	76,5	177,16	135,60	205,14	24,3	108,83
Paris	69,0	173,72	119,82	192,88	44,0	47,51
Prague	58,0	80,74	46,79	92,82	25,0	23,13
Vienna	74,7	136,56	102,04	178,70	33,9	59,74
Zurich	73,7	151,14	111,39	206,67	35,1	63,52

Explanations of abbreviations:

ARR – Average Room Rate (the total bedroom revenue for the period divided by the total bedrooms occupied during the period).

TrevPAR – Total Revpar (the combined total of all revenues divided by the total available rooms during the period).

Payroll - the payroll for all hotels in the sample as a percentage of total revenue.

GOP PAR - the Total Gross Operating Profit for the period divided by the total available rooms during the period.

London, Vienna and Zurich are the cities with hotel occupancy percentage above 70. The highest average room rate was achieved in London, Paris, Amsterdam and Zurich, over 150 Euros. The largest revenue per room was realized in London, Paris, Zurich and Vienna, over 100 Euros. The leading cities of the total revenue per available room are Zurich and London (over 200 Euros), as well as Paris and Vienna (over 150 Euros). The largest share of the payroll in total revenue can be seen in Barcelona and Paris, and the smallest in London and Prague. The highest Total Gross Operating Profit per available room is realized in London, over 100 Euros. It can be concluded that London is the European city with the best indicators of hotel chain business in hotels with 4 or 5 stars. London could serve as a benchmark for the development of hotel industry in European cities. According to indicators realized in London, limited standards required to achieve an adequate level of quality can be set by hotel companies and municipal tourist and hotel associations.

Displacement Calculations

It's usually a safe bet to assume that any hotel would like to increase its revenue and acquire more profits. High-performing hotels foster a culture of constant improvement and regularly ask, "How can we grow and sustain increasing levels of income?" Revenue growth and exploring new revenue resources is the aim for everyone and it is everyone's business, so why can't we make it part of everyone's daily work routine. Every employee wants to be part of a company's growth agenda, but most don't know how. Hotel management needs to provide them with both information and tools, starting with making revenue growth an inherent part of daily conversations, meetings, and presentations.

We have all heard the old motto/pivot of Revenue Management: "Selling the right product, to the right customer, at the right time, at the right price, through the right channel, with the right tools" results in the application of disciplined analytics that predict consumer behavior at the micro-market level and optimize product availability and price to maximize revenue growth.

One of the revenue management tools to make sure you increase your profit is the displacement calculation and analysis, so let us exam what is it and how to use it. What is displacement: in general it could be one of the below:

1. The action of moving something from its place or position.

2. The occupation by a submerged body or part of a body of a volume which would otherwise be occupied by a fluid.

3. The unconscious transfer of an intense emotion from one object to another.

4. The component of an electric field due to free separated charges, regardless of any polarizing effects.

Based on the above, the displacement in hotel revenue management mean you move or not accept some business and replace it with other business i.e. accept group booking and denial some other group, or accept one group and denial some corporate or retail booking, the accepting or denials will be based on some factors, calculation or analysis.

In a scenario happening everyday with the revenue management team the raised questions are there all the time "Should we take the group with 10 rooms at $200 or the group with 20 rooms at $100?, in other scenario " Should we take the group of 30 rooms at $250 or we accept our regular corporate and retail business" And yes it is not that easy question to answer, as there are many factors playing a role to make a proper decision i.e.

- A- How many nights the groups stay?
- B- What days of the week they will stay?
- C- What room types then will choose?
- D- Is the group linked with F&B activities?
- E- Is there are any additional revenues attached to the group?
- F- What is the total group revenue will generate

And here it is the most important question "Do I displace any other business?"

Displacement Calculation

Groups displacement: Those revenue people with the proper tools, understanding with knowledge those outsmarting the competition. They might decline many groups, which competition later accepted, because they thought it is 'good' business. At the end of the day completion lost money and were behind in RevPAR ranking For revenue management a wrong decision might cost you money, sometimes a lot of money! You have to do some maths before making a decision. A blank excel sheet gets us started as shown below: As it show, we just calculated all expected revenues for each group together and show the difference, so it is very clear the tendency to which group to accept .

Transients Segments Displacement Calculation: The same calculation can be made for the transients segment, with a raise question "are the revenue/sales team contracted non-yieldable segments adding to your bottom line? Or are they displacing revenues that can be generated by selling public transient rates? See the below example:

In a daily scenario if one of your LRA (Last Room Availability) account send a request to books 2 nights arriving 09 March, the hotel will have to accept the reservation. In mean time the hotel receive another request from individual guest for the same period for 2 nights as well, who would the hotel to accept. Let's say that the account contracted rate is $100. The hotel will lose with that stay $200 (corporate room value minus the BAR rates).

Some revenue managers will say they would accept the individual request since it is the same stay patterns and generate more revenue, others will say no, they should keep their regular LRA account as it is and provide the hotel with regular business all the year round. We will leave the answer to your best judgment, but it would be better if a displacement calculation regularly performed on the hotel main accounts to evaluate the revenue gain: revenue displaced on identified dates minus the positive revenue on non constrained dates.

In hotel revenue management it is highly recommended extracting the day by day production of top accounts (Retails, Tour Operators & Wholesalers, Corporate, Consortia, and Groups etc) and evaluating day by day the possible displacements.

Transients and Groups Displacement Calculation: Group business is the segment of hotel business that is transacted in a negotiated fashion. Types of group or negotiated business include: Associations (national, regional, governmental, educational, etc.) By their negotiated nature, group bookings are different from transient bookings. For example, groups negotiate blocks of rooms at specified, discounted rates. Group rates are established well in advance of the stay date-often a year in advance or more. Group packages are for blocks of rooms (typically ten or more). Group contracts often stipulate a cut-off date, the last date at which the group can book rooms at their discounted rate. Beyond that date, rooms are booked at the standard transient rate.

It's critical to create the right mix of negotiated group rate customers and transient customers. Generally, the posted prices offered to transient guests are higher than those offered to groups. Transient guest revenue, however, is not guaranteed.

In the above example we compare 100 group rooms with F&B versus 100 transient rooms. Even though the transient rooms pay an $80 higher rate, but the group including the profit of its F&B components is the more profitable business.

Unconstrained Demand

Today's revenue management system (RMS) tools help hotels forecast overall occupancy and rate for future arrival days largely based on historical data from previous years. That's where current tools come up short. They don't go beyond the hotel to see the bigger picture of market opportunity. Right now, RMSs provide no insight regarding true demand available from the significant transient segment, including both leisure and unmanaged business travel.

Unconstrained demand is a term in revenue management to mean total demand you have for a specific date with no constraints, such as number of rooms in the hotel or the price needed to make money. Obviously, the concept cannot be taken too literally as GMs and revenue managers have to put some reasonable boundaries around what is possible, and even desirable.

RMSs do very good job of constructing this view from the past data, such as denials and regrets, of various demand channels:

- Group,

- Wholesale,

- Negotiated corporate business,

- GDS,

- OTA and third-Party,

- Online Direct,

- Call Center.

Additionally, RMS platforms account for factors such as how on-the-books production is pacing by channel, demand drivers such as major events within the destination, and changes in supply as additional inputs.

But what if this year is different than last? What if there is new political/economic unrest in the market? Or new competitors, e.g. Airbnb, that are changing the market dynamics. Then hotels need revenue management solutions that look at what's happening in the market right now to capture the broader opportunity inherent in real unconstrained demand:

- Hotel demand for future arrival dates – unbooked,

- Competitive set demand for future arrival dates – unbooked,

- Overall market demand for future arrival dates – unbooked,

- Hotel share of overall consumer demand – unbooked and booked,

- Consumer response to prices for the hotel and comp set for future dates, e.g. comp set pricing is generating higher volumes of search and bookings for future arrival dates.

Having this type of information helps hotels make smarter rate and distribution decisions for future dates. For example, if a hotel knows from forward-looking shopping data that market demand is strong – even higher than last year or last month – and competition is lowering rate in a panic because lead times are shorter than in the past, the hotel can opt to hold rate and ultimately increase ADR in the long run.

Insight to true unconstrained demand helps hoteliers increase profitability based on the following advantages:

- Improved forecasting: Unconstrained demand data shows consumer shopping peaks and valleys for future arrival dates, based on specific hotel and comp set rates.

- Optimize ADR: An integrated view of future rate and demand tells hoteliers when to hold, raise or lower rates based on consumer behavior.

- Increased certainty: actual demand available for future patterns is important because it gives a level of certainty in uncertain situations.

In a new environment, hotels have to make decisions in new ways. That means no longer relying on trends based on historic data, but putting unconstrained transient demand for future dates into the mix.

Importance of Revenue Management

Similar to larger hotels, smaller ones are constantly generating data. Especially if the property has a restaurant, spa, bar, or other ancillary sources of revenue. Without automation, it is difficult to compile and analyze all this continuous information.

Furthermore, smaller hotels frequently have fewer resources and don't have a dedicated revenue manager; thus, leaving the revenue strategy up to the general manager, director of sales and marketing, reservations manager, or a revenue management team – all of which already have hectic days filled with other responsibilities. Often times, this results in over-pricing and under-pricing room rates, which leaves independent hotels at a competitive disadvantage.

The human mind (or even a team of minds) can only process so much information in its decision-making process. One of the biggest challenges with manual revenue management practices is the inability to collect quality data in a timely manner while being able to use it before it is obsolete. Hotel data comes from a multitude of sources, changes rapidly, and is critical to making proper pricing decisions.

Smaller hotels need an RMS more than larger ones. Here's six reasons why a revenue management system is important to small independent hotels:

1. Every room counts in a smaller hotel;

    Pricing rooms incorrectly has a much more noticeable impact on ADR & RevPAR performance. If there is a pricing error at a larger hotel, it is easier to 'bury' the rate mistake. Simply stated, larger properties can hide a multitude of sins in volume.

2. Smaller independent hotels compete with branded hotels;

    Branded hotels use a proprietary revenue management system. If an independent property has branded hotels in its comp set, every single day, those branded hotels have a competitive advantage by having data 'visibility' and technology tools the independent hotel likely does not have.

3. Understanding demand via analytical forecasting;

    All hotels, big and small, benefit from recognizing demand present, demand yet to come, and where demand books. Doing so enables setting the right price, for the right guest, at the right time, via the right channel.

4. Balance of business mix and length of stay;

    With fewer rooms, managing booking pace and capturing optimal reservations by accepting the most valuable demand across arrival dates and lengths of stay is even more critical to maximizing revenues. As opposed to focusing on peak nights and accepting lower-rated business when it isn't needed, which simply trades down revenue.

5. Appropriate staffing levels;

    Being able to effectively deliver a positive guest experience is impacted by proper hotel staffing. Dependable forecasts help hotels ensure appropriate staff levels.

6. Determining profitable group business;

Generally, in addition to having fewer guest rooms, smaller hotels often have limited meetings and events space. So, accepting groups under the right conditions, at the right price, over the best set of dates, while understanding transient displacement, is important to driving additional profitability and contributing to increasing occupancy.

Regardless of hotel size, revenue management principles apply for all hotels. But for smaller-sized properties, there's less margin for error due to having fewer rooms.

By utilizing an RMS, smaller properties level the playing field of competing with larger ones with automated revenue management tools. An RMS helps independent hoteliers make fact-based, data driven decisions on what one *knows* will happen versus making decisions on what one *thinks or feels* might happen. Such knowledge only comes from incorporating the art and science of revenue management automation – with hoteliers providing the art and the RMS bringing the science.

References

- Rate-fences-revenue-management: hotelquest.com, Retrieved 20 April 2020

- Six-reasons-why-revenue-management-technology-is-important-to-small-independent-hotels: ideas.com, Retrieved 12 June 2020

- Market-segmentation-know-hotel-demand-comes: bernerbecker.com, Retrieved 29 July 2020

- Why-revenue-management-systems-fall-short-on-identifying-unconstrained-demand-for-hotels: nsightfor-travel.com, Retrieved 10 April 2020

- Target-market-segmentation-in-travel-and-hospitality-2297028: thebalancesmb.com, Retrieved 19 March 2020

Permissions

All chapters in this book are published with permission under the Creative Commons Attribution Share Alike License or equivalent. Every chapter published in this book has been scrutinized by our experts. Their significance has been extensively debated. The topics covered herein carry significant information for a comprehensive understanding. They may even be implemented as practical applications or may be referred to as a beginning point for further studies.

We would like to thank the editorial team for lending their expertise to make the book truly unique. They have played a crucial role in the development of this book. Without their invaluable contributions this book wouldn't have been possible. They have made vital efforts to compile up to date information on the varied aspects of this subject to make this book a valuable addition to the collection of many professionals and students.

This book was conceptualized with the vision of imparting up-to-date and integrated information in this field. To ensure the same, a matchless editorial board was set up. Every individual on the board went through rigorous rounds of assessment to prove their worth. After which they invested a large part of their time researching and compiling the most relevant data for our readers.

The editorial board has been involved in producing this book since its inception. They have spent rigorous hours researching and exploring the diverse topics which have resulted in the successful publishing of this book. They have passed on their knowledge of decades through this book. To expedite this challenging task, the publisher supported the team at every step. A small team of assistant editors was also appointed to further simplify the editing procedure and attain best results for the readers.

Apart from the editorial board, the designing team has also invested a significant amount of their time in understanding the subject and creating the most relevant covers. They scrutinized every image to scout for the most suitable representation of the subject and create an appropriate cover for the book.

The publishing team has been an ardent support to the editorial, designing and production team. Their endless efforts to recruit the best for this project, has resulted in the accomplishment of this book. They are a veteran in the field of academics and their pool of knowledge is as vast as their experience in printing. Their expertise and guidance has proved useful at every step. Their uncompromising quality standards have made this book an exceptional effort. Their encouragement from time to time has been an inspiration for everyone.

The publisher and the editorial board hope that this book will prove to be a valuable piece of knowledge for students, practitioners and scholars across the globe.

Index

Lightning Source UK Ltd.
Milton Keynes UK
UKHW052205140922
408888UK00002B/34